How to be a Writer in the E-Age: A Self-Help Guide

by

Catherine Ryan Hyde

&

Anne R. Allen

Praise for *How to be a Writer in the E-Age: A Self-Help Guide*

"I so wish there had been a book like this back when I first started to consider writing for e-publishers....The moment I started to read *"How to be a Writer in the E-Age"* I knew it was a winner in every sense. The information is not only valuable to new authors, it's relevant to published authors who might be thinking about making the switch to e-publishing, too."

— Ryan Field, author and blogger

"...This comprehensive, humorous and down-to-earth guidebook covers our ever-changing industry, our growing choices, and lays down what we can expect at the end of our road so we plan our travels well."

— Joanna Celeste, author

"...Whether you're a neophyte to publishing, a wannabe writer, or one familiar with the ins and outs of getting you book out there in print, there's a lot of excellent info in these pages."

—John Williamson, writer

CONTENTS

FOREWORD

PART 1—GETTING STARTED

PART 2—THE INEVITABILITY OF REJECTION

PART 5—BEGINNING THE QUERY PROCESS

PART 6—TRADITIONAL OR SELF-PUBLISHING?

PART 7—EDITING: THE KEY TO GOOD WRITING

PART 8—THE WRITING LIFE

PART 9—AFTER PUBLICATION

CONCLUSION

ABOUT THE AUTHORS

A FOREWORD FROM CATHERINE

LIKELY YOU HAVE NOTICED THAT THE WORLD IS FULL OF BOOKS to help you through the thorny challenges of writerdom...by teaching you how to write. Everything from hacking through your first draft, to building multi-dimensional characters, to crafting heroic story arcs, to teaching your dialogue to sing. How nice to know your work-in-progress has so many therapeutic options. Now what about you? The draft is in better shape with every how-to book you read. But you're a mess.

Won't anyone tell you how to pick your way through the land mines of your chosen profession? How to weather rejection without feeling like you've been left out in a hurricane? How to discard the folly of your critique group's misguided advice without losing that one gem that could potentially pay you back for all their abuse?

So many voices tell you how hard it is to get an agent (true), how hard it is to sell a novel (truer), how hard it is to get anybody to read your novel even if you do sell it (sadly, truest). Yes, the woods are dark and deep, but how about a few voices suggesting a good path to find your way out into (at least dappled) sunlight?

I still remember the time someone asked if I'd considered becoming a stand-up comic. I was speaking to a big audience at the Junior League in Toledo, Ohio. They'd been looking for a speaker on short notice. Someone had dropped out. I happened to be free because I'd set those days aside for my vacation, which involved day-hiking to the bottom of the Grand Canyon and back. I put work first, and then, amazingly, was able to change my reservations and do my Canyon hike one day early.

My calves were still seized up like granite the whole time I was on stage.

After the talk, I met with a smaller group over luncheon, and for some Q&A. I didn't know that, after I'd left the stage, the moderator had told them all about my hike. So that was one of the questions I was asked: Tell us about your Grand Canyon hike.

After closing my gaping jaw, and being filled in as to how they even knew about that, I shared some of the vaguely funny—I hoped—thoughts that go through your mind during eleven hours on a tough trail.

I said the scenery was beautiful, but by five in the afternoon you find yourself thinking, "I've been looking at those same rocks since sunrise. Now I want to look at a sirloin steak with some garlic mashed potatoes on the side. Now that would be scenic." Seriously, one can only be happy for just so long on trail snacks and Gatorade.

I shared some of the problems I'd had trying to explain my hike to friends and acquaintances who couldn't seem to grasp the concept of hiking the entire canyon all in one day—as evidenced by their inquiries regarding exactly where on the bottom I would camp.

I said there was one woman who, after I'd fully explained the day-hike concept, asked me if I'd be taking "one of those mules."

"No," I told the Junior League crowd. "I don't think I could rightly consider it hiking if I took one of those mules. I think the mule could consider it hiking. In fact, the mule could consider it hiking with a heavy pack. But it would be disingenuous if I did."

And I'm sure there were more, but this was a few years ago.

That's when a woman in the crowd asked me if I'd ever considered becoming a stand-up comic.

"Thanks," I said. "Thanks for suggesting possibly the only occupation on the face of the planet that's harder than mine."

I'd be tempted to say there's no harder way to make a living than as a working writer, but I can't. Because there are stand-up comics. At least authors suffer our ego deflation in the privacy of our own homes. Imagine receiving your worst rejection slips on stage, with an audience watching you squirm, heavy lights causing beads of sweat to roll down between your eyebrows.

See? Take heart, fellow writers. It could be worse.

Although, in all honesty...not by much.

Won't anyone tell you...not just how to write a book...but how to be a writer, sanity (mostly) intact?

Yes. Anne and I will try.

A FOREWORD FROM ANNE

WHEN CATHERINE RYAN HYDE FIRST SUGGESTED I COLLABORATE WITH her on a book for writers, I was flattered and a little terrified. I've been in awe of her work for years.

I met Catherine a couple of decades ago when visiting a local critique group. I'd already published my first novel as a serial in an entertainment weekly, and although Catherine's short stories had appeared in lots of prestigious journals and won some impressive awards, she was still struggling to get recognition for her book-length fiction.

I found her prose electrifying, but most people in the group didn't seem to get it—and made what I thought were harsh and unhelpful comments. Because I was a guest, I wasn't allowed to critique, but when I ran into Catherine later in the post office, I told her I didn't agree with what had been said.

She just smiled.

"I always consider the source," she said. "If a criticism is valid, it will bring an 'ah-ha' moment. Otherwise, I let it go."

That piece of wisdom has helped me through some rough

patches in my own career. It taught me how to keep improving my writing without losing my own voice and creative integrity.

A few years later, Catherine zoomed to superstardom with *Pay It Forward*, but she has always taken the time to nurture new writers—especially those who might be in the same situation she was in with that critique group.

There's a whole lot of information out there on how to write. But there's very little about how to be a writer—how ride the roller-coaster of the rapidly changing publishing business and deal with the overload of conflicting information.

You'll find thousands of blog posts every day on the subject of writing and publishing, and you can't read them all. Which ones do you trust? Who do you believe? So much of it is negative and snarky.

Making a living as a writer seems to get more difficult by the day—does that mean you should give up your dreams?

Our answer to the latter is a resounding no. The life of a creative writer can be the most rewarding in the world. A writer lives a life of the mind—an examined life.

Whether you become the next Stephanie Meyer, get published in a few literary journals or even just write for family and friends, your life is infinitely enhanced by the process of creating worlds out of words. Never let anybody take that away from you.

This book is about helping you learn how to navigate the publishing business as it zooms into the future, to learn to be the best writer you can be—and keep on writing, no matter what.

PART I

GETTING STARTED

ANNE
HOW DO YOU LEARN TO BE A WRITER?

I'M OFTEN APPROACHED BY PARENTS OR GRANDPARENTS OF CHILDREN who've shown a talent for writing. They ask how a child can learn to be a writer. Or sometimes a person going through a mid-life job change will ask my advice about going back to college to pursue a long-deferred writing dream.

I have to tell them the truth: Learning to write is hard. And earning money from writing is harder.

I'm not saying certain types of writing can't be lucrative. For example, "content providers" can find careers in advertising and various tech fields. But that's not usually what the doting grand/parents or career-changers are thinking. They might be imagining plays or screenplays, or even journalism—fast-fading professions too—but mostly they're thinking memoir or novels.

But the truth is, writing book-length narrative is one of the toughest ways to earn a living—and it's getting tougher all the time. The average book advance is less than half of what it was ten years ago. Almost all writers need day jobs.

I

So the question arises: how much money should people put into educating themselves to be writers?

Anybody who visits a lot of writing sites has probably been followed around the Web by ads for college-level creative writing degrees. Do those give students a jumpstart or prepare them for a writing career?

Unfortunately, they usually don't. They're often based on very old ideas of what the publishing industry is like.

If you have the privilege of attending college, by all means take courses in creative writing. Also take courses in business management, advanced string theory or Athenian red-figure vase painting—whatever interests you.

A lot of writers major in literature—in their own or other languages—because that's where their interests lie. Studying literature—as opposed to writing—may be the best training. It gives students the chance to soak up the works of the masters without trying to compete with them until they're ready.

If you do get to learn about writing and literature in the groves of academe, enjoy every minute of it. None of your time spent learning will be wasted, and a well-rounded college education is massively helpful to any career.

But don't go to college expecting to be taught how to be a professional writer who can enter the workforce and earn back the cost of college like somebody studying accounting or medicine. It won't happen.

I'm not saying degrees in creative writing will hurt—not at all—but they're not necessary for a writing career. And they're usually expensive.

Keep in mind: the number one thing that's NOT necessary to any creative career is…DEBT. Debt is a prison that can keep you locked into a job you hate, living in noisy, crowded circumstances, and plagued with anxieties that are the enemy of creativity

"But, wait!" says Aspiring Young Writer, "What about a master's degree in creative writing? That gives you a leg up into the publishing business doesn't it?"

Um, not really.

Not with most agents and publishers (although a prestigious school can provide valuable contacts). What an advanced degree will do is steer you in the direction of literary writing, which tends to be less lucrative for a publisher (and you).

An MFA (Master of Fine Arts) will qualify you to teach creative writing at the college level, and as a day job, college teaching is a pretty good one. But be aware of the implied trade-off.

Compare an advanced creative writing degree with the advanced study of ballet or classical music: you're entering a fiercely competitive field with a niche audience and not much remuneration…but a lot of prestige. For those who love it, there's also the fulfillment that can come no other way. If writing and teaching literary fiction is your bliss—follow it! The world needs people to carry on that tradition.

But if your goal is writing popular fiction, treat your education more like preparing for musical theater, playing roots music, or ballroom dancing—and take a more eclectic route in your training. (And prepare to work a day job.)

Of course, you first need to learn the basics just as a literary writer does: grammar, sentence structure, spelling, and word usage. If you didn't get that in high school or college, you need to take some brush-up classes. Language is your instrument, and you need to learn to play before you can get into the band.

NOTE: Don't count on some hired editor to clean up your stuff after you write it. Editors cost a bundle and they can't do it all. Good language skills are essential. You wouldn't try to be a carpenter if you couldn't pound a nail.

But once you have that down, what do you do?

There's still a whole lot to learn. Straight-A grammar skills don't help you with learning how to tell a story. You need to educate yourself on story structure, how to create compelling characters, pacing and all the rest.

For that, the best approach is to study widely. Get as much education as you can from many sources as you can find. There is no one right way. You can enroll in inexpensive classes at your local adult education r community college extension programs. Short online courses can be really helpful, too, especially ones that concentrate on structure and story-telling techniques. Read the classic books on writing. Go to writers' conferences, especially local ones where you don't have to pay for room and board.

Sometimes professional writers will offer workshops in person or online. A short course from a well-known author is usually worth the price, because a big name will hold weight in a query and you may be lucky enough to have them mentor you.

If you live in a place where there's a local writer's club or chapter of organizations like Romance Writers of America/Australia, the Society of Children's Writers and Book Illustrators, or Sisters in Crime, join. Clubs like those can be amazingly valuable resources. A good critique group can sometimes teach you as much as a college class about how to write.

However, you want to beware group-think. Critique groups are only as good as their members, and ignorant people can spread bad habits. (For more information on this, see our section on dealing with criticism.)

The truth is that these days, a whole lot of what you need to learn is available on the Internet for free. I know people who have learned a huge amount by working with other writers in various writers' forums.

To become a professional, it is as crucial to learn the business side of publishing as it is to master grammar and story structure. Business skills are equally important to the contemporary writer. Agent blogs are a valuable resource here. Agents and former agents like Rachelle Gardner, Nathan Bransford, Kristen Nelson, and Janet Reid offer mini-courses in publishing in their archives that are valuable to aspiring writers all over the world.

Also, you'll need to learn to use social media. It's as important to a writer today as it is to know how to use an apostrophe. More on that in our chapters on "Getting Your Geek On."

If you ask most professional writers what's the best way to learn to write, they're going to tell you two things:

1) Read

2) Write

And some will add:

3) Live

The New Yorker's Malcolm Gladwell wrote in his book *Outliers* that you need to do something 10,000 hours in order to learn to do it well. That's a valuable number to keep in mind.

ANNE

THE #I TALENT YOU NEED TO BE A GOOD WRITER

THE BRILLIANT COLUMNIST/PHILOSOPHER/LITERARY OUTLAW MICHAEL Ventura famously said the most important talent required of a writer is the ability to work alone. In his much-reprinted 1993 article, *The Talent of the Room*, Ventura wrote:

"Writing is something you do alone in a room. It's the most important thing to remember if you want to be a writer... Unless you have that, your other talents are worthless."

But it occurred to me recently that writers no longer have to be as isolated as we were when Ventura wrote those words two decades ago. With the click of a mouse, we can communicate with fellow writers all over the world. One of the ways technology has altered our universe is that we can now emerge from a session with the muse, pop onto the Internet and tweet, blog, email or whatever and be part of a community.

We're not so alone in our rooms any more.

But there's another talent that may be even more important than a capacity for solitude—and that is the ability to get out of our rooms and *listen*.

Without knowing how to listen attentively, we can only write about ourselves. All our characters will act and sound like us. And the truth is that readers care a lot more about themselves than they do about us.

As Margaret Atwood said in a *Narrative* magazine interview: "Nothing interests people so much as themselves."

All writers may need the talent of the room, but good writers need the talent to shut up and listen.

Our technological culture does not listen well. It's hard to go anywhere and not be assaulted by the sound of some Bozo talking loudly on his phone. Talking. Not listening. Often they hardly even stop for breath.

I sometimes wonder if the other person in the conversation is compulsively talking as well. Maybe I'm hearing one of two lonely Bozos: both loudly failing to communicate.

Most people do a whole lot more talking than listening.

But as writers, we must do the opposite.

I think a lot of people become writers because they're not big talkers. Their early lives may have been dominated by noisier friends or family members. (How many writers are middle children, I wonder?) They write because they want to have their say—to get somebody to finally listen.

But during the process of writing, we come to realize our best stories are mosaics of the voices and stories we have listened to—all those snippets of other people's lives that have been thrust upon us by the loud and Bozoid. We take the raw material of their non-communications and make it into something that truly communicates.

A good writer offers readers an echo chamber in which they can hear themselves.

In *The Sirens of Titan*, Kurt Vonnegut invented a life form he called Harmoniums, who could only communicate two messages: "here I am, here I am, here I am," and "so glad you are, so glad you are, so glad you are."

Maybe Earthlings aren't so different. Noisy Bozos with cell phones are the "here-I-ams" and writers are the "so-glad-you-ares." Out of their seemingly pointless noise, we make art that reflects the truth of their own existence.

It is our way of being heard. And our reward for listening.

ANNE

12 MYTHS ABOUT BEING A WRITER

WHEN YOU'RE BEGINNING TO WRITE, YOU'RE LIKELY TO BE BOMBARDED with advice from all quarters—your family, your friends, your hairdresser, and that know-it-all guy at work. I don't know why, but everybody who ever watched a few minutes of Oprah's book club show seems to think they know all about the publishing business.

But chances are pretty good they don't.

And chances are even better that whatever they may have heard is out of date. This is a business in a state of rapid change.

If you don't want your heart broken in this ever-more-difficult, soul-crushing process, you need to keep those myths and outdated ideas from infecting your brain.

Here are twelve things to disregard when you hear them from those well-meaning friends and relations. Be polite, but you might be forgiven a slightly condescending smile.

1) Writers make big money.

How many times do you hear stuff like this? "You're a writer! Will you still talk to me when you're rich and famous?"

Tell them to rest easy. It's not likely to be a problem. Even "successful" writers need day jobs these days. Royalties and advances are shrinking at an amazing rate. Yes, J.K. Rowling is richer than the Queen, James Patterson lives in movie-star grandeur in Palm Beach, and indie superstars Amanda Hocking, Hugh Howey and John Locke made millions self-publishing. (John Locke chronicled his success in a book that became a phenomenon of its own: *How I Sold 1 Million eBooks in 5 Months*—but was later disgraced when he revealed much of his success came from phony reviews purchased from review mills.)

But these stories are the exceptions that prove the rule. Of course you (or your hairdresser) can fantasize you'll become a superstar, too—we all do—but the odds are mighty slim.

2) Genre fiction is easy to write.

People will tell you to start out with something "easy" like a Romance/Mystery/kid's book. Don't even try. If you don't love a genre and read it voraciously, you'll never write it well enough to publish.

3) Never write for free.

Professional freelancers will tell you this with the ferocity of union organizers, and they are absolutely right...when they're speaking to seasoned journalists (although even they aren't getting paid much these days).

But it's a long way from writing your first essay to publishing in the *Times*. During your learning process, writing for free is good practice and a great way to get your name out there. Think of it as if you're being paid in clips and platform-building. And if you write literary fiction or poetry, you may never be paid for it (most literary writers make their money teaching).

The lack of paying markets doesn't mean your work doesn't deserve an audience.

Plus, it's important to remember that literary agents work for free a lot of the time—sometimes for years when they're getting started, just like writers.

4) Don't waste time on short fiction.

People tell you short stories are a waste because you won't make any money, but that's all changed with the ebook and the advent of stand-alone ebook shorts like Kindle Singles.

Also, short stories are the best place to hone your skills. Publishing shorts makes you more attractive to agents and gives your self-confidence a boost. And it's a whole lot easier to publish a short story than a novel. There are many thousands of literary magazines and contests in the English-speaking world but only five major book publishing houses.

More on this in the chapter "Why You Should be Writing Short Fiction."

5) Don't reveal your plot, because somebody will steal it.

Everybody's got a story. It's how you write it that matters. Since the copyright law reforms of the 1970s, copyrighting your work before it's published (especially a first draft) has been the mark of a paranoid amateur. It's copyrighted as soon as you type it onto your hard drive (and BTW, you can't copyright a title).

6) With talent like yours, you don't have to jump through all those hoops.

The old saw about 10% inspiration/90% perspiration is 100% true: talent without skill is useless. That means skill at writing AND hoop-jumping. Learn the rules and follow them or nobody will ever find out about that talent of yours.

7) Spelling and grammar don't matter.

The only thing that's important is creativity, right?

When you're seven, maybe. Words are your tools. If you can't use them properly, nobody's going to hire you for the job.

8) Be extra creative so you'll stand out.

Sorry, but you won't get a book deal if you write your query with animated emoticons, invent a new genre, or try to bring back the papyrus scroll (at least not when you're a newbie). If you have any hopes of getting traditionally published, follow genre and word count guidelines. It's a very stodgy business and if you don't follow the rules, you won't get in the door.

And even if you're self-publishing, follow the three-act structure, and skip the show-offy rule-breaking, or you won't get read.

9) Don't read other writers' work or you'll imitate them.

Reading widely is essential to the growth of your craft. The more you read, the better your own work will be. If you imitate a bit when you're a beginner, no harm done. Traditionally, painters were trained by copying the masters. It's not a bad exercise for writers, either. Your own voice and style will emerge as you grow as an artist.

10) The sadder your personal history, the more publishers will be moved to buy your book.

In spite of what you've seen on Oprah, readers are not likely to be interested in your personal tragedies, unless you write beautifully and have something new to say that will benefit THEM. Do you enjoy listening to strangers complain about their problems?

Yeah. I didn't think so.

11) Sell yourself. Show them you're confident!

Confidence combined with cluelessness will not help your career—unless you're Will Ferrell and you do it in an elf suit.

In publishing, tooting your own horn is more likely to make you the butt of nasty agent snark on Twitter.

So when the office know-it-all claims you're "not trying" unless you query with lines like, "my poignant and exquisitely-written memoir will be bigger than *the Hunger Games* and Harry Potter books combined," smile politely and change the subject to his impending mortgage foreclosure.

12) You wrote a whole book! It deserves to be published!!!

Uh, no. Almost all successful writers have a few practice books hidden away somewhere. Getting something published—especially book-length fiction—is like getting to Carnegie Hall. It takes practice, practice, practice.

ANNE

THE SUCKY FIRST DRAFT

IF YOU'RE A BEGINNING WRITER, YOU'VE PROBABLY HAD AN IDEA rattling around in your head for years. It may be a novel, a story, a novella, a memoir or piece of creative nonfiction. You may not even know which. How do you find out—and where do you start?

Try this: Butt in chair. Fingers on keyboard. Type three pages. Don't think about grammar, spelling, or rules. Don't look anything up. Just type. Does it suck? Good. The first draft usually does.

Anne LaMott wrote in her classic book for writers, *Bird by Bird*, "the only way [most writers] can get anything done at all is to write really, really, really shitty first drafts."

So try to resist revising those first awful pages. Instead, type three more the next day. And the next. Pretty soon you have a chapter. And a head full of ideas for what comes next.

Here are five tips for getting those first words on the page:

1) Don't agonize over your first chapter. You'll hear endless carping about how the first chapter has to hook the reader, introduce all the major themes and plot elements, begin with the world's most exciting sentence, etc. But when you're writing the first draft, none of that matters. You're introducing yourself to your characters and their world. You only need to think about your reader when you revise.

2) Don't spend too much time on research before you start writing. I know this sounds counter-intuitive, but writers who do years of research tend to want to put it all into their work. It will have to be cut out of the final draft or you'll bore your reader silly. Get a general knowledge, then write the book and see whether you really need to know how they cooked cabbage in 13th century Scotland or what kind of underwear Cleopatra wore. Research the specific details you need after you've written the first draft.

3) Don't worry that you can't write about THAT because your brother–in-law/former science teacher/ex-girlfriend will recognize him/herself. You can always change some characteristics later. Besides, you'll be amazed how characters who are inspired by real life take off on their own and become very different from the way you first imagined them. And excuse me, when did your brother-in-law last read a book?

4) Don't save some of your ideas for later. I used to do this, terrified I'd use them up. That was silly. Put your best ideas on the page. You'll have more, I promise.

5) Don't try to control the process. If it goes somewhere you didn't want it to go, or won't stick to your outline, let it. This is your muse talking—don't make her angry.

And then, just do it! Make yourself write at least three pages a day no matter how much they may resemble dung. You can fix everything else later.

ANNE

WHAT IF SOMEBODY STEALS YOUR PLOT?

I OFTEN HEAR FROM NEW WRITERS WHO ARE AFRAID THEIR PLOTS WILL be stolen if they talk about their books online or in critique groups.

But I tell them to rest easy. Writers have a lot to be wary of these days—faux agents, bogus publishers, draconian contracts—but plot-purloiners should not be high on the list.

Consider the old saying: "There are no new stories, just new ways of telling them."

Experts don't agree on the exact number of narrative plots, but there aren't many. In the 19th century, Georges Polti listed 36 "Dramatic Situations." In 1993, Roland Tobias counted 20 "Master Plots," and in 2005, Christopher Booker compressed the list to seven "Basic Plots." The legendary agent who used to blog as "Miss Snark" said there were six, and I found a recent article in *Author* Magazine that listed only five. The number seems to be shrinking.

But everybody agrees it is finite. So—no matter how original your story feels to you, somebody has probably told it before. Maybe last week. And they didn't steal it. They thought it up just the way you did.

It's amazing how often an idea that sprouts in your brain from the seeds of your own imagination can take root in other people's brains at the same time. Human minds often respond in similar ways to prevailing news stories, music, weather patterns or whatever—and end up generating similar thoughts.

Evolutionary biologists call this phenomenon a "meme." The term—from the Greek *mimema*—meaning something imitated—was coined by biologist Richard Dawkins in his 1976 book, *The Selfish Gene*. He observed that certain stories, melodies, catch phrases and fashions can flash through a whole culture in a short amount of time, changing and mutating as they go. Darwin and Wallace simultaneously came up with the theory of evolution while on different sides of the world. Newton and Liebnitz simultaneously invented calculus.

This explains why we can't copyright ideas. Everybody has them. Very often the same ones at the same time.

Unfortunately, new writers don't always realize this, and they can embarrass themselves with plot-theft paranoia. That's why you never want to mention copyright in a query letter: it red-flags you as an amateur.

Of course, if you're having severe anxiety about it, and you're sure nobody ever thought of mixing classic fiction with B-movie paranormal creatures, you can copyright your logline for "*Pride and Prejudice* meets *Poltergeist*." Just don't mention this to industry professionals.

This is because delusions about the uniqueness of story ideas can get pretty off-the-wall.

Victoria Strauss at the all-important "Writer Beware" blog wrote about some poor deluded guy who was trying to sell his plot idea on eBay for ten million dollars. He said, "It can be compared to stories like Star Wars, Harry Potter, Lord of the Rings, Matrix, Indiana Jones...and will bring in endless fame and money to anyone who takes it."

And he's not the only starry-eyed doofus who has combined delusions of grandeur with total cluelessness about the effort required to actually write a novel or screenplay.

In the thread of the same post at Writer Beware, children's author Kathleen Duey said, "I have been approached so many times by people who want me to buy a story, or who are willing to share half the proceeds if I will just do the writing. I never know what to say. I am not rude, but...really? Try that split on any other kind of business person. 'I think that a colony on Mars would be awesome and I am willing to give a 50% share of all eventual proceeds to anyone who can make it happen.' I am always careful to walk away, if that's what it takes, to keep anyone from telling me the idea...just in case I ever write something similar by accident."

I'll bet a lot of writers have been approached in a similar way. I sure have.

In fact, I have a feeling this delusion is as old as writing itself. I imagine Virgil probably met a guy at the Emperor Augustus's orgy who said—

"You're a writer? Hey, I've got this idea for a book about a guy who sails around the Mediterranean. Meets up with big storms. Monsters. Some hot nookie. You can write it down and we'll split the proceeds 50-50."

I hope Virgil had a good lawyer. Kathleen Duey's instinct to run is a good one. Clueless people can get scary.

When somebody approaches me with this "proposition," I say, "The going rate for ghostwriters is $50-$100 an hour. I don't provide that service, but I can get you a referral."

I don't want to be mean, but they need to understand that most writers have plenty of story ideas of our own. Our biggest fear is not living long enough to write them all.

But what do you do when somebody does publish a book that's similar to yours? Even if they didn't literally "steal" it, you can feel kind of ripped off.

Don't despair. Memes can work in your favor. If you're writing the final draft of your version of your *Pride and Prejudice/Poltergeist* mash-up, and somebody else sells a *Pride and Prejudice/Gremlins* mash-up, you're now part of a trend. Publishers tend to be sheep. If the first book is popular, they'll want another.

And if yours is better, you're way ahead. As the above quote says, you can't tell a new story, but you can tell it in a new way. It's not about being first. You can be pretty sure you're not.

In fact, I'll bet some guy told Virgil when he first pitched the *Aeneid*, "A lost dude sails around the Mediterranean after the Trojan War having adventures? Sorry, that's been done. Haven't you heard of that Homer guy's story, *The Odyssey*?"

Did Virgil steal Homer's plot? I suppose you could say he did. But it doesn't seem to have hurt sales for either of them for the last couple of millennia. It's the telling that makes each story unique. And that's going to be true of your story, too.

It's not about the plot. It's about the writing. Nobody can steal that.

ANNE

HOW DO YOU KNOW YOU'RE REALLY A WRITER?

I THINK PRETTY MUCH EVERY WRITER GETS THE "OMG I'M-NOT-really-a-writer, why-am-I-kidding-myself?" blues. Former Curtis Brown agent Nathan Bransford called them the "Am-I-Crazies."

You know how it is. Rejections are pouring in. Your Work in Progress is stalled. Your BFF has refused to listen to one more word about the unfairness of the publishing industry.

So, after a sleepless, agonizing night, you decide you're unworthy to call yourself a writer.

Q. So how DO you know if you're a writer?

A. You write.

That's all there is to it. If you go off by yourself at regular intervals to create stuff using words, you're a writer. Maybe you haven't written anything publishable yet. Maybe you've written a bunch of first chapters that lead nowhere. Maybe you've never shown your stuff to anybody but your cat.

But you're a writer.

Some people are born to it. If you're one of those, your early years went something like this:

1) You gave names and backstories to the characters in your coloring books.

2) You wrote a whodunit in third grade in which you killed off the assistant principal who gave you detention that time when it wasn't even your fault.

3) You poured your adolescent angst into verses that relied heavily on rhyming the word "rain" with "pain."

4) After your first romance ended, above the emotional agony, a tiny voice narrated in your head, "So this is what a broken heart feels like, she thought, as she trudged on leaden feet toward her empty room..."

Some of you came to it later. After taking an inspiring class, reading an extraordinary book, or experiencing something that begged to be shared in written form, strange things started to happen:

1) Both your roommates went off to a party. You weren't invited. But you couldn't have been happier. Time alone to write!

2) You could no longer join workplace chat about TV, because you didn't even recognize the names of the shows. Who has time to waste on television?

3) When your friends exchanged funny stories about their kids, you chimed in with an anecdote about what your protagonist did last night.

4) Writing took on the urgency of a bodily function.

Other writers are just getting started. You've always loved books and wanted to write, and you've just set up a blog and are finally getting concrete ideas for the book you know you've got in you. So you find yourself doing odd things:

1) You pretend to be looking for jobs online, but instead you're doing research for a story or interesting things to post about.

2) You haven't told a soul, but you've kind of written three chapters and sketched out a couple of scenes that might work into a novel.

3) You used to tune out when the old lady next door droned on about her tragic life. Now you eagerly note all the details for use in future fiction.

4) Your most titillating fantasies involve books in a Barnes and Noble window with your name on the cover.

Q. Yeah but... sez you. I want to know if I'm a REAL writer—can I make a living at it?

A. If you write—and you're not a wooden puppet carved by an old Italian guy named Gepetto—you're a real writer. Most writers don't make a living at it. Not creative writers, anyway. Journalists are having a hard time of it these days, too. Only a handful of superstars can quit their day jobs.

Of course every one of us hopes to be a superstar some day, and nobody should give up the dream, but there's no point in going all either/or.

Think of it like this:

Q. How many people play golf?

A. How many of them are Tiger Woods?

Should everybody else give up golf?

Nobody starts at the top. Every star was a clueless beginner once. Learning takes time. We have to spend years—maybe decades— taking classes, studying how-to books and blogs, joining critique groups, and learning the ins and outs of the publishing business—the way a golfer works to perfect a swing. It's a process. A really, really long process.

So before you give in to the I'm-not-really-a-writer blues, remember:

1) If your queries are coming back with form/silent rejections, you're a writer.

2) If your WIP is refusing to come to a satisfactory end and you kind of hate your protagonist right now, you're a writer.

3) If your neglected spouse suggests you take up something more lucrative and less time-consuming, like making a model of the Taj

Mahal out of toothpicks, you're a writer.

4) If you're questioning your worthiness to call yourself a writer—welcome to the club.

Don't give up because you don't have an agent yet, or your mother-in-law calls you a slacker who "sits around on your butt all day," or your mechanic keeps asking why you don't have the money to replace that clunker.

You're a writer. Go write.

PART 2

THE INEVITABILITY OF REJECTION

CATHERINE

EDITORS (ALSO APPLIES TO AGENTS IF YOU WANT IT TO)—WHAT IS THEIR PROBLEM?

WHAT IS IT WITH THESE EDITORS, ANYWAY?

They send form rejections. They don't deign to comment. Or they scribble a mortal wound of an insult. Or you hear nothing for nine months. Or your novel or story disappears entirely.

Who are these people? Don't they appreciate what we go through?

Years ago, I worked as an editorial assistant for a small literary journal. And more recently, for a regional commercial magazine. So let me ask you a question from another perspective: Do writers appreciate what an editor goes through?

Picture this: The "slush pile" is taller than I am. Half the submissions are from people who know little about their marketplace. Their stories belong in *Field & Stream* or *Cat Fancy*, not a journal that publishes only literary fiction. Most are awash with typos and punctuation errors. Often they arrive with no personalized cover letter—just a small strip of paper listing a few credits. I am to take half an hour of my life to read the submission. The author apparently wouldn't take five minutes to compose a letter addressing it to me.

I'm careful not to say anything kind, lest I receive a furious note that reads, "If you like it so much, why won't you publish it?"

Okay. You asked. So let me give you a few possible reasons.

We already have too many first-person stories for this issue. We ran a story about a dog last season. The Big Cheese editor is going through a messy divorce. Your story on divorce was swell. I don't want to show it to him. Do you?

Or, more likely, I've narrowed it down to six stories. And I have room for four. End of story.

That's the world of short fiction.

Now let's visit the world of novels, which is hard.

In this world, the agent's or editor's job is to second-guess what the public is or is not ready for, and how much money they will spend on it at a bookstore. And if they don't do their jobs well, they'll soon be looking for new ones.

But no pressure.

There is an element of good fortune involved in getting your story to the right editor on the right day. Learn your market well, and accept that your odds are better here than in the lottery—but not by much.

Then buy a lot of tickets.

ANNE

HOW TO DECREASE YOUR REJECTIONS ON A FIRST NOVEL: EIGHT DOS AND DON'TS

I'M NOT GOING TO LIE TO YOU: MOST FIRST NOVELS NEVER SEE PRINT. Editors call them "practice novels." Like any other profession, writing requires a long learning process. But there are a few things that will give your first novel a better chance in the marketplace. These are guidelines for getting traditionally published. But even if you self-publish, it's good to be aware of what's most likely to sell.

1) DO write in a genre that's being read. You may have always dreamed of writing a sweeping Micheneresque saga, a Zane Grey Western, or a stream-of-consciousness Kerouac ramble, but the sad truth is it's not likely to find a lot of readers. Publishing has fashion cycles.

I'm not telling you to follow every hot trend—what's sizzling now will be over by the time you've got the book finished—but do be aware of what might be a tough sell down the road. Read lots of book reviews. Be aware of what's selling and read, read, read.

NOTE: A number of genres that aren't popular with the big New York publishers may still be viable with a small publisher or have an audience in the indie world. This is true of some genres that have been oversaturated in recent years like Chick Lit and Vampire Romance or small-audience genres like Westerns. A rejection in one of these genres doesn't reflect the quality of the book in any way, but you'll probably have to look to smaller publishers.

2) DON'T write a novel that imitates a screenplay. If you're under 65, you probably have the TV screenplay format seared into your consciousness. This means that when you're writing a first novel, you have stuff to unlearn. In a novel, we don't have to rely so heavily on what the characters say. In fact, they often don't say what they're feeling at all. A reader perceives the action from INSIDE the head of the character/s rather than viewing it from OUTSIDE.

In a movie, we're peeping toms, watching the action through a camera lens; in a novel, we're experiencing it. A novel is a mindscape, not a landscape.

3) DO avoid an omniscient point of view or constant head-hopping. Choose fewer than three point-of-view characters and you'll save yourself a ton of grief later on. Omniscient and multiple points of view aren't "wrong" but they're old-fashioned and tough to do well. They tend to slow and confuse the reader and turn off agents because so many amateurs do them badly.

4) DON'T depend on a prologue to initiate tension. There's much debate about prologues in the publishing business, but a vast majority of agents and editors dislike them. Why shoot yourself in the font? (As the late Miss Snark would say.)

5) DO make sure your story has a protagonist and an antagonist. Sounds simple, but this is where most first novels fail. There has to be one main character. Equality is ideal in the real world, but in narrative, one person has to dominate. If another character walks in and tries to take over, tell her you'll put her in a short story later. Otherwise, change the focus of your novel. (Not always a bad idea. Sometimes we start with the wrong point-of-view character.)

And remember an antagonist isn't necessarily a mustache-twirling villain. It can be a situation, a disease, or society itself—anything strong enough to thwart your character for the whole narrative. You can't have a different antagonist for each scene. There has to be one big, major problem-maker to keep the story from being a series of episodes rather than one long narrative.

6) DON'T choose a protagonist who's easily satisfied. Your main character has to want something. Badly. Satisfied people make lovely companions in real life, but as soon as your characters get what they want, your story is over.

7) DO activate your inner sadist. Never let your characters get what they need. Throw as many obstacles into their path as possible. Hurt them. Maim them. Give them cruel parents and girlfriends who are preparing to kill them for alien lizard food. It's OK. You'll solve their problems in the end. Then won't you feel good?

**8) DON'T put something in a novel because "that's the way it

really happened." Even if your story is based on your own experiences, remember real life is mostly boring. That's why we read fiction.

NOTE: I'm not saying you shouldn't write fiction inspired by real life—that's what most writers do. Just don't tether the story to mundane facts, or you may avoid reaching more universal truths.

I based two of my novels on real episodes in my own life. *The Gatsby Game* is about a college boyfriend whose mysterious death on a movie set caused one of Hollywood's most notorious sex scandals, and *Sherwood Ltd.* is based on my misadventures publishing my first novel with some outlaw erotica publishers in the wilds of the English Midlands. Both stories took off in hilarious directions I never intended and have very little to do with the incidents that triggered them. But the writing gave me powerful insight into what really happened.

If I'd tried to stick to the facts, I don't think I would have been able to tell the underlying truth half so well.

CATHERINE

A REJECTION STORY

BETWEEN THE TIME I WROTE MY FIRST NOVEL (MY CRITIQUE GROUP didn't much like it) and the time I wrote my third novel (ditto), I was unable to interest an agent in my work. Sound like anybody you know?

I sent out about 25 queries with synopses and sample materials, just like they asked me to do. And I waited. And not one single one of those agents wanted to know anything more about me or my novels. They either were not accepting new clients (or claimed they were not) or were "unable to give my work the enthusiasm it so obviously deserved."

Right, I know. It's incomprehensible. It's not just you.

In an effort to batter down that brick wall, I decided I would market my own short fiction. Much easier. Right?

Over the next year or so, I received 122 rejections on about a dozen short stories. And no acceptances.

How did I keep going? A little bit of mentorship. A couple of authors in my critique group were much better published, and they said things like, "This happens to all authors," and "It's right around the corner for you."

Finally…finally, finally (did I mention that it was after a bit of a wait?), I received my first short story acceptance.

Five days later I received my second.

Nine days after that I received my third.

So, a year of nothing but rejection. Followed by three story acceptances in the span of two weeks. What does this say about the pattern of acceptance and rejection? So far as I know, nothing. There's not much to be said, because there really is no pattern. A lot of it is just the luck of the draw. Getting the right story to the right editor on the right day.

Here's the most important thing I want to tell you about my short story rejections: every one of those stories went on to find a home. And I did not rewrite them based on what each editor said.

It's a good thing I didn't, too.

That first acceptance was from a magazine called *South Dakota Review*, for my short story *Earthquake Weather*. *South Dakota Review* was a pretty darned good magazine for my first time out. Based in a reputable university, they'd been publishing stories for over 20 years.

Just before I sent *Earthquake Weather* to *South Dakota Review*, I got it back rejected from a magazine of much smaller reputation. It was called the *Belletrist Review*, may it rest in peace. They said they liked the story as a whole but felt there was a "hollowness" to the characters.

The editor at *South Dakota Review* was one of a very few who was nice enough to write an actual acceptance letter, telling me why he chose the story. He said I showed poise in the way I depicted the characters with brief brush strokes.

Hear what just happened?

The characters have a hollowness. The characters are depicted with brief brush strokes.

One editor took it for the same reason the other editor rejected it.

Now picture me getting it back from *Belletrist Review* and revising it. After all, I don't want the characters to be hollow. Then I send it to *South Dakota Review*, and the editor shakes his head. Because I've shown no poise in the way I depict the characters. Because I used far too many brush strokes.

Yes, I do mean to say you should not revise based on rejection. If you had a first date with someone who didn't fall madly in love with you, would you just keep changing yourself until they did? And, as a follow-up question, do you think they ever would?

You should fix a story if you agree that it's broken, but for no other reason.

In the meantime, just keep looking for someone who loves it for what it is.

Even if you have to weather 122 editors who don't.

CATHERINE

ANOTHER REJECTION STORY

THIS IS ONE OF MY BETTER REJECTION STORIES. I'M NOT PATTING myself on the back here. I'm not suggesting that I just love the way I tell this story. It's more that I have a rating system for rejection stories. The more they completely redefine rejection, the better I like them.

So this is a good one, in my opinion.

This is the one about the agent—not just any agent but *my* agent at the time—who rejected *Pay It Forward*.

I was already under contract with her for *Walter's Purple Heart*, which she had sent out many times, to many rejections. I had already shown her *Funerals for Horses* (to which she responded, "I love this, but it doesn't work." I'd shed light on that comment if I had any). And now, contractually, I had to show her *Pay It Forward* when I finished writing it.

But I should mention that I had another agent at the time. Yes, another one. You see, technically, if my agent passes on a novel, I have a right to seek representation for it elsewhere. And I had been approached by a younger, newer, hungrier agent who had read one of my stories in a small literary magazine. Agent #2 was enthusiastic about representing me. Enough so to be willing to take on *Funerals for Horses* without first right of refusal on any of my other works. And Agent #1 confirmed, with only the slightest prickle in her tone, that so long as I was doing so with full disclosure, I did have that right.

What could possibly go wrong?

Ever heard it said that an author's relationship with an agent is something like a marriage? I always took it to mean that you plunge in thinking life will be beautiful from here on out and in less than a year you've deteriorated into arguing over who has to take out the trash. To the extent that having an agent is something like having a spouse, having two agents is a bit like bigamy. You spend a lot of time telling one or the other that she is the only one you truly love, that the other agent means nothing to you. (It was one book. It meant nothing.) As my relationship with Agent #1 began to fray, I could always make Agent #2 laugh by saying, "My other agent doesn't understand me."

Of course, I wanted to give *Pay It Forward* to my agent who understood me. But I couldn't. She didn't have the "first right of refusal" contract.

I mailed the manuscript to Agent #1 and waited. She called me and left a message. It said, "We need to talk."

Have you ever noticed that after people say, "We need to talk," they never go on to share any good news? Ever? I've noticed that. And I thought maybe you had, too.

I wish she had sent me this in a letter. I would have saved it. And we'd have a merry little laugh over it now.

Short version: she hated it.

She asked me why all the people in it had to be "so awful." I told her I didn't think Trevor, Reuben and Arlene were awful. She admitted that perhaps awful was the wrong word, but noted that everybody had something wrong with them. They all had problems. (Unlike life, I was thinking, where nobody ever has any issues.) She asked me why nice people couldn't pay it forward to other nice people. (Should I even comment? No. Too easy.)

She got angry because she said I wasn't listening to her suggestions on taking it apart and putting it back together. She was right. I wasn't. Because I knew I wasn't going to take it apart and put it back together. Because I didn't think it was broken.

I asked her to send it, and *Walter's Purple Heart*, back home to me. And I gave them to Agent #2, who had never sold anybody's first fiction. She went on to make me her first. She and her partner-husband sold my first five novels and three movie deals—including selling *Pay It Forward* to Simon & Schuster and Warner Brothers films—without revision.

Maybe you think the point of the story is that Agent #1 was wrong. But the point of the story is that there really is no right and wrong in fiction. She didn't like it. That's her prerogative. But I'm awfully glad I didn't believe her, get discouraged, and slide it into a drawer.

Next time you get a rejection, picture the manuscript of *Pay It Forward* gathering dust in one of my desk drawers. And assume that the next person you ask may offer a wildly different opinion.

ANNE

HOW TO DECREASE YOUR REJECTIONS ON A MEMOIR: 12 DOS AND DON'TS

THEY SAY WE ALL HAVE A BOOK INSIDE US—OUR OWN LIFE STORY. THE urge to put that story on paper is the most common reason people start writing. Adult education programs and senior centers everywhere offer courses in "writing your own life." Memoir is the most popular genre at any writers' conference.

Unfortunately, it's the hardest to write well—and the least likely to be published.

Agent Kristin Nelson blogged that she's seen so many bad memoirs that she avoids pitches from memorists whenever possible. Author J. A. Konrath once offered the simple advice: "Unless you're one of the Rolling Stones, don't write anything autobiographical." The legendary agent who blogged as "Miss Snark" pronounced, "every editor and agent I know HATES memoir pitches...I'd rather shave the cat."

But memoirs like *Eat, Pray, Love, Gypsy Boy,* and *The Rules of Inheritance* top the bestseller lists.

In this age of "reality" TV, there's a huge audience for shared real-life experience. Readers are hungry for true stories: look how angrily they reacted to writers like James Frey and Herman Rosenblat, who passed off fiction as memoir.

So keep working on that masterpiece-in-progress. But hone your craft—brilliant wordsmithing and/or stand-up worthy comedy skills help a bunch—and follow some basic dos and don'ts:

1) DO read other memoirs. Before you put pen to paper, it's a good idea to read some currently selling memoirs. See what works and what doesn't. Know the genre and the market

2) DON'T write an autobiography. An autobiography is a list of events: "I was born in (year) in (place) and I did (this) and (that.)" Konrath is right—unless you're Mick Jagger, nobody cares. (Except your family. Don't let me discourage you from self-publishing a chronicle of your life as a gift to your descendants.)

3) DO tell a page-turning story. A book-length memoir is read and marketed as a novel. It needs a novel's narrative drive. That means tension and conflict—and ONE main story arc to drive the action. Most memoirs fail from lack of focus. Choose a basic storyline, like: "Orphan kids save the family farm during the Depression," or "A cross-dressing teen survives high school in the 1950s."

4) DON'T confuse memoir with psychotherapy. Writing a book about a traumatic personal event may be cathartic for the writer, but there's a reason shrinks charge big bucks to listen to this stuff. Put the raw material in a journal to mine later for fiction, poetry, and personal essays.

5) DO remember that a memoirist, like a novelist, is essentially an entertainer. A memoir may be nonfiction, but it requires a creative writer's skill set. Always keep your reader in mind. Never fabricate, but only tell what's unique, exciting and relevant to your premise.

6) DON'T expect a big audience for medical journaling. If you or a loved one has a serious disease, chronicling your experiences can be invaluable to those suffering similar trials. To the general public— not so much. You may find it's best to reach your audience through online forums, blogs, and magazines (See #7). Remember that publishing is a business, and no matter how sad your story, if it's not an enjoyable read, it won't find an audience.

7) DO consider non-book formats to tell your story. Beginning writers often make the mistake of jumping into a book-length opus. It's smarter and easier to start with short pieces—what a writer/editor friend calls "memoiric essays." Nostalgia and senior-oriented magazines and blogs are great venues for tales of life in the old days. Some niche journals and websites focusing on hobbies, pets, disabilities, veterans, etc. even provide a paying market. These will also give you some great publishing credits, and you won't have to slog for years before reaching an audience.

This is one area where a blog can provide you with a fantastic forum. Consider blogging your book and monetizing the blog, rather than trying to sell a book in the crowded marketplace.

8) DON'T include every detail because "it's what really happened." Just because something is true doesn't mean it's interesting. Your happy memories of that idyllic Sunday school picnic in vanished small-town America will leave your reader comatose unless the church caught fire, you lost your virginity, and/or somebody stole the parson's pants.

9) DO limit the story to an area where your experience is significant and unique. If you gave birth in the mud at Woodstock, dated Elvis, or helped decipher the Enigma code, make that the focus of your book. I knew a musician who worked with some of the great legends of American music. His memoir of those jazzy days was gripping, but because it was buried in his "happy ever after" life story, he never found a publisher.

10) DON'T jump into the publishing process until you've honed your skills as a creative writer. Unless you're only writing for your grandchildren (nothing wrong with that—but be clear in your intentions), you need to become an accomplished writer before you can expect non-family members to read you work. Even the most skilled editor can't turn a series of reminiscences into a cohesive narrative.

NOTE: There are ghostwriters who specialize in memoirs, so if you want to get your story into book form and aren't interested in becoming a writer, you can hire a professional. Many editing services offer ghostwriting—a much more expensive process than editing— but worth the cost if you don't have expertise in writing narrative.

11) DO look at small and regional publishers. A national publisher may not be interested in stories of the vanished ranch life of old California, but a local publisher who has outlets at tourist sites and historical landmarks may be actively looking for them. Another plus: you don't need an agent to approach most regional publishers.

12) DON'T get discouraged. You're not alone. It's hard to interest Big Publishing in a memoir, but many memoirists find success with self-publishing. Start by building an audience online with a blog or other social media and network with other writers in your demographic. They'll give you the feedback and encouragement you need. These days, no writer needs to feel isolated.

If you're working on a memoir, do these three things and you'll avoid the cringe-making amateurishness that agents, editors and readers fear:

1) **Polish your creative writing skills.**

2) **Remember publishing is a business.**

3) **Always keep your reader in mind.**

CATHERINE

YET ANOTHER REJECTION STORY

HERE COMES ANOTHER REJECTION STORY.

It's the story of my first short fiction acceptance.

Right. I know what you're thinking. Then this should be an acceptance story. Shouldn't it now? No. It's a rejection story. Trust me.

I already told you a little bit about my first short story acceptance. It was South Dakota Review. It was submission number 123.

Here's what I haven't told you yet:

The last story I'd sent to *South Dakota Review* had been returned with a written rejection so mean, so vile, so dismissive, that my plan was never to send them another story again as long as I live. (Which is proving to be a long time.)

It was a note from a woman editor whose name I have blessedly (and probably quite purposefully) forgotten. But I still remember the note.

45

Every. Single. Word.

"First sentence decision in the negative. You have the wrong market here."

Now, you're smart. And you can probably catch the full import of that all on your own, without needing me to translate for you. But let's compare translations anyway, just for fun.

She said she only read one sentence of my story, and, based on all that information, was asking never to hear from me again.

Is that what you heard? Yeah. Me, too.

Oooh. Oooh. Oooh. I fumed. I paced. I mumbled to myself. I was right ticked.

I scratched the *South Dakota Review* off my submission list so hard I went through the paper. As far as I was concerned, there was no literary journal by that name. I lived in a happy—if somewhat artificial—world, quite thoroughly lacking any such publication.

I can't say for a fact how long this went on. Maybe three weeks.

Then I woke up one morning, and it hit me.

That's not me. That's not the way I do things. I'm petulant. I'm pathologically stubborn. It's part of my charm, to phrase things in the best possible way. In any case, I'm stuck with it.

I sent them another story, "Earthquake Weather." And I didn't duck what had happened, either. Right up front, in my cover letter, I said, "Enclosed please find my short story, 'Earthquake Weather.' If you still think I have the wrong market in the *South Dakota Review*, I won't ask you to read more."

About six weeks later I received my first acceptance. From the *South Dakota Review*.

The moral of the story, on the off chance you haven't caught it already, is that tenacity counts. Also neatness. But I'd give higher points for tenacity. Talent is also helpful. But tenacity without talent will get you a lot farther than talent without tenacity. If you don't believe me, read some airport bestsellers.

Non-pathologically-stubborn individuals need not apply.

CATHERINE

THE ULTIMATE REJECTION STORY

THIS IS THE ONE I CONSIDER TO BE MY ULTIMATE REJECTION STORY.

Each of these stories is meant to illuminate rejection, to show that it doesn't mean what you think it means. At first you think it means the work is no good, you're not a good writer. But then how can you reconcile the fact that my short stories were rejected an average of 17 ½ times each before going on to find a good home (without further revision)? Okay, so then you figure the work may be good, but you're trying to place it with the wrong publisher. But if that were true, I wouldn't have placed my first short story with the same magazine that issued my most vicious rejection.

Now, hopefully, you're almost where you need to be, thinking rejection really only means that this particular editor won't publish this particular work. Hold onto your socks for what comes next: It doesn't even mean that much.

Remember the agent who marketed *Walter's Purple Heart* to no avail (25 rejections!) and wouldn't even take on *Pay It Forward*? Remember how I told her to send both home to me, and then gave them to my newer, hungrier agent?

Agent #2 sold *Pay It Forward* to Chuck Adams at Simon & Schuster, who then immediately asked what else I might have. Out of the drawer came *Walter's Purple Heart*. He bought it in a six-figure deal right before Christmas.

Why is that a good rejection story? Because one of *Walter's Purple Heart's* 25 previous rejections was from...wait for it...Chuck Adams at Simon & Schuster.

And he knew it.

His statement on why: He said Simon & Schuster had changed. They didn't used to let him take on the smaller, more literary works. Now they did.

My statement on why: My career had changed. A book he might not have successfully marketed as a debut could be much more saleable as a follow-up to *Pay It Forward*.

So there you go. The true story of rejection. It doesn't even necessarily mean that any one particular editor won't buy that work of fiction. It just means he (or she) chose not to buy it *on that day*. Later, things can change: reader tastes, the book industry, or your name recognition.

Here's a final question before I move on from the subject of rejection.

I once received a plain, printed rejection on my story "Nicky Be Thy Name" from a small literary journal. But they accepted the next story I sent. In a phone conversation with the editor, he remembered "Nicky," and referred to it, saying he'd come within "a hair's breadth" of taking it.

Now, I hadn't known that. He hadn't said. I'd just figured he didn't like it.

When we get a rejection back in the mail, we usually don't know the process the work has gone through. We don't know if one paragraph was read by an editorial assistant (translation: first reader, probably straight out of college) or if our work made the rounds of all editors and survived everything but the final cut.

Here's the question:

Why do we always assume the editor(s) hated it, that we have been branded as hacks? Why don't we ever assume that it came within "a hair's breadth" of acceptance, and is being returned with deep regret?

PART 3

GETTING USEFUL FEEDBACK

ANNE

CRITIQUE GROUPS AND BETA READERS

THERE ARE A LOT OF WAYS TO STUDY WRITING. YOU CAN TAKE CLASSES, go to workshops and conferences, join critique groups and online forums. Or read a lot of books like this. Or immerse yourself in writing blogs. They will all teach you lots of good stuff.

But there's only one way to learn to write well.

Write.

Regularly. You don't necessarily have to write every day, as the classic rule prescribes, but you have to do it for years: Gladwell's 10,000 hours. Yeah. Sorry. It's the only way. And you can't do it in a vacuum. The only way to find out if what you're doing is working is to find readers who can critique intelligently without squashing your dreams. I know—easier said than done.

A "beta" reader is simply a person who reads your manuscript after the "alpha"—that would be you—has finished reading it over. I've seen all sorts of complicated stuff on the Internet about alpha, beta, kappa and all manner of Greek readers, but when most people talk about beta readers, they mean a careful reader you can trust to give feedback on a work in progress. This can be a professional editor-for-hire, a friend, or a writing buddy you meet online. The term comes originally from SciFi fan fiction but now has been adopted by the whole industry. Anyone can be a beta, but it's wise to choose yours carefully.

Family and close friends are not the best choice. Your primary relationship with them will usually color their comments. A family member will either be terrified of telling you anything is wrong, or slash it to bits because she wants to look smart.

...or because you forgot her birthday last year.

...or you told him those pants *did* make his butt look fat.

It's very hard for a person who is close to you to be objective.

The best reader is a fellow writer—and you'll probably get the best help from writers in your own genre. Joining a genre-specific club like RWA, SCBWI or Sisters in Crime is a great way to meet possible critiquers.

Other great beta-hunting grounds are online writers' forums like Nathan Bransford's or Kristen Lamb's We Are Not Alone (myWANA.) Or use a social networking site to advertise for one.

I'd generally advise against asking non-writers, unless they read a lot in your genre and are capable of being objective but diplomatic. A reader needs to have some knowledge of the writing process to be able to critique a first draft.

And never, ever ask your spouse or significant other. The only thing a wise spouse can say after reading your work is "Great! Wonderful! You know I love everything you do and say, sugarbearloveofmylife." Anything else is likely to take you down a dark road. I speak from experience here.

CATHERINE

MAKING SENSE OF CRITICISM

YOU MAY RECALL THAT MY FIRST SHORT STORY ACCEPTANCE PRAISED the way I "depicted the characters with brief brush strokes," while same story had just been rejected by another magazine because of the "hollowness" of the characters.

One story was accepted with such enthusiasm that the editor thanked me for sending it to his magazine, citing such work as his reason for being an editor. He went on to nominate it for *Best American Short Stories*, the O. Henry award and the Pushcart Prize. The last editor to have read the same story rejected it, saying it did not hold the reader's interest and was told, not shown.

When my novel *Pay It Forward* came out, *Time* Magazine called my dialogue tinny and my characters stunted. *The Chicago Tribune* called my dialogue believable and my characters well-drawn.

It starts the day you join a critique group, it intensifies when you get an agent. Every time your agent sends out the work, the rejections get more confusing. One editor says it's too this, the other says it's too that. In the face of such conflicting opinions, what do you keep and what do you throw away?

I like to say that you must never, ever, under any circumstances, change your work just because someone tells you to...unless, of course, they're right.

The writers in the group usually laugh. Because, of course, knowing who is right was the problem to begin with. I can't sum up this thorny situation in a handful of words and make it all come clear. But I can offer a few ideas for consideration:

1) There is no "right" and "wrong" concerning art or creativity. Everyone's opinion is just that. An opinion. I despise the work of Ernest Hemingway. If I had been a contemporary, I might well have told Papa not to quit his day job. Would he have been wise to accept my opinion as fact?

2) Lichtenberg said, "A book is a mirror; if an ass peers into it, don't expect an apostle to peer out." This is not cited to characterize those who disagree with you, only to make the point that people bring their own experiences and perceptions to your work. You can't stop them. No two people will have the same experience with what you write.

3) Our egos tend to dictate that all the advice given us regarding our work is wrong. This is what I like to call the "You just don't get it" syndrome. Sometimes that same advice sounds a lot saner and more workable a few days later. In a critique situation, it helps to write down everything that's said and sleep on it for awhile.

4) Try saying nothing when faced with advice. When you begin to argue you stop listening. Even if the person really is saying stupid things, arguing will only make him or her say more stupid things. Right or wrong, just listen.

5) Your reader is important. If your reader doesn't get it, you're not done. Then again there will always be someone who doesn't get it. If it's one in ten, you can't please everybody. If it's nine in ten, it's time to listen.

6) Important as your readers are, their names do not go on the finished product. It is your own sensibility that you ultimately have to please. No matter how strongly someone disagrees with the direction of your work, it must remain your work, or you've lost everything worth having.

One of the biggest breakthroughs I ever had was when I learned to stop saying, "Is it good or is it bad?" and switched to, "What is the market for this? Who would like this kind of work?"

Dealing with the opinions of others is, in my estimation, the hardest part of being a writer. I don't know that anything I've said makes it all that much easier. But there's a question you can ask yourself at times such as these, and the answer will tell you everything you need to know. The catch is that you have to ask it on a deep level and answer honestly.

The question is, "Do I agree?"

When you can answer that question honestly, a great deal of initial confusion will fall away. When you base changes—or the refusal to make changes—on that answer, you will be honoring your reader, your work and yourself.

ANNE

BEWARE THE AUHORITY OF IGNORANCE: BAD ADVICE TO IGNORE FROM YOUR CRITIQUE GROUP OR BETA READER

ALTHOUGH READERS OR CRITIQUE GROUPS ARE ESSENTIAL TO YOUR development as a writer, it's important to remember not all the advice you'll hear will be useful. As Victoria Strauss says on the Writer Beware blog, "never forget that people who know nothing are as eager to opine as people who know something."

Even worse than know-nothings are the know-somethings who turn every bit of advice they've ever heard into a "rule" as ironclad and immutable as an algebraic formula. Follow their advice and your book will read like an algebraic formula, too. They have what John Steinbeck called "the authority of ignorance."

"I am never shy about it when a professional is doing the reading. But God save me from amateurs. They don't know what they are reading but it is much more serious than that. They immediately start rewriting. I never knew this to fail. It is invariable. They have the authority of ignorance, something you simply cannot combat."

Here are a few critique group "rules" I find more annoying than useful:

1) Eliminate all clichés. Unless your characters are wildly inventive poets, space aliens, or children fostered by wolves, their dialogue and thoughts will include familiar expressions. Don't rob your Scarlett O'Hara of her "fiddle dee-dees" or deprive your Bogart of "doesn't amount to a hill of beans."

2) More! Make it vivid! Would we really improve *Casablanca* with "a hill of Moroccan garbanzos, yellow-pale and round, of the kind the English call chick-peas."

3) Avoid repetition. Beware what H.W. Fowler called "elegant variation".

OK: "It was a good bull, a strong bull, a bull bred to fight to the death."

NOT: "It was a good bull, a strong animal, a male creature of the bovine persuasion bred to do battle..."

4) Eradicate the verb "to be," especially in the past tense. People seem to believe "was" is the enemy.

It's true that it's generally wise to avoid the passive voice, which uses "was" in the past tense:

"The cat was laundered by me" is passive and sounds lame.

"I laundered the cat" is active and stronger.

But sometimes the passive voice makes the clearest statement: "The cat was abused."

Real problems arise when amateurs confuse passive voice with the progressive tense, which also uses "to be" (with the present participle.) These two sentences mean very different things:

"I was just sitting there when the cat owner punched me."

"I just sat there when the cat owner punched me."

Eliminating "was" changes meaning instead of "strengthening."

5) Put your protagonist's thoughts in italics. When you write in the third-person-limited viewpoint, it's read like first person: no italics or "he thought/she thought" necessary.

"I walked away from the 'In Crowd'. They were just a bunch of ill-bred alley cats," can be changed to third person with just a switch of pronoun/noun: "Pufferball walked away from the 'In Crowd'. They were just a bunch of ill-bred alley cats."

6) Characters must behave predictably. Don't let anyone tell you a character "wouldn't" behave in a certain way. Only the writer knows if this particular truck driver would read Proust, this bride would run off with the florist's mother, or that Maine Coon cat would pee in your Jimmy Choos.

7) Describe characters in detail. When your English teacher told you to beef up that "Summer Vacation" essay with colorful descriptions of Uncle Louie, she was looking for a complete page, not preparing you for publication. Brevity is now and ever shall be the soul of wit. The only thing Jane Austen told us about Elizabeth Bennett's appearance was that she had "fine eyes.")

8) Protagonists must be admirable. Ignore comments about your characters "morals." Saints are boring in fiction, unless they liberate France and get burned at the stake, and that's been done.

9) If we don't point out everything wrong, we're not doing our job. A group should tell you what's right with a work as well as what's wrong. No one can hear endless negativity. The brain shuts down to protect itself.

Even so-called professional resources aren't always reliable—the writing and editing question forums at LinkedIn, supposedly a place for business and professional networking, are absolute pits of bad advice and misinformation—and as for writers' message boards, always keep Ms. Strauss's dictum in mind: *"people who know nothing are as eager to opine as people who know something."*

I'm lucky to live in an area where we have a writing organization that is an umbrella for many critique groups, so finding the right group is relatively easy. Libraries and bookstores are the best place to look if you want an in-person group. There are also a growing number of groups online. Or if you want to work with a series of one-on-one beta readers, there are forums where you can meet other writers looking for first readers.

CATHERINE

THE CARE AND FEEDING OF CRITIQUERS' AGENDAS

Each and every person who comments on your work has a personal agenda. This is not to say that anybody has a conscious agenda to change the course of your writing for personal gain/satisfaction. More that nobody does anything without an agenda, conscious or not. If you are being critiqued by a writer, then the agenda springs from the way this person critiques him- or herself. In other words, a writer is so used to directing his or her own work as to tend to direct your work in the same...well, direction. If you are being critiqued by a non-writing reader, the agenda is basically what that person likes to read. That is, personal taste. Which is not always relevant to you as the author. Ideally, you would first achieve a match in the personal taste department, then go on to see what misses with this person who is generally on board with your kind of fiction.

There are advantages to both (writer/reader). A reader will

generally approach your work with less concrete agenda. Then again, they may identify weaknesses without being able to provide specifics or advice. That is, they may say a certain portion of the book dragged for them, but a writer can say that if you edit out certain unnecessary portions and lose the passive verb tenses you can create a much faster pacing. This is how they (hopefully) pay you back for all that agenda.

Another strong factor of agenda is opinion/life experience. A staunch feminist will have a very different opinion of your book than would an old-school male Republican. Don't bother to try to point out such prejudices. You will not be heard. The important thing to know about agenda is that the owner of the agenda has no idea it exists.

So, as an old spiritual teacher of mine used to say, "Don't spook the locals."

If you pay attention, you can learn a lot about your critics as they ostensibly comment on what they think is about you. A classic example would be my novel *Electric God* (called *The Hardest Part of Love* in the U.K.). Lots of readers adored Hayden, no matter what he did, which included a good bit of breaking of jaws. Others refused to forgive him, even after he forgave others and himself. The latter tells me that the reader is an unforgiving person. It was also clear from reader comments which readers had been victims of angry males in the past. It would be nice if you could get the reader to put aside such life experiences, but they can't, and even if they could, they wouldn't on principle.

Occasionally an agenda will spill over into a more obvious transgression we call "critiquing on content." An example would be if someone tells you, "Oh, but that's so violent," or, "I find that offensive." Life is often violent, and art reflects life. And any book incapable of offending someone isn't worth the time it takes to read it.

A really good editor will identify what he or she feels are weaknesses in the work, but not how they are to be repaired. If they suggest how it should be written instead, they are doing the job of the author, and leaving too many fingerprints on the work. Better to help the author understand what needs fixing and why. Then the author can sleep on those thoughts and come up with a fix completely in keeping with the creative style. A bad editor will actually go through and arbitrarily change sentence length, punctuation, word choice. In other words, rewrite the piece to be more in keeping with how he or she would have written it. A good editor knows that how he or she would have written it is quite irrelevant.

In a looser critique situation, such as a workshop, a good teacher or participant will listen to get an idea of what you are trying to accomplish with the piece. Then the critique will ideally be based on helping you sharpen the effectiveness. In other words, to make it a better example of what they think you're trying to do. But this is only an ideal, because what they think you're trying to do will always be filtered through...yeah, you got it—their agenda.

I'll cite two great examples of teachers I've had (who shall remain nameless). Both are old friends of mine.

One is a deeply religious man who, in his fifties, never had sex with his second wife when they were dating. Only after marriage. Yet you can read him a piece about a pregnant nun in a leather bar, and he'll try to get you closer to what he thinks you want to achieve.

The other is just the opposite, a brilliant, intolerant man who dismisses work that's not to his fairly narrow tastes.

I wish you could see them in action. You'd understand so much.

You might think sometime about adding a different critique group or conference, to read your work to a brand new group. You'll be surprised to learn that even a group can have an agenda.

Other than that, there's nothing special I expect you to do with all this information. Just sleep on it and let it in and see if it clarifies anything. I hope any or all of it helps.

ANNE

EVERYBODY'S A CRITIC

EARLY INTO OUR JOURNEYS IN WORDSMITHING, MOST WRITERS discover our chosen art form has a major drawback: everybody's a critic.

For some reason, folks who happily offer praise to fledgling musicians, quilters, sculptors, or Star Trek action-figurine painters feel compelled to launch into scathing critiques of the efforts of the creative writer.

I remember showing an early story to a boyfriend. He returned the manuscript covered with red-penciled "corrections"—changing characters' names, dialogue, and much of the plot. The man wasn't a writer or even much of a reader, so I asked why he felt the need to edit my story.

He said, "What else would I do with it?"

I said, "The same thing I do when you show me your woodworking projects—say something nice."

He looked at me as if I were speaking Klingon.

Even years of professional writing credits don't deter a compulsive critic. Recently, a visual artist who's always e-mailing me .jpgs of her latest work—which I dutifully download and praise—asked me about my latest project. I sent her the first chapter. She replied with a 100% negative critique.

Maybe this behavior is perpetrated by those grade-school teachers who had us read aloud our poems about "What Thanksgiving Means to Me," and invited class comments—which often devolved into verbal spitball attacks. I don't remember the same free-for-all judging sessions for our construction-paper Pilgrim hats or renditions of "Over the River and Through the Woods." Maybe some grade-school teacher can tell me why.

Gratuitous criticism is often so clueless we can laugh and ignore it. It can even be helpful. An untrained eye can sometimes help us look at problems in a new way.

But if it's derisive, hostile and/or entirely lacking in praise, energize your deflector shields. It has nothing to do with your work and everything to do with the "critic." An amazing number of people, even decades out of adolescence, still think negativity sounds smart. But it's good to remember that any Homer Simpson can look at a Picasso and say, "My two-year-old paints better than that!"

Appreciation takes education.

We do need feedback. If you don't have an editor or trusted beta reader, find a good critique group, preferably writers in your own genre. A good critique is a gift. You know when you hear one. It may sting, but it gives you an "ah-ha" moment that improves your work. Good critiquers know "not my cuppa" shouldn't be expressed as "your story sux."

Plus they'll always give positive comments to balance the

negative. Nobody can take undiluted criticism. The brain registers it as an attack, which triggers a fight or flight response.

Here are some suggestions for dealing with self-appointed critics:

1) Avoid showing first drafts to non-writers.

2) Consider the source. If Mr. Judgmental hasn't read anything but *TV Guide* since he dropped out of Bounty Hunter school, this is not his field of expertise. (And keep in mind what Catherine says: "Each and every person who comments on your work has a personal agenda.")

3) If someone asks to see unpublished work, be clear you aren't inviting critique. Say something like, "My editor prefers that nobody else edit my material. However, I'll be happy to hear about what you enjoy, and please let me know if you catch any typos."

4) Give the critic a sweet smile while plotting her murder in your next novel.

5) Think of this as practice for when you're successful enough to be reviewed by snarky professional critics.

6) If something feels like verbal abuse, consider the possibility that it is. Ask yourself if the critic is:

a) Feeling neglected. Writers can be selfish with our time. Take him out for coffee and catch up.

b) A writer-wannabe: she's dying to write, but too terrified/blocked/lazy. Envy makes people mean.

c) A narcissistic bully. Writers are magnets for them. We pay attention, which is what they crave—and we're solitary, which makes us easy prey. They lure us with praise and fascinating stories, keep us enslaved with threats and/or self-pity, then try to erase our personalities and make us mirrors for their reflected glory. They will do or say anything to destroy a victim's sense of self. Remember that nothing a verbal abuser says has value. Win a Pulitzer, and you'll hear, "What, no Nobel?" You'll never please them by doing better, because nothing pleases them but having power over you.

Good criticism is necessary to any art form, but the unsolicited, negative variety is poison. If comments are unhelpful, ignore them and boldly warp into the next galaxy.

CATHERINE

THE CRITIQUE GROUP'S OWNER'S MANUAL

THESE ARE RULES THAT ALL CRITIQUE GROUPS SHOULD KNOW AND practice to avoid damaged egos, shattered friendships, and the occasional fistfight.

In general:

1) **All egos should be checked at the door.** Hah! Easy, right? Okay, it's impossible. But try. Your critique may carry more weight than anyone else's if it's highly insightful. But your publication credits don't always translate into better suggestions for others. And by the way, this rule also applies to those with abnormally small egos. If you feel like everybody in the world knows better than you, check that at the door as well.

2) **Always establish, before joining a critique group, that its**

members like to read what you like to write. I could elaborate, but I'm hoping this one speaks for itself.

When reading:

3) As an old critique group colleague of mine used to say, "Shut up and read." I would encourage you both to practice this rule and to phrase it more delicately. Why are you prefacing Chapter 1 with all sorts of explanation? You won't be in the agent's office as he or she begins to read, and you sure as hell can't be in every book store that agrees to order it. So it had better be on the page. If it's not, give up on repairing it through verbal explanation.

4) Give the work what's called a "flat reading." Don't act it out with voices, action or dramatics. Just read what's on the page. If you can't avoid dramatics, give your work to someone else to read.

When hearing critique:

5) Cultivate the phrase, "Duly noted." As I've surely mentioned, arguing with someone who is saying stupid things will only inspire him or her to say more stupid things. Write it all down. If it doesn't warrant writing down, write down the person's name with the notation, "Consider the source." As long as they're not close enough to read your notes, it really doesn't matter. This leaves them with the sense that you are giving their advice the consideration it deserves. Only you need to know how much consideration you feel it deserves.

6) Don't argue back. Ever. At all. Once you do, you've stopped listening. Plus, back to rule #3. You won't be there in the bookstore or the reader's home to explain why you wrote that scene the way you did. Never say, "But it really happened!" when someone says an element of your story didn't ring true. It doesn't matter if it happened. You are being told it doesn't ring true.

On the other hand, groups that literally don't allow the author to speak at all may be going too far. If Harry from your critique group says he's confused by the sudden presence of a new character, you should be able to say the character was introduced in the chapter you read while Harry was out with the flu. A question as to what you intended the reader to think or know or feel at this juncture is acceptable, and you should be able to answer. But I wouldn't take it much further than that.

7) Don't decide yet. Sleep on all the advice you receive. Advice almost never sounds right when you first hear it. Write it all down and let it simmer for a couple of weeks. I'm famous for thinking, "Sure, I see that person's point, but there's just no other way to do it." Then, eleven days later, I'm lying in bed just before rising, and there it is. Another way to do it.

8) Bottom line: you are looking for the suggestions you know in your heart are right. This is not easy. I suggest cultivating a good working relationship with your heart.

When critiquing:

9) Though you don't literally need to say it straight out, every time, in these exact words, you really only have the right to say, "If this were my work, the following is what I would change." Also, please bear in mind at all times that *it's not.*

10) Practice the Golden Workshop Rule. Critique others as you would have others critique you.

ANNE

ON WRITERS' CONFERENCES

LITERARY/WRITING CONFERENCES CAN BE FOUND ALL OVER THE world. From venerable institutions like the Adelaide Writers' Week in Australia or The Times Cheltenham Conference in the U.K., to the hip multi-arts "Istancool" in Turkey, they are places for authors and readers to meet and greet and learn what's happening in the world of books.

American and Canadian conferences tend to focus primarily on educating aspiring writers. They involve formal university-level writing classes as well as readings and talks by successful authors. The oldest is probably the Bread Loaf conference at Middlebury College in Vermont, founded in part by the poet Robert Frost in 1926.

In recent years the teaching conference has spread throughout the world, and is often recommended as a way to get a foot in the door of the publishing industry—which is an increasingly international business these days.

At some of the bigger conferences you'll even get a chance to book a personal pitch session with an agent.

Whether they're held in idyllic settings like San Miguel de Allende or big urban hubs like Paris or San Francisco, they provide an educational opportunity and an exciting, vibrant atmosphere where you can learn the latest publishing trends, hang with your peers, and meet successful authors, agents, and publishers.

For a hefty fee.

There's the rub. When you combine the cost of travel, hotel and the conference itself, these lovely retreats are not cheap.

So should you go? Are conferences a shortcut to publishing success? Are they worth the money?

Most agents do recommend them. Many suggest attending a conference or two before even sending a query. In fact they often mention them in form rejection letters, urging writers to "learn about the publishing business by attending a writers' conference."

(I found those a little annoying when I was querying my Mystery *Ghostwriters in the Sky*, which is a satire of writers' conferences. I stated clearly in my query that I'd attended nearly a dozen. Form rejections are the pits).

The conferences I've attended were worthwhile, for the most part, and I'd recommend them to other aspiring writers. However, I need to make it clear the conferences did NOT land me an agent or publisher.

Most agents will admit they don't discover many new clients through conference "pitch" sessions, especially when the pitch comes from the next stall in the ladies' room. (Don't do this.)

What I got out of my experiences was solid instruction in the basics of the industry. I also received some painful reality checks and a couple of ego boosts. But for me, the major benefit was networking with fellow writers. A random sampling of writing blogs suggests that's the general experience. Ours is a lonely profession. Connecting with others of our species keeps us grounded.

If you're thinking about attending a conference, choose carefully. Some of the best known are more like fantasy camps for Scott and Zelda wannabes than training grounds for professional writers.

I've heard it's cleaned up its act, but the oldest and most revered conference, Vermont's Bread Loaf—which rejects 78% of applicants—is also known as "Bed Loaf" for a reason. In a famous 2001 article for *The New Yorker*, Rebecca Mead said, "The triple compulsions of Bread Loaf have, traditionally, been getting published, getting drunk, and getting laid."

Unless you're looking for a party-hearty getaway or an excuse for an exotic vacation, I'd recommend avoiding big-name conferences and starting small. The most cost-effective are weekend conferences offered at many colleges and universities. You may even find one close enough to home that you don't have to pay for lodging.

Most writers I know get more out of conferences that concentrate on their specific genre, not the national award-centered extravaganzas, but smaller workshops sponsored by regional chapters of national organizations like RWA and SCBWI.

But all conferences can have their dark side. I do know people who have had really bad experiences. There's a lot of stress from the overload of information and activities, plus you're likely to run into know-it-all bullies and dream-squashers.

Wear your psychological armor, remember what we've said about critiquers and their agendas, and heed the following tips:

1) DON'T dress to impress. At one conference I attended, a woman came dressed as a tree. Shedding real leaves. Don't do this. Also, dressing as one of your characters WILL get you noticed, but not in a good way. Wear neat but comfy clothes. (No high heels—

you'll thank me.) The days will be long and intense. Try wearing a distinctive scarf, hat, or jacket every day that will help people remember you.

2) **DO Google the presenters** and learn as much about them as you can so you'll have good subjects for conversation if you have a chance to chat. (Don't pitch your project unless you're in a specified pitch session!) But it's smart to offer to get a presenter a cup of coffee or ask how she's enjoying the conference. It will give you great material for your query letter.

3) **DON'T expect to get representation at a conference.** It does happen in rare cases, but it won't 99.9% of the time it doesn't.

4) **DO get business cards printed** if you don't have any yet. They are essential for networking. Something that can be helpful—if requested—is what's called a "one sheet". It's mostly a convention in the Christian book world, but it's useful for any kind of book gathering. It's a printed page with your photo, bio, contact info and a short pitch for your book including word count, genre, target audience, and a short synopsis.

5) **DON'T cart around all 800 pages of your magnum opus** and try to thrust it upon faculty members, or compete for faculty attention like a needy two year old. If you're attending a hands-on critique session workshop—bring a first chapter, story, or a few poems. (Full disclosure: I schlepped my own first novel around a writers' conference for a whole weekend before I realized nobody else had one.)

6) DO perfect your pitch beforehand, so you can tell an agent or editor in three sentences what your book is about. (See the chapter on "Hooks, Loglines, and Pitches.") Then ask if you can query. (If you're querying a novel or memoir, make sure to tell her if it's complete.) If she says yes, you can put "REQUESTED" on the envelope. A big plus.

7) DON'T neglect your health. Carry some protein bars and water and maybe an energy drink. Your breaks may be too short to grab real food. If you're feeling overwhelmed, don't feel you have to attend every session.

8) DO take a notebook and several pens as well as your laptop or tablet—wifi can be iffy and batteries die.

9) DON'T forget to have fun. You're there to make friends as well as learn. One of the most important aspects of a conference is meeting fellow writers. But not too much fun—especially at the bar. People talk.

10) DO remember agents and editors are people too. As the late, great Miss Snark said "It's like visiting the reptile house. They're as afraid of you as you are of them. Honest."

PART 4

GETTING YOUR GEEK ON

CATHERINE

SOCIAL NETWORKING: GET USED TO IT

OKAY. WE HAVE TO TALK ABOUT IT. IT CAN'T BE AVOIDED ANY longer. Facebook. Twitter. Pinterest. Shelfari. Red Room. Google+.

"What a waste of time!" you shout. "That's just cutting into my writing time."

Ah. I see. So you just want to write the books. You don't want to assure that anyone will actually read them.

"But Twitter is so silly. All these foolish people telling you they're tying their shoes, or they just ate a salami sandwich."

Only if used improperly. And you won't use it improperly. Of course you won't. You'll use it the way all good writers should.

"But I'm not 'techie.' I'm not a nerd. I'm just not. I don't understand how that stuff works."

Start learning. It's the wave of the future. Do you want the future to pass you and your work by? Didn't think so.

I resisted, too, when my agent suggested a MySpace page. At the time MySpace was king and Twitter was barely breaking on the scene. How things change.

I put it off as long as I could. Then I found a lovely young person to guide me. I strongly advise, if you can't hack your way through the Everglades of social media, that you find a teen. He or she will get you started. Then jump in and get your feet wet. Twitter and Facebook do not bite.

Today, the Internet is the new major media, and social networks are your media power tools. You can use them to share information, and you can also use them to get the latest news on the publishing business. Twitter is brilliant for this. Here's the trick. Don't follow people who tweet that they just ate a salami sandwich. Follow people who tweet intelligent thoughts, book recommendations, and great links to what's going on. (Hint: book bloggers, other authors, agents, publishers.)

Suddenly you will be on the cutting edge of what's going on.

If you have a blog—you do; you have a blog—you are no longer limited to just the people who follow it. You can tweet a link to your blog, then post that same link on Facebook. If you're really smart, you can easily figure out how to get one update to post on, say, Twitter, Facebook, Google+, and LinkedIn, all in one click (hint: Tweetdeck or Hootsuite). If you have really important news, you can ask your followers to retweet it for you, giving you access to not only your followers but your followers' followers.

And how do you get all these followers? Step one, follow. Follow to be followed. Step two, tweet well. If you are interesting, they will come. Step three, be patient. They will find you.

DO:

1) Actually read posts by people you follow on Twitter, and your Facebook friends. Pay attention to what's going on with them. Reply to their posts. Retweet them, or otherwise share them with your friends/followers when inspired to do so.

2) Create a profile on Shelfari and Goodreads. Add the books you are reading. Share thoughts about those books. See (search) which members are reading and enjoying your published book. Make friends.

3) "Talk" to people. Get to know them.

4) Mix it up. Some posts can be personal, geared to letting readers know you better. Some should have hard news of your career. Some should be in support of other books, other users. If it's all about you, this tone will bleed through.

DON'T:

1) Directly tell or ask your social media friends to buy your book. This is too self-serving, and will be seen as such.

2) Directly praise your own book. Does anyone care if the author thinks it's brilliant? Not if they're smart. It's fine to share good reviews, however, blog or otherwise.

3) Send out Goodreads or Shelfari book recommendations for your own book. I get these all the time. John Selfserving recommends you read "The Sky is Blue" by John Selfserving. Sure he does. And I've no doubt he's impartial. Can you say "bad form"?

4) Otherwise give the impression that all you care about is you.

"But that sounds so time-consuming!" you cry, (still not convinced).

After the initial set-up, plan to spend somewhere in the neighborhood of forty-five minutes a day keeping up your social media presence. Are you sure you really have something better to do with that time than build a readership and spread the word about your book?

INTERNET BASICS

Q AND A

"Never, ever let any of the voices on the internet, no matter how helpful or authoritative they aim (or claim) to be, take away from your ability to hear your own unique authorial voice."—agent Holly Root.

Q: Can I really learn writing skills on the Internet?

A: Anne—

Yup. Pretty much everything you can learn at a writer' conference, college class or even an MFA program is available on the Internet. But you need to know where to find it, and that can be daunting.

Probably the best resources for beginning writers are blogs and agent/author websites. You don't have to start your own blog or comment in order to get the benefit of blogs. Writers are naturally shy and it's OK to just lurk for a while until you get the hang of it. There are a few superstar agent-bloggers who put a huge amount of effort into educating us. They change fairly often. Three years seems to be the life span of a lot of blogs.

To keep up with current blogs, we recommend looking at *Writer's Digest*'s annual list of the 101 Best Sites for Writers to start yourself off.

Agent blogs can be very helpful for a beginning writer, whether or not you're planning to go the traditional publishing route. Blogs have a short shelf life, so anything we recommend here may soon die off and others will take their places. Right now we recommend Jane Friedman's "Being Human at Electric Speed" and the blogs of agents Rachelle Gardner and Janet Reid (especially her "Query Shark" blog) plus author and former agent Nathan Bransford. Chuck Sambuchino's Guide to Literary Agents is really useful if you're getting ready to query, and Kristen Lamb's blog has great craft advice as well as the best advice on social media on the Interwebz. And, ahem, "Anne R. Allen's Blog...with Ruth Harris" is one lots of people find useful.

Q: Do You Need a Computer to be a Writer?

A: Catherine—

Yes. If you want to be published, that is. Here are the six basic things you'll need:

1) **A computer that will save a document to Word.** Most submissions are done in Word and won't be read otherwise.

2) **Internet access.** About 99% of communication with editors

and agents is done through email.

3) **A professional email address.** Snookums@hotstuff.com will not get you an impartial read.

4) **Basic search skills.** Google is a writer's #1 friend. Followed closely by Wikipedia.

5) **Some allotted time for reading blogs, joining forums and social networking sites**. This is the only way to keep up with the rapidly changing industry and make the contacts you'll need when you get closer to your goals.

6) **A blog or website.** At least you'll need them as soon as you start to submit manuscripts to agents and editors. You must be reachable. Facebook and other sites that can only be accessed by members don't count.

Q: Do You Need a Website?

A: Catherine—

Yes. It's really only a matter of when.

There are those who advise fledgling writers to go out and get a website now. Right away. As you struggle to flesh out the first draft of chapter three. This seems like a misstep to me. What information will you post on said website? I'm not sure a rundown of what you did before sitting down at the computer that morning—followed by an excerpt from a very rough draft of work that might not be available for purchase this decade—will prove ultimately compelling.

But before you have a book...published, out, available for

sale…even if it's only an ebook in the Kindle store, yes, you need a website. Don't delay.

Now, if I were writing this scrap of advice even five years ago, I'd have told you to brace yourself for what this will cost. A good website used to set authors back in the thousands or even tens of thousands, after which they were often bound to the web designers/webmasters, paying $40-$100 an hour to change the date on their upcoming signings.

Good news for authors (bad news for web designers, most of whom are in a new line of work): The Web is now DIY. Do It Yourself. The unreasonably complex world of HTML code still exists, but you don't need to learn much, if any, of it. Because websites can be built in programs employing WYSIWYG (pronounced something like wizzy-wig, an acronym for "what you see is what you get" technology. If you want to add an image, you drag it onto the page, or hit "add image." If you want a block of text, you place a text block on the page and start typing.

That's the good news. Now for the bad news. You have to do it yourself.

Well, that's not entirely true. You don't have to. There are still plenty of web designers in business for those who don't want to. If you have a spare few thousand lying around, feel free.

If, like the rest of us, you have other uses for that money (groceries and the mortgage spring to mind) the advice is much the same as for social networking. Get used to it. Find a teen, or even a kid. Learn one site-building program. Go into the tutorials if you have to. Go into the user forums if you have to. Hire a pro to get you started if you have to. Do what you have to.

Believe it or not, I created my own first website in the late 90s, in actual HTML. Not that I know HTML *really*. I just learned as much of it as I had to. I lost a few hairs in the process, and the ones I didn't pull out turned a bit grayer, but it was a website. It was, however…to put it as kindly as possible…basic.

Then things took off, and I just hired somebody, period. And paid him. And paid him. And paid him. For every tiny change. When money was tight, there were few changes. My site became outdated, static. Flat. Because I couldn't afford to make it sing.

Then one day (well, one two months) I buckled down and built a new site on (the now discontinued) iWeb. I put a lot of myself into it. Literally. Photos, videos. Book cover images that doubled as audio players, to "read you" an excerpt from the book. A welcome video. It didn't look like a professionally designed site. But it looked like me. And it was ten times more interesting than what it replaced.

Now I have a site that looks much more professional, but is still DIY. It's built on Squarespace, but my domain names point to it. I had some initial help from a friend who knows the platform well. That saved me a lot of frustration. But I did most of it, so I know how it was done. And I can—and do—change it anytime I need to.

There are more programs out there than I can mention. GoDaddy allows you to purchase (or use a basic free version of) "WebSite Tonight" to design a site for your GoDaddy domain. Similar situation with Network Solutions. Bloggers use Blogspot and Wordpress for little or no money. Windows users traditionally had access to Front Page, which has since been replaced by Expression Web and Sharepoint Designer. That's just the tiniest sampling.

Be brave and go forward. To the best of my knowledge, no one ever died from WYSIWYG. It's just one of those things that sounds worse than it is.

A: Anne—

And remember that a blog is a website. Many writers do fine with a free blog as their only website. Even Nathan Bransford does that. With WordPress it's even possible to have a static first page and put the blog in an inside page, so it works just like a hosted website. Which leads us to the next chapter...

ANNE

HOW TO BE A SUCCESSFUL BLOGGER (IN FIVE PARTS)

Does a writer absolutely need to have a blog to get published?

Nope.

But it sure helps.

Even a couple of years ago, only nonfiction writers needed "platforms," but that's changed. Even big name publishers expect authors to do most of our own publicity.

And what is a platform?

It's the network of people who know you well enough that they might buy your book. All social networking sites contribute to it. So joining Red Room, She Writes, MyWANAtribe—or any of the smorgasbord of writer schmooze-rooms—will help build platform. So pick a few and join up. But not too many: remember this is about promoting your writing, not keeping you from it.

The point is to get your name out there where the Google spiders can find you.

Why?

Here's a quote from Oak Tree Press acquisitions editor Sunny Frazier that I think will answer your question:

"I don't read the query (sorry aspiring writers!). I look for two things: genre and word count. I then Google the author. I'm looking for the number of times the writer's name appears on the Internet. I'm searching for a website or any attempt to build a platform."

Sad but true. So what's a platform?

It's how many people know your name before you launch your book. The three major pillars of most writing platforms (right now) are Facebook, Twitter and your blog.

And the greatest of these is your blog.

This is where you get to be 100% yourself. Your blog can be part of your website, like Catherine's, or a stand-alone entity like mine. But the important thing is that you need an interactive website where people can communicate with you, not just read about you.

Here's what publishing guru Jane Friedman says: "All serious writers need this kind of hub so they can start learning more about their readers and formalizing a connection with them. Facebook, Twitter, and other sites help you find readers and connect, but those connections can disappear at any moment, or gradually over time – but with a blog, they can always find you."

That's why a website you have to pay somebody to update for you isn't as useful. People want to connect with you—not your web designer. The difference between a static website and a blog is the difference between putting an ad in the Yellow Pages or personally giving somebody your phone number. Blogs are friendly. And if you have a blog, you don't need an expensive website. Here's what

Nathan Bransford said about formal websites:

"The thing about author websites is pretty simple, in my mind. They're expensive. Are they worth the return on investment? I don't know. I can't think of a time I've ever bought a book based on a visit to an author's website. But I have definitely bought books based on author blogs. I know I may not be the average reader, but I still have a hard time seeing how it's worth the investment unless the website is really spectacular."

Does a blog sell books?

No it does not. Not directly.

But it helps in lots of indirect ways. It's how I found both my publishers, and how I got a blog partner (Ruth Harris) who has been at the top of the *New York Times* bestseller list and worked at the highest levels of New York publishing—somebody I'd never have met any other way. And because I'm known in the blogosphere, when it's time for a blog tour, I only have to ask a few friends. Networking pays off.

A lot of blogging advice is aimed at professional bloggers who are looking to make money selling ads on the actual blog. That's probably not what you want as an author. Most beginning authors just need a fun, inviting place where people can visit and get to know you—a home rather than a storefront.

#1 HOW TO BLOG

I HAD TO LEARN BLOGGING BY TRIAL AND ERROR—LOTS OF ERROR. SO here's the stuff I wish somebody had told me:

1) Read blogs. If you don't do it yet, spend a couple of weeks reading a bunch of writing and publishing blogs before you jump in and create your own. See what you like and don't like. Agent blogs and some of the popular indie-publishing blogs are good for meeting people at all stages of their careers.

I especially recommend reading Kristen Lamb and Nathan Bransford. Kristen is a skilled teacher and social media guru and Nathan is a publishing insider as well as successful author. Plus they both have well-moderated forums where you can get to know people without being attacked by trolls.

2) Comment and interact with other commenters. You only have to say a few words of agreement or disagreement, or offer your own experience about the topic. Lots of writers have a "blogroll" in their sidebar with a list of other great writing blogs. Start clicking around. If you like what somebody says, click on their name in the comments and you'll get their profile and you can go visit their blog. Comment there and Bingo, you've got a potential follower.

3) Get an online profile. It's easier to leave a comment if you have an online profile. The easiest way to do this is to sign up with Google+. This is the quickest way to establish a presence Google's search engines will find, and you don't have to do much interacting on the site if you don't want to. (Sign up for minimal email notifications so you don't get nagged to death.)

But if you don't want to join anything, you can sign up at Gravatar.com, owned by Wordpress. This gives you an online profile that's compatible with all blogging platforms, but it's not a social network, so you don't have to do anything with it.

Upload a picture—a smiley one of yourself is best. There's room for a short bio and your contact info. Make sure you post an email address and link to all your sites. That's why you're doing this—so people can find you. If you're on Facebook, Twitter, Pinterest or whatever, post the link so people who see a comment and like it can find you.

4) Choose a blogging platform. The biggest free blogging platforms are WordPress, Tumblr, LiveJournal, and Blogger. Tumblr is a platform for short posts, videos and pictures—something between a blog and Twitter. You can also have a blog on your personal website, the way Catherine does, or on a community site like Red Room. But these aren't as likely to be picked up by search engine spiders, so if your goal is to be more Googleable, I suggest having your own stand-alone blog.

I use Blogger (owned by Google, with addresses that read "blogspot.com") because it's the easiest to set up and use—and has some attractive templates. But Blogger does have some drawbacks. Whole continents get blocked periodically—probably by Blogger's fierce spamblockers. And for a while there, we were all losing our follower widgets, and some people couldn't get into their own blogs. But the glitches eventually get ironed out.

People who are more tech-savvy love WordPress. If you decide to go with WordPress, Google Jane Friedman's directions for starting a Wordpress blog. They're very user-friendly.

4) Decide on a focus and tone for your blog. Blog gurus will tell you to address a niche, but I'm not sure that's the best way to start. I think the most important thing is to develop a strong personal voice and be flexible.

One successful writer/blogger I know pointed out she'd never have the following she does if she'd started with a niche blog. She started out as a YA writer and switched to erotic Romance. Yeah, a tough switch.

Don't plan to blog about writing all the time. There are an awful lot of us out here doing just that and you want to be able to provide something fresh.

Beginning author-bloggers form a wonderful community. That community can help you in hundreds of ways, so don't worry too much about seeming like a "professional" blogger right away. Be real, flexible, open and friendly and you can ease into your niche later.

Remember that the most successful blogs reveal the writer's personality and provide something useful at the same time. Even if you choose to be a niche blogger like me, keep flexible. Don't focus on one book or lock yourself into one genre, especially if you're a newbie.

Zombies could invade the second draft of what started out as a Cozy Mystery. Or a Victorian Romance could veer into Steampunk. Romance writer Rosa Lee Hawkins might decide to become dark Thriller author R. L. Hawk. She doesn't want to be stuck with that pink, lacy blog—or betray her Romance-loving followers. You can always add stuff, but it's harder to take it away.

5) Think of a title and sub-header. Don't get too creative here. Make sure you put your own name in the title. An author's name is his/her "brand." People buy a "Stephen King" novel because of the name on the cover. You want that to happen to you, too.

NOTE: if your name actually is Stephen King—or like a friend of mine, Ann Frank—you need to choose a pseudonym right away. No point in doing all this work for somebody else's brand. You also might want to choose a pseudonym if you have an unmemorable or difficult name. Or if you're well known in some other field that doesn't mesh, like you own an eponymous septic tank-pumping business and also write cookbooks. If you've got a generic name like "Anne Allen," at least use a middle initial.

Yes, I know most blogs you see have names like "Musing, Meandering and Muttering," but this really isn't a good idea.

Anywhere you go online, you want to promote your brand, or you're wasting time (time you could be writing that opus—that's the reason for all this, remember?) It's OK to be unimaginative like me and call it YOUR NAME's blog—maybe reducing the ho-hum factor with something like "Susie Smith, Scrivener." These are the advantages to using your own name—or the one you write under:

a) When somebody Googles you, your blog will come up, instead of that old MySpace page you haven't bothered to delete, or the picture of you on Spring Break in Cabo in 2008. Yeah. That one.

b) You don't get boxed into one genre. (I strongly advise against starting different blogs for different books. One blog is hard enough to maintain.)

6) Choose a couple of photos from your files to decorate the blog. Usually one of yourself for your profile, and another to set the tone. And of course your book covers, if you have them for sale. Try to keep with the same color scheme and tone.

On Tone:

If you write Middle Grade humor, you don't want your blog looking all dark and Goth, and cheery colors will give the wrong message for that serial killer Thriller. Romance sites don't have to be pink, but they should be warm, inviting and a little sexy or girly.

Also, if you have a website or Twitter page, aim to echo the tone and color in order to establish a personal "brand" look.

7) Prepare a bio for your "About Me" page. This is the most important part of the blog, but it's amazing how many people forget to post one. Make your bio intriguing and funny without giving TMI. You can add some more pics—maybe of your dog or your funky car. Keep family out unless it's a family blog. Pseudonyms for kids are a smart idea. Remember the Blogosphere is "in public" and you don't know who's out there.

8) Go to a friend's blog. If they use Blogger or Wordpress, there will be a link at the top that says "create blog."

9) Click on "create blog." Follow directions in the window.

They're easy. In Blogger anyway.

10) Choose a template. Don't mess with the design too much, except in terms of color—a busy blog isn't a place people want to linger. And don't add gifs, really big files, or anything that takes too long to load. Keep with your color scheme and tone.

11) Pick your "gadgets." There are lots. But again, keep it simple. I suggest just choosing the basics like about me, followers, subscribe, share, and search. "Share" is the widget that allows people to Tweet or FB or + your post. You want this to happen. This is how people find out about your blog.

You can go back and add anything you want later. Later you can just go to your "design" tab to find more. If you Tweet, get a twitter button (Google "Twitter buttons"). Think twice before you choose an animated one, though—they're cute but they slow your load time. And make sure that you post your Twitter handle (your @yourname ID) on the main blog page. People who want to quote you will want to be able to use your handle, so don't hide it.

In a little while, you'll want to install the gadget that posts links to your most popular posts. That makes people want to move around the site and not leave after they've read one thing.

I don't recommend putting your stats on the front page, bragging about "X many hits." It will only advertise that you're a newbie and might make you sad. Do keep track of your stats on your own dashboard, but remember it takes about a year to get a blog going at full stride. So don't obsess.

Yes, you will have weeks when you have no hits. My blog had five hits in its first three months.

But checking stats is actually a good idea because you can see where your traffic is coming from. If you suddenly get 40 hits from one address—go check it out. It could be spam, but also could mean somebody's posted a link to you. You may have a new friend you didn't even know about.

12) Set up privacy settings. I suggest making no restrictions on new posts. Don't make every comment wait for your approval before it goes live. You won't get a discussion going that way. Monitor your blog yourself instead. I've personally found that 99% of commenters are friendly in your first couple of years.

Also, I suggest turning off the "CAPTCHA" word-verification thingy. Spambot programmers are learning to get around them and they don't screen out most spam. (That's done by the spamblocker, which will work just fine without Captcha.) But reading those out of focus letters and numbers will annoy people no end and keep them from commenting.

But DO have every comment on posts over a week old sent to you for approval. Old posts attract more spam and trolls.

13) Sign up for email notification of new comments so you can respond to them in a timely way. If commenters give an email address in their profile (always smart) you can respond to them via email, but I prefer to respond in the comment thread to stimulate discussion.

14) Upload those photos. But not too many. One per post is good. This is a WRITING blog. And NO AUDIO!!! People read blogs at work. And on their phones. Even though you're sure everybody on the planet adores the classics of the Abba catalogue, some of us don't. Trust me on this.

It's that easy. But don't forget to:

15) BOOKMARK your blog, or you may never find it again. You'd be amazed how many people set up a blog only to have it disappear forever into cyberspace. It happened to me.

16) When you go back to your blog, click "sign in" and then "new post" to post something new and "design" to get inside the blog—what they call the "back" of the blog.

17) Keep to a schedule. Decide how often you want to blog—I suggest once a week to start—then do it. Preferably on the same day each week. Most blog gurus will tell you to blog more often, but I have a pretty highly rated blog and have never blogged more than twice in one week.

I follow something called "Slow Blogging." It's like the slow food movement. Quality over quantity.

Joining the Slow Blog movement is simple. Start a blog and announce you're planning to post on alternate Tuesdays, or every full moon, or whenever. Or if you already have a blog, next time you miss a few days, tell yourself you didn't FAIL to blog; you SUCCEEDED in joining the Slow Bloggers. All you have to do is skip those boring apologies, and you're in.

18) Write your first blogpost.

So how do you write for a blog?

- A post should be 600-2000 words presented in short, punchy paragraphs.
- Bulleting, numbering and bolding are your friends. Make a

point and present it in a way that's easy to grasp.

- Offer information and interesting observations, not navel-gazing. Direct your focus outward, not inward. (And keep to nonfiction. Blogging your fiction isn't a great idea for a number of reasons, which I'll go into in a later chapter.)
- If you have more to say than fits into a few paragraphs—great! You have material for next time.
- Keep to one topic, because that stimulates conversation. (If you have dozens of short things to say—Tweet them.)
- Always ask a question of your readers at the end. It makes people feel involved and stimulates discussion.

19) Go tell those blogfriends you've made that you've got a blog. Hopefully, a few will follow. Don't despair if you don't get a lot of followers right away. I had maybe ten for my first six months—consisting of my critique group and my mom.

20) Congratulations. You are now a blogger.

Really. It's that easy.

#2 HOW NOT TO BLOG

ONCE YOU'VE SET UP YOUR BLOG, HERE ARE A FEW THINGS YOU'RE going to want to avoid:

1) Ignoring comments. If somebody comments, respond in the thread. Personally, I did not know this for, like, months when I started out. I have no idea how many readers I lost because of it. Email responses are good, too—for commenters who provide emails on their profiles—but responses in the thread stimulate discussion and further comments.

2) Crying in the wilderness. Social Networking is SOCIAL. Nobody coming to your party? Go find one. Visit other blogs. To have a friend, you gotta be one. Follow and comment. It's called social networking. Go out and be sociable!

Tip: Looking for stuff to post about? Respond to other people's blogs on your own. Instead of leaving a long comment in that anti-prologue thread, write your own post on the pros of prologues and leave a link.

3) Using your blog as a personal journal. "Today I went to the dentist, picked up groceries and cooked my husband's favorite meatloaf," will snoozify anybody who isn't a member of your immediate family. It's OK to post personal stuff if it's funny or newsworthy—like how Pufferball won the "ugliest pet" award or how many Kardashian wannabes you spotted yesterday at the mall. But don't use it like a private diary if you're blogging to build platform.

4) Whining: Resist posting rants about the unfairness of the publishing industry. Or how lame that famous writer's work is compared to yours. It's OK when you've had a big disappointment to ask for the emotional support of your friends, but don't give specifics—and never rail against the agent/editor/reviewer who spurned you.

Remember the first thing an agent will do if she's interested in your query is Google you. She probably just had lunch with that editor you called Mr. Poopy Brains.

5) White text on dark backgrounds. Ouch! My eyeballs. Seriously. Every "how to blog" article says this, but still, half the blogs you visit have white text. It's not "cool"; it's a big "go away" sign.

6) Posting unpublished fiction or poetry if you ever hope to publish it. And don't post creative stuff if you're just trolling for praise. Want a critique? Try CritiqueCircle.com, or writing community forums. For some reason, people don't tend to read fiction posted on blogs (even by famous published authors). Save the fiction for the occasional blogfest or contest, but otherwise, keep your WIP to yourself, especially if you're a newbie. You don't want that sucky first draft hanging out there in cyberspace. Trust me on

101

this.

Besides, you'll be seriously limiting your future publishing options. Listen to agent Meredith Barnes:

"Many writers serialize their work on their blogs. I cannot encourage you strongly enough to avoid that. Authors nearly always list 'getting an agent' as the reason they put 'teasers' on their blogs. But there is already a mechanism for showing your work to agents: the query. If you choose to do so anyway you may put yourself breach of the warranties and indemnities clause of the publishing contract that you haven't even signed yet."

Exception: blogfests, flash fiction days, and contests. A blogfest is a non-competitive mass sharing of work. One blogger will announce a topic, say "first-kiss scenes," and anybody who wants to join in signs up. On the given day, everybody reads each other's posts and makes comments. It's a fun way to meet new writers and get acquainted with their work. A blog contest can be anything from a random name drawn from a list of commenters to a competition for the best cat-related haiku. Prizes are usually a book or maybe a critique from the blogger. Rewards for the host blogger are an increase in traffic and more followers.

7)Writing snoozifying headers. "It's Wednesday" and "So Sorry I Haven't Been Blogging" won't snag a lot of readers. If you want examples of good headers, browse Twitter and see what YOU would want to click on. Certain types of headers typically draw in readers.

a) Lists: 10 Lies That Work Better than My Dog Ate My Homework

b) Questions: What if Your Homework Eats your Dog?

c) Answer a Question. A how-to is usually a grabber: "How to Sell Homework-Excuses on eBay"

d) Search Engine Optimized. Use keywords potential readers might use in a search to bring new readers.

8) Pointless tags or none. Tags are the little words and phrases at the bottom or top of a post that tell search engines what's in the text. Use as many tags as possible. This is how Google finds you. Tag your posts with names of anybody mentioned, plus your main topics. (More SEO.)

9) Failure to link. Don't be afraid you'll send your readers off to read somebody else if you include linkage to other sites. Linking is friendly and it also gets the attention of those search engines. In fact, a weekly round-up with links to some of your favorite blog posts of the week is a great way to get readers and notice from the Google spiders.

10) Blogging too often. If you have nothing to say, don't say it. Yes, I know blog gurus tell you to post once a day or more, but their advice isn't aimed at creative writers. We have other priorities. (You've got that novel to write, remember?) I suggest once a week, with an occasional mid-week post for important announcements. Most blogs burn out after two years. But you want yours to be a platform to support you for the long haul.

Personally, I'm relieved when my favorite bloggers cut back to a few posts a week. That way I have some hope of keeping up.

11) Blogging erratically. Keep to a posted schedule. Most agents say they'll look up your blog before they request a partial. If you have an abandoned blog hanging in cyberspace, this says—

a) You don't stick with things.

b) You don't have much to say.

c) You don't have the platform needed to sell your work to an editor.

And if you're a self-pubber who doesn't update your blog, you're abandoning your fans. They don't tend to like that.

It's fine to take blogcations, especially when you're at work on a big project, so if you have to skip a few posts, leave a message letting readers know you've got big things in the works and when you plan to return. And—if you do lapse for a while, don't post a long list of excuses when you get back. Bo-ring.

FYI: Wednesday and Thursday are the biggest blog traffic days. (Worst days: Saturday and Sunday—which I didn't know when I started a Sunday blog. Sigh.)

12) Monetizing a writing blog. If you sign up for Google ads, you have no control over what they advertise, and many of the ads will be for bogus agencies or scam vanity publishers. Besides, they won't pay you more than a few pennies a day and they'll make your blog annoying.

Monetizing is fine if you're blogging for its own sake, and you're blogging on some subject other than writing.

But if you're blogging to build platform for your books, don't clutter things with ads that pay pennies. You're after bigger fish. Like followers, readers and maybe a book contract.

13) Acting like you're a rock star from Mars. Don't act as if you have fans when you've never published a book. Talk to your readers as equals, not adoring minions.

Don't assume all your readers are newbies who don't know the basics. Or that they are fans come to worship at the feet of your greatness. And please: don't make oblique references to your characters as if the reader has been living in your head.

If somebody disagrees with you in a comment, argue respectfully or delete their comment (if it's offensive) but don't say— "When you've written a whole novel like I have, you ignorant pipsqueak, you'll know I'm right." You may be talking to a bestselling novelist— or an agent's assistant who's about to read your query.

14) Trying to maintain too many blogs. One is plenty. Two if the other is a group blog. Anything more and you won't be able to keep them up. If somebody visits your profile and randomly clicks on one of your twelve blogs and it hasn't been updated since you posted that rant about the stupid ending of *Lost*, they are not going to try another—and you just stamped "unprofessional" next to your name.

15) Not listing an email address on your profile. A blog is essentially an advertisement for you as a writer. Why advertise a product that's not available? Unless you're being actively pursued by a cyberstalker, give readers an email address where they can contact you.

16) Making the blog about one book and/or posting cute observations from your character's point of view. Yes, I know some bloggers have managed to sustain this kind of tour de force for a while—but what happens when your editor has you change the character's name? Or that series doesn't sell and you move on to something else? You want a blog to establish your career—not lock you in a box.

17) Focusing on follower numbers. Go for quality, not quantity. This is about making friends who (hopefully) will become loyal fans. If you treat people as a commodity, they're not going to care about you, either.

19) Spamming other bloggers. Visiting random blogs and saying, "This is a swell blog; come visit mine" is creepy. If there's a discussion going on about how not to write an ending as lame as the last episode of *Lost*, by all means mention your post on the subject. But it has to be relevant to the discussion.

20) Writing posts that are too long, dense, or address more than one topic. I've read that 79% of Web users scan rather than read. Break up posts with lists, bolding, and lots of white space. If you want to write about several topics, use separate blog posts.

21) Letting blogging take over your life. You CAN'T read all the top publishing blogs and comment on all your friends' blogs every day. Choose one or two days a week for blogging and let go of the guilt.

22) Forgetting the #1 rule of blogging is the Golden one. Offer the kind of content you like to read. Keep it short, sweet, informative and reader-friendly, and pretty soon you'll have a bunch of friendly readers. Want followers? Follow. Want commenters? Comment. This is social media, get it?

#3 WHAT DO I BLOG ABOUT?

WHEN I TEACH BLOGGING, THE MOST FREQUENT QUESTION I GET IS "What do I blog about?"

A writer starting a blog right now faces two problems:

1) There are already, like, a trillion writers out there lecturing the blogosphere about how to write vivid characters, prop up saggy middles and avoid adverbs. A lot of them probably know more than you.

2) If you're a writer with books to sell, you want to reach a general audience, not just other writers selling books.

So how can you be different? How do you create a blog that somebody will read—somebody besides your stalkery ex-boyfriend and your mom?

The most important thing to remember with any kind of blog is that you need to offer something. It should be fresh, informative, and/or entertaining.

How you approach your new blog is going to depend a whole lot on your stage in the publishing process and your immediate goals.

Stage #1: You're a developing writer.

You're working on your first or second novel, and maybe have a few stories in literary journals or a couple of contest wins. You want to be a published author sometime soon, but you're not quite ready to focus on writing as a career.

Your goal: LEARNING THE PUBLISHING BUSINESS AND NETWORKING.

You want to make friends in the writing community for career help and mutual support. You want to learn the best writing techniques, network with publishing professionals, and educate yourself about the business.

Stage #2: You're ready for the marketplace.

You're querying agents and ready to publish. You've got a couple of books polished and ready to go. You've been to writing conferences, taken classes, and maybe hired a freelance editor. Your writing is at a professional level.

Your goal: BUILDING PLATFORM

You want to get your name out there to the general public. When you query an agent or ask for a blurb or review, you want a Google search to bring up ten pages of listings about you.

Stage #3: You're a published author

Your agent/marketing dept. says, "Get thee to the blogosphere!"

Or you realize the brilliantly blurbed *oeuvre* you've self-published is sitting there on Amazon with only two sales in three months (both to your spouse) because nobody has heard of it—or you.

Your goal: FINDING AND CONNECTING WITH READERS

***

If you're a Stage #1 writer...

It's OK to blog about writing. (I know social media guru/Jedi Master Kristen Lamb says you shouldn't do this but I think her caveat is aimed more at people at stage #2 and #3.)

I'm not talking about lecturing on craft as if you're a pro when you're not. But an equal-to-equal post about something interesting you've discovered about pantsing vs. outlining, point of view, or what agents are looking for this month—that's great stuff to talk about when you're reaching out to other writers.

Why do you want to reach other writers? Because writers help each other. (We're kind of a nice bunch, in spite of our stereotyping as depressed substance-abusers.) I know a number of authors who got their agents through a referral from a fellow blogger. I found both my publishers through blogging. I'm not sure I would have made it through the darkest rejection phases if it hadn't been for the support of writer blogfriends.

In fact, blog and book marketing guru Bob Mayer said recently, "authors need to build community more than focusing on marketing. Especially new authors or those that plan on publishing in the future. Too many people are looking at sales, when what you really want are relationships."

When you have a writing blog, you get to participate in blog hops, flash fiction days, contests and all kinds of networking events that help you meet people who can be important in your future career.

But do make sure the blog has something interesting going for it—something that's helpful. There are all sorts of ways you can help:

1) Author interviews

2) Profiles of small publishers or agents who are interested in your genre (take them from websites—you don't have to bother the agents and editors)

3) Info on contests, giveaways and blog hops

4) Links to great articles and posts in your genre or field of interest.

5) Book reviews. If you write thoughtful, useful reviews, you'll immediately become everybody's best friend.

If you're a Stage #2 writer...

This is when you should heed Kristen Lamb's advice to avoid blogging about your writing process. If you're starting a blog right now with the goal of building platform, writing is definitely not the best choice of subject matter. You've got a trillion competitors and you're limiting your audience to other competitors.

So try something that's related to your writing but has a unique slant. Here are a few suggestions:

1) Focus on your genre or subgenre (unless you're still experimenting with different genres). You can discuss movies, videogames, TV shows, even jewelry and costumes—as long as they relate to your niche. A great example is SciFi writer Alex J. Cavanaugh's super-popular blog that specializes in all things SciFi.

2) Blog about your home town or state, especially if they're the setting of your novels. Travel sites that link to local landmarks and Chamber of Commerce sites will help you make friends locally that can be a big help later on.

3) Choose a writing-related subject that has a broader audience. A general-interest writing blog is *The Wordmonger*, where YA writer C.S. Perryess gives a fun, in-depth study of the etymology of one word per week. I learn something with every post.

4) Offer links to important information. If you're writing a memoir or fiction about certain health issues, promote organizations that help with those issues. Link to support groups and they might even link back.

5) Provide people with the benefit of your research. If you're writing historical fiction about a certain time period—post the research on your blog. (This is doubly useful because it will help keep you from cramming it all into the novel at the expense of story.) Have to research guns for a Thriller? Poisons for a Cozy? Are you basing the story on a real case? There are people who would love to read about this stuff.

6) Appeal to another Internet community. If that historical novel is based on a real person or your own family history, you could target readers from the genealogy blogosphere and links to historical research sites. If your heroine loves to fish, sew, or collect stuff, connect with blogs for fly fisherpersons, quilters, or collectors of floaty pens.

7) **Provide a forum** for people in your target demographic. If you write for a particular group—single urban women, Boomers, stay-at-home moms, or the just-out-of-college dazed and confused— focus on aspects of life of special interest to them.

8) **Offer recipes or how-tos**. Have a character who's an expert at something? Give readers the benefit of his expertise in the woodshop, garden or kitchen. Have some great recipes that relate to your character, time period, or region? Write about the food in your books, or food in fiction generally.

If you've reached Stage #3…

You can be more eclectic. People will be coming to your blog because they want to get to know you and find out about your books—so focusing on one subject isn't as important. The blog becomes a place to showcase who you are. Think of it as your own version of *Oprah* magazine: not a place to toot your own horn as much as share things of interest to you that will also be of value to your readers. So you can continue whatever you've been doing in Stage #2, plus add stuff about you and your books.

Yes, you can talk about your books. I think people are silly who say you shouldn't use your blog for self-promotion. That's why you're in the blogosphere in the first place. It's fine as long as you don't use hard-sell tactics and you don't project an attitude of "I'm an author and you're not."

Each type of blog can evolve into another as your goals change.

6 Tips for the New Blogger

1) Make a list of topics you might like to explore before you begin, so you have a running start. If you visit other blogs regularly (and you should) you may find yourself making long comments on some subject that gets your hackles up/juices flowing. That's the stuff you should be putting in your own blog.

2) I STRONGLY advise against having more than one blog. It saps your energy and fragments your audience. (It also annoys the hell out of them: I hate hitting somebody's profile and finding six blogs. Unless one is clearly marked "author" I don't even try to wade through them: you've lost me.) Blogs have many pages. Use them.

3) Put your own name in the blog title! Yes, I know I've said it before, but I'm saying it again: your name is your brand. Also, you'll find it easier to transition from Stage #1 to #2 and #3. Subtitles are easy to change. Titles, not so much. "Susie Scrivener's Blog" can go from "writing and ranting" to "Floaty Pen Collecting" if Susie decides to change the blog's focus. But "Floaty Pen Central" can't be changed to "Susie Scrivener's Amazing Books" without a lot of confusion. And you want to keep the same blog. The longer a blog exists, the higher it ranks with the Google spiders.

4) Write an inviting "About Me" page with clear contact information. The whole purpose of blogging is to let people know who you are and how to find you! (And don't just post your resume. Be informal and friendly.)

5) Don't succumb to pressure to blog more than three times a week. Posting once a week on a regularly scheduled day is better than posting often but erratically. Allow yourself time to write your books. Remember you're in this for the long haul. Quality over quantity. Slow blogging works.

6) Be friendly. The way to build an audience, no matter where you are in your writing career, is to be likable and helpful.

#4 TWELVE MORE DOS AND DON'TS FOR NEW BLOGGERS

THERE'S NO WRONG WAY TO BLOG—BUT IF YOU'RE AN AUTHOR WHO wants to get published, you need to be professional about it. If you want to be taken seriously in the industry—and we have to remember it is an industry—you need to create a helpful, reader-friendly place that's an easy-to-navigate hub for your online presence as a writer.

Here are some more dos and don'ts I've learned along the way that will make that job easier:

1) DO post your Twitter handle somewhere prominent on your home page if you tweet. I know I've said this before, but it's important. Don't just use one of those birdy icons. Make sure you put your whole @twittername up there. I spend way too much time using Twitter's iffy search engine (why is it so useless?) trying to find the handle for somebody I'm quoting or want to reach. If it's right up there on your blog home page, people are much more likely to be able to tweet you or follow. Don't make it difficult for people to be nice to you.

2) DO post a Facebook link, (or "badge," or "Like" button) so people can join you on Facebook. (Unless you've managed to resist the pressure to venture into Zuckerland. For which I applaud all three of you.)

3) DO provide an email address. I don't know how many blogs I visit and find no contact information. The place most people will look is on your "about me" page. So that's a good place to put it. If you're afraid of spambots picking it up, write it this way : "myname (at) gmail (dot) com" –but do it! Imagine an agent or editor reads that short story that won the online contest and loves it. She wants to find out if you've got any full length fiction (yes, this does happen) so she Googles you, finds your blog, and...no contact information. Opportunity is knocking and nobody's home.

4) DO post your blog schedule. Under the header of my blog are three little words: "Updated Sundays, Mostly" They keep us disciplined and keep readers coming back. Ruth and I have never missed a post, but if we do, that "mostly" covers our derrières—we're not running a boot camp here. On the other hand, it's very important to remember it's your professional profile. When you're trying to get published, you're basically applying for a job. You don't want a sloppy blog any more than you want to show up late for an interview, wearing stained sweats and smelling like last night's party.

5) DO learn to write 21st century prose. Writing for the Interwebz is very, very different from what you learned in school. It's light, punchy, and easy to skim. The vast majority of online readers are skimmers. They want:

- lists

- major points highlighted

- bullet points

- **Bolding**

- lots of white space

See where your eye went? There are a couple of important publishing industry blogs I hardly ever read because they're written in the dense, repetitive prose of the old paid-by-the-word, pre-electronic era. I wait for somebody else to post excerpts or summarize those posts, because sweetie, I have things to do....

6) DON'T let yourself get pressured into too many blogfests and bloghops and blog awards and other blogmania. Just because somebody gives you an award doesn't mean you have to drop your WIP and spend a day visiting 80 blogs to tell them all the most embarrassing thing you've ever done with a book or whatever today's game is. Thank them politely, tell them you're honored and do as much as you have time for. Same with invitations to blogfests. No matter how much fun it sounds, just gathering a lot of blog followers isn't as important as getting that novel written!

7) DON'T die intestate. No matter how young and healthy and immortal you feel, appoint a blog executor. Make sure that somebody besides you has the passwords to your blog so if anything dire should happen, they can attend to it and/or take it down. Yes, it's kind of icky to think of, but stuff happens. Not just kicking the bucket. You could get in a parasailing accident while you're on that vacation in Mazatlàn. Be attacked by angry bees. Get stuck without power for two weeks in darkest Connecticut. You don't want your blog hanging unattended in cyberspace as it collects Ukrainian porn and fake Viagra ads.

8) DON'T neglect your "About Me" page. Keep it updated. (I'm speaking to myself here. I've let mine get sloppy at times.) Make sure it's friendly but professional. As I said earlier, you don't want a resume snoozefest. But you also don't want to use it to post pix of yourself after your tenth margarita at Señor Frog's or photos of your puppy learning to go potty outdoors.

This is about you, the author. Even if you aren't published, you want this to be about your writer-self. Give a short bio, a list of what writing organizations you belong to, your genre if you've settled on one, plus links to any short pieces you've published, or contests you've won—anything that relates to you as a writer.

Make sure you include links to all your social media pages, especially book-related ones like RedRoom, AuthorsDen or Shelfari. You can talk about your favorite books, your philosophy, or your life goals as long as it's short and not preachy. You can mention your family, but even if you're a devoted stay-at-home parent, don't make this all about the kids. This is for you.

9) DON'T try to maintain too many blogs. OK, I'm kind of hammering this, but I see a lot of misinformation about this on the

Interwebz. To me, two is too many. If you don't have a day job, and you aren't in a hurry to finish that WIP, maybe you can handle two—especially if the second is a group blog. Or if one is the blog for your XXX- rated erotica and the other is for your sweet Christian Romances. But please, don't try to do any more. Multiple blogs don't only take too much of your time—they also fracture your follower count and really annoy publishing professionals trying to reach you.

Imagine you're that editor I quoted earlier who Googles a writer before reading a query. She finds four blogs listed, so she clicks on one: It's your stream of consciousness self-help blog called *Sobbing and Sighing*, which has exactly three followers—your BFF, your therapist, and your stalkery ex-boyfriend. Do you think the editor is then going to go on to find out you have 60 followers on your *Sweetie Snookums, Vampire Slayer* blog, 143 on *Sassy Susitude,* and 15 *on Storytime Snippets?*

Probably not.

Why not make things nicer for her—and your career—by having one blog called *Susie Smith, Scrivener* with all 221 followers in one place?

A Blogger blog has 20 pages. Count them: twenty. You can have one for your vampire stories, one for your musings and scribblings, one for giving yourself pep talks, and one for writing about being a storyteller—and still have 16 to go. So don't start another blog until you've filled them all, OK?

10) DON'T make commenting difficult. This is another thing I've been hammering on about, because it's important. I just read a new study of customer habits and discovered the #1 motivation for the contemporary customer is "ease of use." They're not so worried about fancy or special. They want things to be easy. That's why Amazon is so successful. First they invented a way to buy books with the click of a mouse, and then they offered us a way to publish them with a few more. "Quick and Easy" wins the day, hands down.

So remember those CAPTCHA word verification things do NOT make it easy to comment. You can remove robo-spam yourself, which is a little harder for you and a lot easier for your potential customers. And as for insisting on moderating all new comments—especially if you don't get around to them for days—that's pretty much saying, "I don't need no stinking comments/customers."

Try being open to comments on new posts for a while. If you get a robo-spam attack, by all means go back to moderating, but with a small blog following, it's less likely you'll get spam. If you moderate (I moderate comments on older posts myself, because that's where the spam shows up), DO check many times during the day so you don't send people away mad.

These are your potential customers. Saying "prove you're special enough to buy my books" isn't going to make the sale.

NOTE: Blogger loves to play Big Brother. It often turns your CAPTCHA back on after you've turned it off. It's happened to me. So ask a good friend to let you know if it's on.

11) Don't delete a blog you've neglected. Bring it back to life by giving it your own name (you can't change the url, but you can change the header very easily.) The older a blog is, the higher its rating with search engines. So remember that blog about *Lost*? You can delete content and change the title, but keep the url and you'll have much better SEO.

12) But: if you have 42 blogs, delete all but one. Seriously. Did I mention multiple blogs are annoying?

13) Don't let yourself be pressured into letting somebody guest blog just because they asked. Good guest posts are informative and target your audience. Somebody with a book or service to sell may approach you with what is essentially an advertisement. Even if you're just starting out, remember your blog is about presenting yourself to the world, and if something doesn't work with your audience, politely decline. Good guest bloggers should already have relationship with you: they should have been by to comment a few times, or know you from other blogs.

#5 TROLLS, SOCK PUPPETS AND CYBERBULLIES—DEALING WITH DIFFICULT BLOG VISITORS

BLOGGING IS FUN, AND A WONDERFUL WAY TO NETWORK AND BUILD your author platform. But it's not always rainbows and unicorns. Sometimes a visitor may disagree with you or be confrontational in some way.

Nothing wrong with that.

If it's done in a friendly manner, disagreement can be an excellent way to stimulate conversation and learn to see things from another point of view. I've learned a lot from people who have pointed out my mistakes and blogging faux-pas.

But the occasional commenter crosses the line from polite disagreement to a verbal attack or full-on temper tantrum.

Starting a blog is like opening a shop. Anybody out there on the street can drop in. Most people who come by will be great. But some might be substance abusers or suffer from mental illness. Some might be looking for a fight. Others can be just plain mean.

Do remember it's your blog, and it's your responsibility to make it a safe place for your commenters, so if one of your followers is attacked, speak up.

Problems can be compounded by the fact that online we can't see the dangerous ones coming. When you meet somebody in person, you get a lot of clues about how to interact with them. A woman wearing a tinfoil hat and muttering about the invaders from Betelgeuse probably won't be the one you choose to chat up as a new friend, and most of us aren't going to worry much whether some guy sporting racist tattoos and an Aryan Nation baldscape likes us or not.

Age is a major clue, too. When you meet somebody in her seventies, you won't expect her to have the same world view as somebody of seventeen.

But when people comment on blogs, we treat them all as peers. This can be good or bad, depending on the type of interaction.

Here's an example. Recently I used the word "Luddite" in a short, friendly blog comment. Another commenter found the word highly offensive. (In case you were wondering, actual Luddites were an early 19th cent. group in the English Midlands who resisted the Industrial Revolution and revered a mythical Robin-Hood type figure called King Ludd.)

When a Boomer like me uses the word, we usually mean somebody who thinks the Internet is a fad and still takes photos with the Instamatic he bought in 1976. To the young woman who had the melt-down, apparently it means somebody who doesn't have the latest Kindle Fire. If she'd seen my matronly, aging self, she might not have assumed I was attacking her lack of youthful geek-chic.

Although you can't be sure. She also might have been one of those people who surf the 'Net looking for ways to feel insulted. Insults generate self-righteous rage, which produces endorphins that some people find addictive. They will ferret out anything that can set off their anger triggers, so they'll feel justified in beating others to an emotional pulp.

Insult Ferrets are just one of the disruptive types who might wander into your blog.

Your first instinct will be to delete an out-of-line comment, but that's not always the best solution, especially if you're dealing with Cyber-Taliban types. They may feel you haven't properly submitted to their will, so they'll launch a coordinated campaign against you on other blogs and forums and the problem will escalate.

I've made suggestions on when to delete comments below. Do immediately delete anything that is bigoted, libelous, or deliberately hurtful to any of your readers.

It helps to remember you can't please all of the people all of the time. Humor is subjective, and some people will feel offended by any kind of joke. There are common brain conditions that leave people unable to understand whimsy, hyperbole for comic effect, or irony of any kind, so a lot of humor is a mystery to them.

Remember people tend to judge other people's characters by their own. Happy, friendly people assume others are happy and friendly until proved otherwise. Angry, nasty people assume everybody else is angry and nasty, too.

When they accuse you of bizarre things, they aren't saying anything about you; they're telling you what is in their own heads.

And the truth is—no matter how nice you are, some folks are just not going to like you. You have to ignore them and concentrate on the people who do.

Here are some of the disruptive people to watch out for:

1) Trolls. "Troll" is an all-encompassing term that means pretty much anybody who's looking to cause trouble and might be lurking under a cyberbridge. Trolls thrive on creating conflict for its own sake. If they happen on a Christian blog, they'll post an atheist manifesto. Then they'll go to an atheist site and tell them they're all going to Hell. Their posts are often obscene or bigoted. They're probably living in their mom's basement and haven't had work since they lost the dishwashing job at Krusty Burger in 2008. These are people who feel pretty helpless in the world, and this is how they make themselves feel powerful.

Solution: Don't feed trolls! Any engagement at all will be perceived as encouragement. They crave attention and don't care if it's negative or positive. Delete the post and try to laugh about it with offline friends. No matter how nasty the remark, remember it's not aimed at you. It's the whole world these people hate.

Tip: Trolls usually post as "anonymous," so if you're hearing from them regularly, you can change your settings to require a name in order to comment.

2) Sockpuppets. On the Interwebz, "sockpuppet" means somebody using a false identity to praise himself or attack his competitors, posing as an independent third party. The term first originated in Internet communities and spread when customer reviews started gaining importance on shopping sites.

Somebody using a false name might post comments praising his own product or knocking competitors. Sockpuppet reviews are sometimes offered for sale. I saw a site recently that offered positive one-line reviews on Amazon for $5, or negative ones for a competitor's book for $10. That explains why you sometimes see Amazon pages with 25 or 30 nearly identical, generic reviews. (I don't think they fool very many readers.)

People also use sockpuppets for blog comments that promote their own agendas. Bogus, fee-charging agents, for instance, sometimes pose as clients to talk up their agency on writing blogs.

Solution: Use your judgment and delete as necessary. If you know the puppet's true identity, you can respond with the person's real name, and that may deflate them. If you see an obvious sock puppet review on a writer's Amazon page, report abuse.

Tip: If you have a tech-savvy friend, they can usually find the identity of a puppet visiting your blog through their IP address.

3) Insult Ferrets. These people are rage addicts looking for a fix. They're surfing the 'Net looking for things that make them feel insulted, so they can justify going on the attack. If the young woman I mentioned above is one of them, she'll have a whole list of trigger words besides "Luddite." She might go off on a blogger for using the word "Heffalump," because that's what her cheating ex-husband called her when she was in her third trimester. Or the word "blue" will send her into a wild temper tantrum because everybody says her eyes are blue, but they're really blue-green, kind of, when she wears that green blouse.

Insult Ferrets tend to be narcissistic and think everything is about them.

Solution: Try to soothe ruffled feathers, but realize you've done nothing wrong. If a Ferret attacks one of your commenters, call her on it in a friendly but firm way. If you're attacked on your own blog, apologize, even if you're clearly not in the wrong, but only respond once. Don't engage in conversation. Don't delete unless the comment is seriously over the top, because that will anger the Ferret further and anger is what they feed on. They'll come back for more.

Tip: You can block addresses by reporting them as spam.

4) The Politically Correctibot. This is a version of the Insult Ferret—people who browse blogs looking for perceived insults—not to themselves, but some downtrodden demographic. They often have the linguistic sense of Spellcheck software. I've seen them attack a blogger for using the word "fatuous," calling it an insult to fat people. Or they'll attack anybody who talks about Seinfeld's "Soup Nazi" as being unsympathetic to the Holocaust. I once got attacked for being "ageist" because I suggested that some of us Boomers have trouble learning the latest ways of the Interwebz.

I can guarantee the attackers weren't Boomers, because we KNOW how hard it is to keep up with this stuff.

Solution: If they're berating you, it's probably best to simply ignore them, but if it's one of your commenters being dissed, speak up. But sometimes you can leave an idiotic comment in place, because it doesn't harm anybody but the person who wrote it.

5) The Cyber-Taliban. These are Ferrets and Correctibots who operate as a tribe. They see themselves as the righteousness police—often enforcing a set of rules unknown outside their own niche demographic. I knew an author who had in some mysterious way stepped on the cybertoes of a fanatical online group. The day his next book came out, he got ten one-star Amazon reviews. I sent him a sympathetic tweet and immediately got flooded with DM's warning me not to associate with the "evil" author.

Solution: Report abuse. Then run. Disengage from these people in any way you can. Delete if the comment is libelous, but otherwise, it may be wiser to let it stand so they think they've "won." Simply unfollow, block, and unfriend. There's no way to have a rational encounter with mass hysteria.

6) Cyberbullies. The fanatics above were being cyberbullies. But bullies don't need to be motivated by self-righteousness. Some are just mean. Destroying innocent lives and reputations is fun for them. You've seen the headlines. They often work in packs and can, in some cases, actually cause death by making vulnerable people commit suicide. Teens are especially susceptible to this, both as victims and perpetrators, but adults can be victimized too. I have personally received death threats from some Cyber-Taliban bullies. Scary stuff.

Solution. Report them to the FBI and get help on the National Crime Prevention Website if you're in the U.S. They are breaking the law. There is no reason to put up with criminal behavior, even if it's "only on the Internet." Delete seriously offensive comments, but you might want to leave some up if you can stand it. A self-incriminating post will catch up to the perpetrator eventually and will get you lots of support and sympathy from sane people.

If you see somebody being bullied on a blog, try to reach out to them through their own blog or other social media. They may be newbies who could end up seriously hurt.

Some bloggers are cyberbullies themselves and can cause real pain to unsuspecting people who think they're in friendly territory.

I've encountered a number of them. They usually have a group of sycophantic minions who can turn into a CyberTaliban on cue. Victims may think they've somehow done something to deserve the snark or personal attacks. They almost never have.

NOTE: If you feel you're in real, physical danger from a cyberbully who shows knowledge of where you live and work, contact local law enforcement immediately.

The most important thing to keep in mind when dealing with blog meanies is: DON'T TAKE IT PERSONALLY. Remember it has nothing to do with you. You're just a random victim. How you should deal with them individually depends on the severity of the attack and how strongly it affects your blog and your followers.

Monitoring your comments will keep the nasty comments from appearing on your blog, but it also prevents conversation in the thread, and comes across as a little amateurish and paranoid, so I don't suggest monitoring comments on your newest posts unless you're under a severe meanie attack.

CATHERINE

HOW AUTHORS BENEFIT FROM RED ROOM, PINTEREST, GOOGLE+ AND OTHER SOCIAL MEDIA

NOW THAT WE'VE (HOPEFULLY) CONVINCED YOU TO GET OUT THERE and get your feet wet (or wetter, as the case may be), I want to go into more specifics on how these social media tools can help your career.

Joe Konrath, on his blog A Newbie's Guide to Publishing, advises his readers to go slowly in these areas, and I think that's good advice. I agree it's better to take these sites one at a time, and get comfortable before adding more facets. You don't want to risk becoming the proverbial jack of all trades but master of none. (Sorry. That's a cliché, isn't it? Serving our point that real people do sometimes use them.)

Let's face it. A full range of social media takes time to learn. Each site is a little like learning a new language.

Do practice every day, but don't overwhelm yourself.

I'll start with examples of sites I've used successfully. I'm leaving out Twitter and Facebook only because I said so much about them in my last chapter. Also because they're the ones you're most likely to already know.

Red Room: Personally, I just love Red Room. I love the people who run it. I love using their site. You can create a great little online space for yourself, adding an amazing array of photos, videos, reviews and more.

And they list all your books with buying links.

Red Room will send you a newsletter with a topic they invite you to blog about. If your blog post on that topic is one of the ones chosen and highlighted, this will bring you a lot of traffic.

If you check out the Red Room home page, you'll see a number of features. Featured blog post, featured review, featured author conversation. In the three or four years I've been a member, I've been on their home page more than half a dozen times. And you can let them know when you have a new release, a great review, big news. There are actual people there, who will interact with you. Try to find that on Twitter or Facebook. Yet Red Room is an important and well-respected site.

They'll Tweet your book news to their big Twitter following, and their newsletter can be helpful in featuring you as well.

Once again, I suggest you copy your blog posts, or at least the ones you most want seen, to your Red Room blog.

I could go on and on, but do make contact with these lovely folks and find out for yourself what the Red Room community has to offer.

Pinterest: There's always a new social media darling, and, as of this writing, it's Pinterest. People will warn you it's quite addictive, but I have a classic addict's personality and I have yet to find myself unable to stop pinning. I do like it, though, because I feel that putting together a dozen boards really reflects one's personality.

But how does it benefit writers?

This took a little figuring on my part, too.

Again, as with all other social media sites, please resist the temptation to turn it into a commercial for yourself. People don't like ads on the Internet. Take a hint.

I began by using it just to let people get to know me better. I made up a board for my favorite books (by *other* authors), my favorite movies, things I think are generally cool, places I'd like to go, etc.

Then I started wanting to post my own photos. I take a lot of travel, hiking, nature, and outdoor shots. So that fit well with boards like, "Favorite places and spaces." I made a board for places I still want to go. (A word of caution: you are on the hook for copyright violations. Pin responsibly.)

I had the option of either uploading a pin, or pinning from the Web. Most of the photos were not on my site yet, so I uploaded them. Then I realized that every pinned image (or video) clicks through to the source. I was wasting potential traffic to my website!

I updated the photo gallery pages on my site, then redid my Pinterest boards so that all of the photos were pinned from my site, and therefore linked back to my site.

Then I realized all my travel blogs have photos, so I made a board of my travel blogs.

Then I realized I could do the same with all my author interview blogs. So I created a "Fellow authors I have interviewed" board. Then I did a blog series on book bloggers, and created a board for my favorite book bloggers. With their photos. Linking back to my own blog.

So, out of more than a dozen boards, at least four of them contain valuable link-backs to my site. And lots of others don't. They're just other interesting things to help readers know me better. No hard sell. But more Web traffic is good.

Amazon: ...is not a social networking site. You're right. But learn to use Amazon Author Central. Post photos and videos on your Amazon author page, work on your bio, and teach it to import your latest blog post and your latest tweet. Where will you find a bigger pool of potential readers than on Amazon? And your author page is becoming more important in the digital age, because Amazon is adding a new feature that allows ebook readers to click directly to it from their Kindles. Don't waste the opportunity.

Google+: It doesn't seem that it's unseated Facebook, does it? But then again, there are signs that it has gained a lot of ground.

I have both a personal profile on Google+ and an author page. And I confess that I simply copy the same information onto them that I post on Facebook and Twitter. I can't give you dozens of compelling reasons why you must do the same. But I will say that literally hundreds of people have found me and followed me on Google+, with no particular effort on my part. So my same words can reach a new audience.

I also see some potential in their video "hangouts." Book group discussions with the author spring to mind. You can do the same on

Skype, but hangouts might be technologically easier for all, or Google+ might be a great place to find the book group.

YouTube: I've been able to use it fairly successfully by posting video excerpts (like a book trailer, but with less negative baggage) for most of my books. It's simply an audio of me reading an excerpt, with an original video or a series of stills to accompany the reading. Then I mix the video excerpts with travel videos and other more personal stuff on my "channel." Again, more get to know me, less hard sell.

Do search your name and your books now and then on YouTube. You never know what you might find. I've found book trailers and vlog reviews made and posted by readers.

Next: Now. Breathe deeply. Because they'll just keep inventing more social media sites. You don't have to get involved with every one that comes over the horizon. But keep your mind open and your ear to the ground.

This is free publicity. It doesn't pay to fear or resent it. Just say thank you to the Internet gods and keep learning.

ANNE

TWITTER FOR SHY PERSONS—15 STEPS TO STRESS-FREE TWEETING

TWITTER TERRIFIED ME AT FIRST. IT'S BEEN DESCRIBED AS THE WORLD'S biggest cocktail party and that sounds about right: a cacophonous, shallow, time-consuming Hell for shy, writerly persons.

But most experts say authors who are serious about publication MUST be on Twitter. So I steeled myself and crashed the soirée. I tweeted my new blogposts, and suddenly, my blog went from 40 followers to 400. And then 1400. Many more readers find my blog through Twitter than click through Google.

BUT I HAVE NEVER ONCE TWEETED WHAT I HAD FOR LUNCH. And I only spend about five minutes a day on the site.

So how did I do it?

After making a lot of mistakes (and probably annoying a lot of people—sorry if I stepped on cybertoes) I finally realized that since it's like a Hollywood party, I had to follow the rules of the classic Hollywood schmooze:

- Smile a lot
- Be helpful and/or funny
- Never look desperate or needy
- Accept there is a caste system, and you will never be a Brahmin
- Remember you can't go wrong with, "kiss, kiss—love your work!"

Here are my shy-person secrets for Twitter-schmoozing:

1) Get a good head shot. Nobody follows an egg, so you gotta get a picture up there right away. Actually, it doesn't have to be of you. I used my Mad Men caricature for six months. But a fun, smiley picture of yourself is best. Skip the glamour shots or you may be taken for a porn spammer.

2) Inform, amuse, but never offer TMI (too much information). A profile like: "Retail slave, Romance writer, seeker of chocolate" is better than "I'm an English major and overweight single mom who has been a greeter at Walmart for 20 years." But do let people know something about you that makes you worth following. N.B.: If you write, ALWAYS put "writer" in there, even if you've never published a thing, so you'll be tagged as part of the writing community.

3) Use your @ownname for your "twitter handle." Your "handle" is your Twitter id, which is preceded by the @ sign. Why use your own name? This is about building platform, remember? I know you're tired of me harping on it, but the majority of author-Tweeters don't seem to get this: unless you're writing books under the pseudonym @shysuzi, you're wasting your Twitter time if you don't use your name. If it's long, shorten it, since you want to get retweeted, and you're limited to 140 characters.

4) Remember paranoia is creepy. I have no idea why people "protect their tweets." It's like going to a party in a burka. It doesn't make you invisible; it makes you weird. If you don't want people to read what you write, just stay in your cave and keep pounding out those 350K word literary neo-Nazi Thriller/Chick Lit/Westerns. When you want twittering, you can get a cuckoo clock. But if you want to be read, put yourself out there. It's the only way.

5) Don't just stand there: say something. In 140 characters or less. It's best not to use "txt spk" unless really necessary. (Twitter will shorten urls for you if you want to post a link.) Trying to get followers with zero tweets can make you look like a spammer, so tweet before you follow. Not about your two-for-$20 lunch special at Applebee's. Just say something cute and helpless like "Hi there, Twitterverse. I have no idea what I'm doing." People love to help newbies as long as they're humble and not selling anything. And as soon as you've followed somebody, respond to one of their tweets. If they post a link to a great blogpost on prologues, tweet "@suzyscrivener Thanks for the link! I like prologues, too." That's all there is to it.

The formula for tweeting is supposed to be 33% original tweets (stuff like "I just finished Catherine Ryan Hyde's *When You Were Older*. What a great book!"), 33% responses like the one above, and 33% retweets. But I've discovered that about 70% retweets and 15% each of the others has worked just fine to get started. Retweets take the least amount of time and people like you for retweeting them.

Now you're ready to party:

6) **Start by following people you know.** Like me. I enjoy following people who only have one follower. If I'm 50% of your audience, I feel special.

7) **Then follow some you don't know.** Like agents, *The New Yorker*, and Twitter deities like Nathan Bransford and Jane Friedman. They will NOT follow you back. But now that you have a couple of followers, that won't hurt your feelings, right? You'll learn a lot from their god-like tweets. I like to follow the news agencies like Reuters, too—that way I get breaking news. Retweeting news stories can establish you as a reliable tweep.

But don't follow too many stars. Twitter won't let you follow more than a certain number in ratio to your followers because people who follow a ton of people who don't follow back are usually spammers.

8) **Whenever you open your home page**, check for @connect and REPLY. Old Twitter did not have an obvious @message button, so I didn't see any of my messages for, oh, probably a year. People must have thought I was the most awful snot. Don't do this. And be sure to send your reply through the "reply" window, not a direct message. Direct messages should be sent sparingly. They sort of infringe on personal space. I think that's why the newest version of Twitter hides the DM button in the drop-down menu next to the header (on the top right of your screen.)

9) You don't have to thank somebody for a follow. And if you must, do NOT ask them to like your Facebook page or buy your book. It looks spammy.

10) Follow people back. I follow pretty much everybody who follows me unless they're obviously follower-collectors who plan to sell you to the morons who buy followers. (Collectors have usually been on Twitter for 8 hours and follow 500,000 people.) I also tend to avoid anybody with no tweets or profiles, people who tweet random nonsense phrases, represent car dealerships on other continents, and writers with no tweets except "buy my book." I also don't follow writers who have nothing in their feed but odd random quotes from their own work. (This is amazingly common, so I assume some publicity guru thinks this is a good idea. It isn't.)

11) Make lists. These aren't anywhere near as important as they used to be. There was a kind of contest to see how many people you could get to list you and it got really annoying. Now lists are buried in the drop-down menu. But it's still worth it to list people who belong to different groups—like actual personal friends and family, fellow writers or fellow floaty pen collectors or whatever. Once you start gathering followers, you don't have to wade through every single boring tweet to find the relevant ones. Later you'll probably want to use something like TweetDeck to help you sort followers, but I'm not going to complicate this with too much tech at the beginning.

12) RETWEET, RETWEET, RETWEET. Every time you click on a link to a great blog or read something inspiring, click the retweet button. Also tweet links to articles or posts of interest to your followers (there's almost always a "t" button somewhere on a Web page). This makes you a fountain of knowledge and inspiration. And everybody's grateful for a retweet. They'll often thank you and give you a follow.

13) Skip the personal stuff. Social media gurus will probably have me twit-canned for saying this, but you don't really have to tweet personal stuff at all. I don't—unless you count my daily tweet about my blog and stuff about books I like. I learned this from Mystery author and social media goddess Elizabeth Spann Craig. She reads 100s of publishing blogs and tweets links to her favorite posts. And: I've never seen her tweet anything personal. But she has like, 25 thousand followers.

14) Use #hashtags. A # sign is called a "hashtag" on Twitter. Using that symbol creates a searchable category. You're much more likely to get read if your Tweets are listed in a category. It took me way too long to learn this. If you want to Tweet your blog post about editing, leave space for the 10 characters in #amediting, and people who are currently editing their WIPs will be able to seek you out. Other popular writing categories are #amwriting #writequote #writingtips #pubtip #indie #bookmarket, and #writegoal.

And there are many more. Followers of social media guru Kristen Lamb use the tag #myWANA (for her book *We are Not Alone—the Writer's Guide to Social Media*) which I find very useful for info on writing. It's also an automatic entry into a vibrant writing community. You can create your own categories, too. Look around to see how tweets that interest you are tagged. Then when you're looking for info on a topic, put the #topic into the search window and you'll see what people are currently saying about it.

15) Spread the love. If you have favorite tweeters, give them a mention on #WW, (Writer Wednesday) or #FF (Follow Friday.) But don't do it the way you see it done most of the time—with eight or ten names strung together and no other information. The best #FF recommendation says something unique about one or two people you're recommending. Say something like "#FF @walkingdead and @ilovebrains have the best tweets about #zombies."

No lunch menus. No sobbing about rejections. Just be helpful.

I'm not going to lie to you. Twitter isn't always fun for non-party persons. And it's full of ruthless corporate types who are only there to use and manipulate you. People will follow you, then unfollow the minute you reciprocate. (Although an app like Tweepi can help you weed those out.) Others will spam you unmercifully. Or tweet inanities every two minutes. The A-listers will never respond to your messages, even if you're congratulating them on a recent triumph.

But, like a huge Hollywood party, it provides a chance to meet interesting people who are useful to know. They're probably not celebrities, and are more likely to be carrying trays of canapés than flashing bling and touting their latest project. But they may visit your blog later and you might even become friends.

Friends are good. Even if you have no interest in publishing that book.

PART 5

BEGINNING THE QUERY PROCESS

ANNE

PUBLISHERS—WHO ARE THEY? AND WHAT ARE AN AUTHOR'S PUBLISHING CHOICES?

THERE'S MUCH TALK ON THE INTERWEBZ ABOUT "BIG SIX", "SMALL presses", and "indie publishing." But a lot of people who are newer to writing aren't quite sure what these terms really mean.

None of us wants to sound dumb, so we usually don't ask.

So I'll pretend you did.

Here's a quick guide:

The Big Six-Five-Four

The "Big Six" has become the Big Five since we first published this book less than a year ago, and will soon become the Big Four or Three.

These are the six (now five) multi-national corporations that controlled most of the Western world's publishing for a couple of decades:

1) **Simon and Schuster**

2) **HarperCollins**

3) **Random House**

4) **Macmillan**

5) **The Penguin Group (Pearson)**

6) **Hachette**

Two are American: Simon and Schuster and HarperCollins, (although Harper is a division of Rupert Murdoch's NewsCorp, so it's pretty international).

Two are German: Random House is owned by Bertelsmann and Macmillan is owned by Holzbrinck.

One (Penguin-Pearson) is British.

One (Hachette) is French.

But in October of 2012, Random House merged with Pearson to form Penguin House (or as many Tweeters jokingly suggested "Random Penguin".) A month later, HarperCollins started making moves on Simon and Schuster.

So as of this writing, we may have the Big Four. Many are predicting it will be the Big Three before long.

Meanwhile, Macmillan has been dosey doe-ing with a new powerhouse boutique digital publisher (see below) called Entranced, which a lot of us hadn't even heard of a year ago.

Most books you see in stores still come from the Big

Six/Five/Four/Three. They have hundreds of imprints with familiar names like Little Brown, Knopf, Viking, NAL, Pocket, Scribner, St. Martins, Dutton, Avon, William Morrow, Crown, Tor, Zondervan, Grand Central, Dell etc., but they're all owned by one of those six corporations.

You used to need an agent to query the Big Guys. There were a few exceptions, like Tor/Forge/Tom Doherty—which is a division of MacMillan—and some children's divisions of the big houses.

But that is changing very fast. Most of the big houses are now branching into digital-only imprints, and some of those accept—even welcome—unagented manuscripts. Avon Impulse—an imprint of HarperCollins—started an online submission form for authors in 2012, and a number of others have followed their lead.

Five of the Big Six—all but Random House—ran afoul of the U.S. Department of Justice because of their attempts to keep the price of ebooks artificially high. A lot of people thought this meant Big Publishing was doomed.

I think that's highly unlikely. Like ocean liners, bigger companies take longer to change course, but they will.

Mid-Sized publishers (sometimes called "small" just to confuse you)

This covers a lot of territory, from university presses to big international operations like Canada's Harlequin, and the U.K.'s Bloomsbury (which has branches in London, New York, Berlin, and Sydney), and Scholastic, the powerhouse that published J. K. Rowling's Harry Potter books.

When Mid-sizers are successful, they've tended to be bought up by the Big Six. (Thomas Nelson, the largest independent Christian publisher, was bought by HarperCollins in 2011.)

But some Mid-Sizers are dying out in the digital age. The ones who relied mostly on the "supermarket paperback" have been going under. Dorchester is one that fell recently. (Although some of its imprints were bought up by Amazon, the new kid on the Big Publisher block.)

There are scores of mid-sized houses. They often address particular niche markets. Here's a sample list—by no means comprehensive:

- **Kensington**: Most genres except SciFi and Fantasy.

- **Llewellyn**: New Age nonfiction and mysteries (under their Midnight Ink imprint).

- **Chronicle Books**: Art, food, pop culture (and some illustrated fiction like Griffin and Sabine).

- **Perseus Books**: Travel and other nonfiction genres.

- **Workman Publishing**: Tends toward the literary. Imprints are Algonquin, Black Dog & Leventhal, Storey Publishing, Timber Press, Artisan Books, HighBridge Audio, Fearless Critic.

- **Scholastic**: Children's and Young Adult.

- **Sourcebooks**: Formerly a publisher of financial guidebooks, it's grown to include fiction in all genres in the last decade.

- **Sunset**: Gardening, cookbooks and how-to.

- **Poisoned Pen**: (Maybe on the cusp of small and mid-sized.) One of the largest Mystery publishers.

- **F + W Media/Writer's Digest Books**: How-to.

- **Titan Books**: U.K. publisher of movie and TV tie-ins as well as graphic novels. Took on Dorchester's crime fiction imprint, Hard Case Crime.

- **Houghton Mifflin Harcourt**: Textbook publishers. (Declared bankruptcy in May 2012.)

Most Mid-sized publishers want agented submissions, but not all. Kensington still accepts unagented queries as of this writing. Check websites for submission guidelines. Midnight Ink no longer accepts unagented queries, but some Harlequin lines do.

NOTE: Mid-sizers tend to pay smaller advances and lower royalties (that includes Harlequin). They also tend to be the most financially precarious. So expect some of these to go the way of Dorchester if they don't keep up with the times.

Retailer/Publishers

Amazon is a bookstore that has become a book publisher. It has a number of lines in different genres:

1) Amazon Encore: Reprints of self-published and out of print books

2) Amazon Crossing: Books in translation

3) Amazon Children's Publishing

4) Thomas and Mercer: Thrillers

5) Montlake: Romance (Which has bought out Dorchester's Romance line).

6) 47 North: SciFi

7) New Harvest: General Fiction—some published in conjunction with Houghton Mifflin Harcourt (see how convoluted this all gets?)

You need great sales as a self-pubber to be approached by Amazon's publishing wing, so most sales to Amazon come from agents.

Amazon has some of the most author-friendly deals around, BUT other bookstores are reluctant to carry their products because of the obvious conflict of interest.

Other online retailers like iTunes/Apple may follow suit.

Brick-and-mortar bookstores are also producing their own books. This isn't new. City Lights in San Francisco has had its own publishing wing since 1955, but with POD technology, this may become a trend that will help bookstores stay alive.

Boutique Ebook Publishers

These are new publishers like Entangled, Ellora's Cave and Samhain Press (with more start-ups every week). They publish primarily ebooks and usually appeal to a particular niche.

Expect to see more and more of these.

Because ebooks have low overhead, they can be more author-friendly and often provide some marketing help for their authors. (Samhain is branching into print, although the bulk of their titles are ebooks.) They usually pay no advances, but offer much higher royalties.

These generally do not require an agent for submissions. But because this is a new industry, check them out thoroughly and try to get referrals from satisfied clients.

Small Presses

These are sometimes called "indie presses." (Ten years ago, this is what people meant by "indie" publishing, but now self-pubbers have kind of taken over the word.)

There are thousands of them. It's hard to find useful listings because the number is never stable. They spring up and get knocked down like a literary version of Whac-A-Mole.

Some, like Beacon Press, GrayWolf, and Copper Canyon Press are extremely prestigious and have been around for decades.

Others are regional and publish books specific to one area.

Others address niche genres, like Canada's SciFi publisher Edge, and noir Mystery publisher Bleak House Books.

A large percentage focus on poetry and literary fiction. *Poets and Writers* magazine has a great database for literary small presses at www.pw.org.

They are usually labors of love and nobody gets rich, but they're often a good way to break in to print and lots of authors are very happy to stay with a small press where there is a more personal interaction with editors.

Authors are responsible for their own marketing and there's generally no advance, but higher royalties.

These publishers generally don't want to deal with agents—writers should query the editors directly. (Remember to check for submission guidelines on their websites.)

But beware: Check them out thoroughly with sites like Writer Beware and Preditors and Editors—and if they're not well-established, contact other clients before you sign. It's a good idea to have a lawyer or publishing professional look at the contract before you sign.

Micropresses

These are a tiny version of the small press—usually one or two-person operations, generally oriented toward the literary. They often publish chapbooks of poetry. They operate on a shoestring, and are usually run as a hobby.

Often these are run by authors who are essentially self-publishers who also take on a few colleagues and friends. A micropress can be a friendly, supportive place for a writer to start out. But beware: they can also be clueless and unprofessional.

Some of these can be a great first step into publishing, but look for red flags. Grandiosity, unrealistic promises, negativity about the industry, and bad spelling/grammar on the website are tell-tale signs.

Vanity Presses

These are publishers who make their money from services to authors rather from sales of books.

Before ebooks and POD (print on demand) technology, vanity presses were mostly pricey self-indulgences—although every so often a vanity-published book like the 1990s phenomenon *The Celestine Prophecy* made it to mainstream readers.

Two of the best known of the traditional vanity presses are Vantage and Dorrance.

But as prices came down and self-publishing took off, the line between real publishers, printing services, and vanity presses blurred. A lot of authors got taken in by vanity publishers posing as real publishers.

But others successfully used them as printers for self-publishing and with a lot of promotion, made the bestseller lists with books like *The Christmas Box* and *Legally Blonde*.

The problem is that most vanity publishers overcharge for services, which means their books are too pricey to be profitable for the author. Some of them, like PublishAmerica, even tie up the author's copyright for seven years.

In the mid 2000's, most of the best known vanity publishers were bought out by one company, AuthorHouse. They kept the imprints' names but offered the same thing: pricey packages that produce books that are too expensive for the author to make money from.

In what seemed to some like a misguided move, Simon and Schuster teamed up with AuthorHouse in late 2012 to form a vanity imprint of their own, called Archway. And things got even iffier when Penguin bought AuthorHouse outright and soon merged with Random House. This meant the biggest of the Big Five, Penguin Random House, became the owner of the world's biggest vanity press.

Authors may be led to believe using AuthorHouse services means they're published by the Big 5, but it's not the case. It's still a vanity press. Writer Beware and many other author watchdog groups do not recommend using any of AuthorHouse's services in spite of their ties to the Big Five

Indie Publishing

True DIY publishing. You do everything yourself or hire somebody to do it for you. You can do this several ways:

1) Get help from a publishing facilitator like Smashwords, D2D, or BookBaby, who for a flat fee or a small percentage will format your ebook and upload to different retail platforms and keep track of royalties. They also offer inexpensive cover design and other services.

2) Get shepherded through the process by an agent. A number of agents are actually helping authors become indie publishers these days—usually existing clients. Some industry purists consider this a conflict of interest, but the agented authors I know who have published through their agents have nothing but good things to say about this.

3) Hire your own private editor, cover designer, and formatter and keep complete control.

NOTE: "Complete control" does not extend to Amazon. Author-friendly as it is, the 'Zon has glitches that can be a nightmare for the author. Cover art can be wrong, prices go up and down mysteriously, and books can disappear for months at a time. Be prepared for a few catastrophes during Amazon's remarkable growth.

If you're an indie publisher who wants your books printed in hard copy as well as electronic form, you'll need the services of—

P.O.D. Publishing Service Providers

These are printer/distributors who use print on demand technology. This means that instead of having a huge print run for your book that has to be stored in a warehouse, the book is only printed when it is ordered.

Most small presses use these providers, too.

The primary POD providers are:

- **CreateSpace:** Owned by Amazon. Printing with them gets you on Amazon, which owns a huge share of the book market.

- **LightningSource:** Owned by Ingram, the biggest book distributor in the U.S. Ingram supplies bookstores, so if you want to see your book in your local bookstore window, LS has the advantage.

- **BookBaby** and **Lulu** also are reasonably priced POD book printers. BookBaby also has a reasonably priced book scanning service.

ANNE

THE NUMBER ONE MISTAKE NEW WRITERS MAKE

AFTER YEARS OF READING AGENT BLOGS, WEBSITES AND SNARKY tweets on the subject of clueless query mistakes, it occurred to me that most of the complaints can be boiled down to one major offense: querying too early.

It's not just that we don't take the time to give the book an extra polish. We also fail to educate ourselves about the publishing industry before we try to join it. I cringe when I remember the amateurish things I did back in the days before agent blogs.

But these days, the information we need is right there at the click of a mouse, so there's no excuse not to find out how things are done. It will save time in the long run.

Unprofessional gun-jumpers waste agents' time, frustrate themselves, and overstuff the slushpile. Or they publish inferior and/or under-promoted books, "ending careers practically before they start" according to agent Dorian Karchmar of William Morris.

I know about that "ending a career practically before it starts" thing. When I was champing at the bit to publish my first book, I didn't have a clue that if you publish a book or two but don't have the sales numbers—which can be completely out of your control—finding another publisher is close to impossible. I've got the calluses on my soul to prove it.

So don't champ. Take your time. You may not get a do-over.

Ms. Karchmar says: "Don't give in to internal and external pressures to try to find an agent before you've matured as a writer. The book business is very difficult and not getting any easier; most books that are published don't sell well." Her advice? "Write a book that only you could write, and rewrite, rewrite, rewrite."

Agent Janet Reid goes further. She suggests writing and polishing at least two books before you start the query process: "After you've written your first novel; you wait, write a second, revise, then query."

And we also need to pay attention to all those agents whose websites post variations of what agent Andrea Hurst says: "Publishing is a business. It bears repeating: publishing is a business! And we are professionals." Writers have to learn to be professionals too.

But Ms. Karchmar is right about those pressures.

You've got the external pressure:

1) From your mom, who thinks the fact you've written 80,000 words of anything is so noteworthy she's already written up the press releases.

2) From your significant other, who wants to know when exactly his/her years of sharing you with that *&%! manuscript are going to start paying a few bills.

3) From your friends, who are getting kind of embarrassed for you, when you keep telling them you're a writer but have nothing to show for it. How long can it take to write a book anyway? They can type 55 words a minute!

4) From your critique group, who are so tired of helping you revise that WIP ...AGAIN, they're screaming "Send it! Away! Immediately!"

And the internal pressure:

1) From your battered self-esteem: How many more years can you take those eye-rolls you get every time you tell somebody at a party you're "pre-published"... and you're only delivering pizzas until you make it as a writer?

2) From artistic insecurity: You won't really, truly know you have talent unless you're validated by the industry, right?

3) From financial insecurity: It's tough to pay off the loans for the Masters degree when the only paying writing gig you've had since you got the degree is updating the menu for your brother-in-law's fish and chips place.

4) From your muse, who says: "This is some @*&%ing amazing s#%t, man! The world totally needs this book!" (What? A muse can't be a stoner dude?)

We've heard them all. But the trick is learning to ignore them. We have to learn to listen instead for that small inner voice when it finally says:

1) **"I've got a couple of polished, print-ready books** that will stand up to the snarkiest reviewer."

2) **"My ego is enough under control** that I'm willing to rewrite again for my agent (even though he's dead wrong). Then again for my editor (even though she looks maybe twelve years old and the last book she read probably had pop-ups in it). And I will not threaten anyone with homicide when they put Fabio on the cover of my prequel to *The Great Gatsby*."

3) **"I'm a professional.** I know all about how the publishing industry works and I'm ready to turn out at least a book a year, promote it, and live my life on deadline."

I approached my career the hard way, but you don't have to. I'm happy where I am now, but I sure took a rocky path to get here. I know I'd have saved myself a lot of misery if I'd held off with those queries and learned more about the business before I dove into it, soul-first.

ANNE

I'VE WRITTEN A BOOK—NOW WHAT?

THAT'S ONE OF THE MOST COMMON QUESTIONS I GET FROM writers. There's tons of info out there on the Interwebz, but not everybody knows how to access it. And along with the good info, there's plenty of bad—especially from predatory vanity publishers, less-than-ethical service providers, and bogus agents. So here are some basics for newbies.

Your book has been critiqued, edited, and polished to a glittering sheen. What do you do next?

1) Celebrate! Break out the champagne, chocolate, fireworks, old Prince CDs, or whatever puts you in a festive mood. Contact a few people who remember who you are after your time in your writing cave, and toast your accomplishment. 80% of people in the U.S. say they want to write a book. A fraction of one percent actually do. That percentage now includes you. Woo-hoo!!

2) Make sure you know your genre. This isn't always as easy as it sounds, but pick one to three genres as a tool to help agents and publishers—and especially, readers—know what kind of book they're dealing with. When you're querying, make sure you use established categories like "Paranormal Romantic Suspense" not "Vampire Bunny Western." Creativity doesn't work in your favor here.

But you ARE allowed to change genres according to who you query. Genre boundaries are oddly flexible these days. Both Charlaine Harris's "True Blood" vampire books and Lisa Lutz's dysfunctional-family comedies are categorized as mysteries. Women's fiction is an umbrella that covers everything from Danielle Steel to Margaret Atwood. And anything with a protagonist under 19 can be YA (the most sought-after genres are in YA these days).

Two caveats here: A. don't call it "literary" unless the writing is to-die-for gorgeous (and an advanced degree helps). Never use the term "Chick Lit." You'll still find it listed on some query websites, but it's the kiss of death. Call it "Romantic Comedy."

More on all this in the chapter "Let's Play 'What's my Genre?'"

3) Research and read the latest books in your genre(s) if you haven't already. It's important to have an idea of the market. A query letter is more effective if you can offer "comps"—similar titles that are selling (but not blockbusters—that looks like bragging). Also, the authors of these books may blog or Tweet and you can follow them and get advice. Network. Find out who represents them. Eventually you might even get a recommendation, which is a golden ticket out of the slushpile.

4) Write your synopsis, hook, author bio and a basic query letter template. You can find helpful guides in any number of places. AgentQuery.com and QueryTracker.net provide solid basics. Most agents have similar information on their websites. Nathan Bransford's blogpost on "How to Write a Query Letter" provides the info in a fun and friendly way, and Janet Reid's Query Shark blog is a boot camp for query writers.

5) Start a blog or build a website. (Info on how to do this in our earlier chapters on Internet Basics.) You want a nice, professional picture and a simple bio, with your contact information and something about your book and other publications. Nothing flashy or slow to load. No bragging. Nothing is sadder than a pretentious website for an unpublished writer. But you need a site. Facebook or other social networking sites that require membership won't cut it. Be Googlable, reachable and professional.

6) Start researching agents. See our chapter on "How to Query the Right Agent."

7) Send out five queries. You only do this after your book is finished, edited and polished. You knew that, right?

8) Start your next writing project. Yes. Right now. Don't sit around waiting to get rejected and depressed. Start writing when you're feeling great about yourself for sending those queries. Otherwise the waiting will make you crazy. Get involved in a new project right away. It doesn't have to be a book. This is a great time to add to your portfolio of short stories. Short stories are making a big comeback with ebooks (see the chapter on "Why You Should be Writing Short Fiction"), so these will not go to waste.

9) Receive form rejections. Those are the kind that say, "Dear Writer: this project does not fit our needs at this time." Yup. You now are officially a member of the professional writing community. The one thing we all have in common? Rejections.

10) Send out five more queries.

11) See if you've had any silent rejections. Go to the websites of agents who don't send rejections. Under submission guidelines, it will say "if you haven't heard from us within two months, it's a no." There will be some silent "no's."

12) Mourn. Fine tune your query. But NOT your book. Not yet anyway. Chances are your book is just fine, as Catherine says. Queries, on the other hand, are worth taking a second (and third and fourth) look at.

13) Sent out five more queries. Yeah. This time you think you really nailed that puppy. You've got it down to three paragraphs and your synopsis is 250 words of distilled brilliance.

14) Maybe get a request for a partial! (That's the first few chapters of your book.) But before you send it, go to the agent's website and double check guidelines for formatting and sending documents. Most formatting is pretty standard, and they will probably ask you to send it as a Word (.doc or .rtf) attachment. Many people don't take .docx Word documents, so save it as Word

1998-2003 unless you're sure. Some agents are quirky and will request something like "no italics" or "number your pages on the bottom of the page." Do whatever they say, no matter how silly.

15) Get the partial rejected. Probably another form rejection. Or, if you're really lucky—a personal rejection. This will say something like "I couldn't connect with these characters," or "the protagonist wasn't strong/sympathetic enough," or "the plot is too complex/simplistic" or even "this is perfect, but I have no idea where to sell it."

DO NOT take this as a sign you need to start rewriting your book. These are mostly just polite words to say, "It didn't give me screaming orgasms, so it's not worth all the energy it would take for me to sell it."

Mourn.

16) Get a request for the full manuscript!! Remember to check those guidelines. Some agents still want to see a manuscript on paper. If so, put a big rubber band around it—do not bind—and mail it in a flat-rate box from the post office with a letter-sized stamped, self-addressed envelope inside for their reply. NEVER send it in an annoying way that requires a receipt.

Celebrate. Get the really good chocolate this time.

17) Keep sending queries. Don't wait for that full to be read. It may take a year. It will probably first be read by a young unpaid intern. If she likes it, she'll give it to the busy agent, who will put it on her pile of 150 TBR manuscripts.

18) Get another partial requested and rejected. And another. Start building calluses on your soul. But—if the rejections start to sound the same—like everybody says the same thing about your unsympathetic, wimpipotamus hero, this is when you might give your manuscript another once-over to see if you can figure out how to tweak things without doing serious damage to the book.

19) Get the full rejected. Mourn. You may get some more detailed feedback on this one. Pay attention, but don't despair. And don't start a rewriting frenzy: go read Catherine's great rejection stories in our "Rejection" section.

Agents reject books for lots of silly reasons. Maybe they rep a similar book from another author. Or your hero has the same name as the agent's abusive ex. Or it could be you're targeting the wrong agents or pitching your book wrong. Try changing your query and hook before you change your book.

20) Finish project #2. Start all over again with #2, but keep sending out #1 until it collects 100-150 rejections.

If you're luckier than most, you may...

21) Land an agent somewhere along the way here. In which case, you will now graduate from "query hell" to "submission hell" and it will be your agent who gets the rejections as she submits your book to editors.

22) If you don't, you may want to consider a small press, regional press, or self-publishing.

Many writers choose self-publishing over traditional publishing for their first publication. Hugh Howey, the indie phenomenon who sold the print rights to his *Wool* series for big bucks to Simon and Schuster, thinks it's better to start with self-publishing, then try to sell to the trads, but I think it's best to go through the query process if only for the education it gives you in the industry. It's hard to go into the publishing business when you don't know the ropes.

Check out our chapters on self-publishing if you want to give it a try.

Do be aware that getting multiple rejections from agents doesn't necessarily say anything about the quality of your book. Rejection often has nothing to do with the writing and everything to do with fashion trends in publishing. All it means is your work isn't part of the predicted trend curve at the moment and isn't what corporate marketers think is the hot item for next season.

My Romantic-Comedy/Thriller *Food of Love* was multi-rejected, although a lot of agents said they'd "fallen in love with it" during the Chick Lit craze. But they said it was "too complex" for the audience they were targeting. When their type of dumbed-down Chick Lit made the genre toxic to the industry, *Food of Love* was rejected again—this time because it was "too Chick Lit."

But the book has been a bestselling Romantic Comedy since I published it with a small press in 2011.

These days, some agents consider the successful self-pubbed ebook the best query, so if you're good at marketing and you know you've got the best book you can write, consider self-publishing even if you hope to trad-pub some day. You could be the next self-pubbed millionaire. Just make sure you have some inventory before you start (Amanda Hocking had eight books completed before she self-published).

Or if you're a little more traditional like me, you might start querying presses that don't require agents.

Even some bigger presses still take unagented work. If you write SciFi, you can still direct-query Daw (Penguin) or Tor (MacMillan). For Romance writers, a few Harlequin lines also take unsolicited manuscripts. There are also a number of mid-sized Mystery publishers that welcome writers without agents.

Or start researching the smaller presses. You have hundreds—maybe thousands—to choose from. There's a list of presses that don't require agents at spywriter.com. Be sure you talk to other authors, though, and check Writer Beware, Preditors and Editors, and other watchdog sites before you query. They operate on shoestrings and can often go under, leaving your book in limbo and your royalties unpaid.

But I'm happily published with a small press.

Just don't let that book languish in your files!

ANNE

BEWARE BOGUS LITERARY AGENTS— EIGHT RED FLAGS

I BELONG TO THE GENERATION OF WOMEN WHO WERE TOLD WE WERE more likely be shot by terrorists than find husbands. Several decades later, we're all writing books about our fabulous single lives—as desperate now for literary representation as we once were for the white dress/gold ring thing.

I haven't seen statistics about the comparative likelihood of being shot by a terrorist vs. finding a literary agent, but given the global political climate, I'd say odds heavily favor the terrorists.

Maybe we can fantasize that someday we'll be shot by a terrorist who works for Curtis Brown.

We can't blame agents. We're in this situation because there are less than 450 members of the Association of Author's Representatives while most of the 250 million of us who own computers have at least one novel in progress in the files.

If as many people bought books as wrote them, our situation wouldn't be so dire—so if you really want to increase your chances of publication, buy more books.

With such vast herds of us overpopulating the planet, it's inevitable that we've attracted our share of predators. In order to hang onto your dwindling cash reserves during this soul-crushing process, keep an eye out for these red flags:

1) The agency advertises aggressively. Be wary of agents who advertise. When I finished my first novel, a librarian friend forwarded me an intriguing ad from an agency soliciting submissions. He'd found it in a highly regarded literary magazine. I visited the agency's charming, positive website and almost fell into the trap until I Googled them. They appeared on the "THUMBS DOWN AGENCY LIST" at Writer Beware. This agency refers unsuspecting writers to their own pricey editing service and sells books only to their own vanity publishing company. They've changed their name, but they're still in business.

Do the math: agents don't have to advertise. We'll find them no matter where they hide.

2) They badmouth the publishing industry or other agencies, and claim to be "different." Publishing is a business that relies on networking. Anybody can call herself a "literary agent," but the successful ones generally learn their trade by interning for more established agents or working at a publishing company. Putting down their mentors would be just plain dumb. And if they haven't worked with/for other agents—beware. They may mean well, but they probably won't have the contacts needed to make sales.

3) They charge "mailing fees" up front. This has been a popular scam for decades. Bogus agencies sign thousands of clients and charge them each $250 or more per quarter for "copying and mailing." But they never make a sale. I've seen heartbreaking letters from writers who've lost as much as $3,000 before they caught on.

Small agencies may legitimately ask for copying and mailing fees AFTER they've sent out your manuscript—usually every quarter— but in the 21st century almost all submissions are done electronically, so I'd worry about any agency that's still partying like it's 1999.

4) They refuse to forward rejection letters. When your book is on submission, most agents send on your rejections from editors every quarter or so. Some scammers "submit" manuscripts to a publishing house in a mass mailing addressed to no particular editor. Those are not real submissions. They go into recycling without a response. You are not actually being represented. Move on.

5) No client list on the website. If there's no client page on their website, give them a pass. Agents don't keep client lists "confidential." If they represent a literary star, they'll pound their chests and bellow about it.

6) You can find no record of recent sales. Even if somebody in the agency can claim to have represented Steven King, if she hasn't sold anything since *Carrie*, don't go there.

7) You can't find them listed at any of the commonly used databases for writers. If the agency isn't listed with AgentQuery.com or QueryTracker.net, go check Preditors and Editors and Writer Beware for any reports of scamming or bad faith. Membership is free for all these sites. Agent Query and Query Tracker have forums where you can ask other writers if they have had encounters with a particular agent.

I should note that literary forums are far from infallible. They can be rumor mills and/or troll habitat, so don't take every word as gospel. Cross-reference your data.

I often see the advice that you should check an agent's credentials with the Association of Authors Representatives (or the equivalent for whatever country you're in), but that doesn't make a lot of sense to me. An agent doesn't have to be a member of AAR to be legitimate and even top-notch. New agents have to work for a certain number of years before they're allowed to join—and it's the newer and hungrier agents who are reading queries from new writers and actively building their lists.

8) They charge a "reading fee." You know this, right? It's not just about the money. Unscrupulous agents can actually hurt your career, since publishers consider these tactics unethical and won't do business with them. At best, they'll sell you worthless editing advice. If you have to pay somebody to read your book, it's not ready for publication.

If you're a newbie, DO pay a qualified freelance editor if you need a polish, but never with a promise of publication attached.

Don't forget: Google is your friend. Check 'em out.

ANNE

WRITE YOUR AUTHOR BIO NOW

You've been sending out queries. Lots. And you're getting rejections. Lots. Or that slow disappointment of no response at all.

But one day, you open your email and there it is: "I'm intrigued. Please send the first fifty pages and an author bio."

OMG. Author bio? Is that like a resume? CV? A chronological history? A book jacket blurb?

You dash something off in 20 minutes so you can send this agent your pages and show what a great writer you are so she'll offer representation and get this career on the road!

Whoa. You do NOT want to dash off a bio in 20 minutes. Every word you send is a writing sample. And you want ALL your writing to be polished and brilliant, right?

So, write it now. Yes. Right now. Before you send off another query.

Here's what you do:

Title it only with your name. Write in third person. Keep to 250 words: one page, double spaced or 1/2 page single spaced, if you include a photo. I advise against this unless it's specifically requested or you have a great, up-to-date, professional photo that makes you look like a contestant on one of those Top Model shows and you're selling Romance or fashion tip self-help.

You're aiming for a style similar to book jacket copy. Except you're not selling yourself to a reader. You're selling yourself to a marketing department. The purpose is to make yourself sound professional and INTERESTING.

A reader might like to know she can identify with you: "Mrs. H. O. Humm is a stay-at-home mom who lives in Ohio with her dentist husband, 2.4 children and a dog named Rex."

But a marketer wants to know what makes you stand out. "Hermione Oz Humm was born in the Emerald City and follows in her famous father's footsteps as an expert balloonist, ventriloquist and voice-over performer."

Things to consider including:

1) Whatever might make you newsworthy. OK, so you aren't the baby who got rescued from that well forty years ago, and were never married to Britney Spears, but whatever is quirky or unusual about you, trot it out. Keep homing pigeons? Run marathons? Cook prize-winning chili? Put it in.

2) Work history/what you do for money. Here's where you say you're a welder or a fourth grade teacher or whatever, even if it isn't related to the subject matter of your book.

NB: Don't call yourself a "novelist" if you haven't published one.

If you're seriously underemployed and want to keep it to yourself, you can call yourself a "freelance writer," but consider saying what else you do, even if it's less than impressive. I remember when Christopher Moore's first book came out and all the Central Coast papers ran stories about how a "local waiter" had just published a book. If he'd called himself a "writer" there would have been no story.

3) Where you live. Your hometown might make a good focus for marketing. Plus people like to be able to picture you in your native habitat.

4) Education. This includes workshops or conferences as well as formal education—especially if you worked with a high-profile teacher. If you took a playwriting workshop with Edward Albee, even if it was 30 years ago, go ahead and list it.

5) Life experience and hobbies. But only if they relate to the book, or are really interesting. If you collect vintage Frisbees and the book is about angsty teen werewolves at a Frisbee contest, include it. If you invented the Frisbee, it doesn't matter what your book is about: toot that horn!

6) Travel/exotic residences. "Rudy Kipling once lived in India." Meh. But "Mr. Kipling was born in Bombay and spent a year as the assistant editor of a newspaper in Lahore," is something you want them to know.

7) Writing credentials/prizes. Here's where you can list some of those credits in small presses and prizes that didn't fit in your query. Include any books you've published, even if they were in a different field. Some old-school agents say not to list a self-published book unless you had huge sales, but most savvy agents will want to know.

8) Family. Use discretion here. If you write for children and have some of your own, it would be useful to mention them. If your family has an interesting claim to fame, do mention it. (Like your sister is Lady Gaga). And let people know if your family history has made you uniquely qualified to write this book (say your father worked for Siegfried and Roy and you're writing about performance anxiety in tigers).

9) Performing history. It's helpful to show you're not paralyzed by the thought of public speaking. You can mention you're the president of your local Toastmasters, or host a jug band program on a public access station, or you played the teapot in last year's production of *Beauty and the Beast* at the local little theater.

Think like a reporter. What would make you sound interesting in a news release?

ANNE

LET'S PLAY "WHAT'S MY GENRE?"

'

YEAH, I KNOW. WE ALL HATE LABELS. BUT IF OUR ULTIMATE GOAL IS space on a bookstore shelf (even if it's a virtual shelf), we have to be able to suggest to an agent or editor what shelf that might be.

The best place to start is an actual bookstore—either online or brick-and-mortar. Find books like yours and see where they're shelved or categorized (speaking as a former bookstore shelver, I can tell you how subjective this is, so don't consider these hard and fast rules). Some categories are traditionally paired, like Mystery/Crime and SF/Fantasy.

Amazon is a great place to search. Look for books similar to yours and scroll down to "Look for Similar Items by Category."

Here are some basic fiction genres. You'll notice how many overlap or can be combined. It's OK to combine up to three (but not more) in your query. Also, if you don't get nibbles with one category, it's OK to call your work something else. Agents say they do that all the time, depending on what an editor is looking for.

Christian/Inspirational: If you call it "Christian," make sure it supports a Fundamentalist Christian world view and has no explicit language, sex or content. Violence is OK. "Inspirational" can be much broader—spiritual rather than religious.

Commercial: Traditionally, any plot-driven fiction, but now, according to AgentQuery, this means "high concept" projects with a unique subject and potential audience of zillions: stories that can be summarized in one wow-inducing sentence.

Crime Fiction: Stories centering on the physical aspects of a crime or the workings of the criminal mind.

Detective Fiction: Just-the-facts-ma'am details of bringing a criminal to justice. If the detective has a badge, it's known as a **Police Procedural**.

Erotica: A major, growing market in ebook publishing—especially erotica for women that has romantic and/or paranormal elements.

LGBT: This category sort of annoys me, since it segregates 10% of the population, but if your main character has a minority sexual orientation and this label helps you get published, go for it.

Fantasy: Not just about elves, dragons, and talking badgers any more. Dark Fantasy (vampires, were-persons), Urban Fantasy (spawn of Buffy), and Erotic Fantasy (vamps and were-persons hooking up) have been white hot for the last decade, but are now fading. Epic Fantasy (Tolkein-inspired) was a hard sell for adult fiction for a while, but *Game of Thrones* changed that. Epics for Middle Grade are always big. (All of this is subject to change, of course.)

Historical Fiction: A story set fifty or more years in the past that uses the time period as an element of the story. Historical everything is hot right now: Historical Romance and Mysteries especially.

Horror: Scare the pants off your reader — á la King. Not selling so well right now, according to agent Laurie McLean, except for Vampire Horror. And Zombies, which have been trending for a while. Splatterpunk (ick) has a small but steady readership. I guess it keeps them from torturing small animals.

Literary: Language and character trump story. Get a story published in *The New Yorker* first. (I'm overstating there, but it's important to establish your literary credentials with short fiction before trying to get a literary novel traditionally published.)

Mainstream: This once-basic category has nearly evaporated. As Patrick Anderson detailed in his book, *The Triumph of the Thriller*, former mainstream staples like family chronicles, historical epics, and sweeping Micheneresque sagas have gone out of fashion.

Multi-Cultural: Anything NOT about middle-class characters of northern European heritage. Generally family sagas. Big plus if it's set in a current war zone.

Mystery: Crime-solving puzzles. Classic Whodunits, Cozies,

Private Eye, and Noir are still going strong, and Historical, Supernatural, and Literary Mysteries are hot. Cozy series with craft and hobby themes are steady sellers, although the genre is a bit saturated. It's hard to come up with a hobby that hasn't been done.

Romance: Must follow specific publisher guidelines and provide happy endings. (One agent blogged bitterly about love stories submitted as Romance—those are considered Women's Fiction.) Paranormal, Urban Fantasy, and Time-Travel have been the hottest sellers in the last few years, but agents now complain of "Paranormal burnout." Regency, Elizabethan and Scottish Medieval are perennial favorites. Western Romance still sells. *Fifty Shades of Grey*-style Erotic Romance is also suffering a bit of burn-out.

Romantic Comedy/Chick Lit: If you can picture Julia Roberts or Hugh Grant in the movie version, it probably fits here. These books can fall under the broad category of Romance, but can also qualify as Romantic Suspense (if the protagonist is in jeopardy), Mystery (if she's sleuthing), or humorous Women's Fiction.

If the protagonist ends up at the altar, it's Romance, and if she ends up drinking pink beverages with her girlfriends, celebrating the departure of a bad boyfriend, it's Women's Fiction.

NOTE: People in the industry still use the term "Chick Lit," but I've heard you're not allowed to put it in your query or they'll make fun of you in a meeting. On the other hand, Chick Lit is very big with indies.

Romantic Suspense: Combines elements of Romance and Mystery with a fast-paced, protagonist-in-constant-jeopardy plot. This is sometimes considered a sub-category of Romance. Romantic comedy-mysteries can be categorized here if the Romance is as equally important as the mystery. For Romantic Suspense of any kind to be under the Romance umbrella, there must be a Happy-Ever-After (HEA) ending.

Satire: A very hard sell. If you write funny, try to sneak it in as another genre.

Science Fiction: The plot should be based on science rather than myth or make-believe. Subgenres include Social, Cyberpunk, Alternate History, Military, and Apocalyptic (HUGE since *Hunger Games*). "Hard" Science Fiction—the kind where you have to know a whole bunch of physics—still sells, but not in the quantities it once did.

Speculative Fiction: Any fiction that plays with reality. Popular subgenres: Steampunk (set in a faux-Victorian/Edwardian alternate universe), Time-Travel, and Slipstream (surreal Literary-Fantasy).

Suspense: Fast-paced adventure with a protagonist in constant peril.

Thriller: Save-the-world, fast-paced adventure. The stakes must be high—not just one person in jeopardy, but civilization itself. Flavors include: Spy, Political, Military, Conspiracy, Techno-, Eco-, Legal, Medical, and Futuristic.

Westerns: Horses, guns, and stoic agricultural workers in the late 19th/early 20th century American West. Kind of a dead horse in New York, but surviving in indie publishing.

Women's Fiction: Women struggling against adversity. Can be literary, gritty, weepy, or funny. If you've seen similar storylines on the Lifetime Channel, chances are it will fit in here. It usually, but not always, includes a realistic love story. Endings can be sad.

NOTE: Middle Grade, Young Adult, and New Adult are not genres, but categories. Most of the above can be written for the under 18 set or 20-somethings.

Middle Grade means novels in all genres for tweens (age 8-12). Increasingly sophisticated these days, but doesn't have romantic elements. Think the first Harry Potter books and the Wimpy Kid books.

Young Adult—Any of the above categories written for teens. Literary novels with teen protagonists sometimes sneak into print as YA to avoid the hasn't-published-in-*The New Yorker* police. Almost any coming-of-age story is best published as YA. Young Adult books are widely read by adults these days, which is why it's the fastest growing area of publishing.

New Adult—A fairly new category, not recognized by all publishers. It's like Young Adult, but set in college rather than high school and the protagonist can be in his/her early 20s. Sex can be very explicit.

Mix and match as you hone your query, and with luck, you'll find a genre label to reach your potential readers.

ANNE

SEVEN TIPS ON HOW TO QUERY THE RIGHT AGENT

OK, SO THE RATIO OF LEGIT AGENTS TO NEWBIE NOVELISTS IS approximately one to twenty-five gazillion. So what do we do— throw mass queries at big-name agents, perhaps employing the services of a Mafia henchperson or Voodoo practitioner?

That would be a no.

One of the reasons the process is so gruesome is that beginners clog the query pipeline with clueless mass-mailings, making agents harder to reach (and way crankier).

A little research saves everybody grief, and it doesn't have to cost you. In the old days, writers were instructed to buy huge tomes like *The Literary Marketplace, The Writers' and Artists' Yearbook, Writer's Market* or Jeff Herman's directories. They were pricey and pretty much obsolete on delivery.

You can still subscribe to these online, and many writers like

Writer's Market online, which costs about five dollars a month. But there are ways to research that cost you nothing.

For A-list agency addresses in the U.S., the member list of the Association of Author's Representatives is up-to-date and free, but it doesn't give guidelines, and it doesn't list new agents, who are the ones most likely to be looking for clients. To find hungry agents who haven't been in the business long enough for AAR membership, **QueryTracker.net** and **AgentQuery.com,** which I've mentioned before, are the most comprehensive sites. They give guidelines, indicate which agents are actively looking for clients, and screen out the scammers.

Then follow a few tips:

1) Know your genre. (See the chapter "Let's Play 'What's My Genre'.")

One of the most common mistakes new writers make is querying agents who don't represent what they write.

If you write Romance, YA, Science Fiction or Fantasy, the writers' organizations for those genres (RWA, SFWA, SCWBI in the U.S.) offer lists of agents looking for your genre, which is a big help.

If you write stuff with murkier definitions, like Literary, Commercial, Women's, or Mainstream, browse Amazon entries for books similar in tone or subject to yours. Usually Amazon lets you look at the first few pages, where authors may thank their agents (or peruse your local bookstore). Also, authors often mention their agents on their websites. Or you can do a search with the author's name and keywords like "agent" or "represented." You can also look at the Amazon "also-boughts" for a similar book.

If you don't know your genre, you're not ready to query. This doesn't mean your book isn't good enough. It means you need to learn more about the business. Go to writers conferences, browse every writing site you find, and read, read, read.

2) Visit the agency's website. This is imperative. The closer to the source, the more up-to-date the info. An agent who accepted queries last quarter may now have a full client list or an Everest-high mountain of partials she has no time to read. Submission guidelines change weekly. Someone who took e-queries six months ago may only accept snail mail after a barrage of spam. One member of an agency wants a synopsis with the query; another likes a few pages of text (pasted in the body of an e-mail—NEVER as an attachment unless specifically requested).

3) Look for new agents in established agencies who rep your genre and are "building a clientele." They're more likely to have time to read their slush piles.

4) Read agent blogs. OK, this can become something of an addiction, but blogging agents provide precious insider info—not just about their own likes and dislikes, but about the industry in general. They can be cranky and snarky, and you may see your own query ridiculed in front of the entire blogosphere, but they give up-to-the-minute news of sales and trends. They'll tell you what markets are overfilled, what's on their wish list, and what sort of faux pas will get their panties in a bunch.

5) Look at their clients' titles. There's a broad spectrum within genres: if an agent's Romance sales are mostly to Christian publishers, your gay vampire-demon erotica probably won't float her boat; and if all the mysteries sport pink lacy covers, your hardboiled noir won't make the list.

6) Check recent sales. The agency that sold mass quantities of paranormal Romance last year may only be selling post-apocalyptic steampunk now, and they'll delete your vampire Romance query without a glance.

7) Search for interviews and profiles of the agent. Narrow your list further with a quick Google of the agent's name with keywords like "interview" or "profile." Interviews, articles and guest blog posts can give valuable insight into an agent's personality and needs.

If you write YA, a lot of the research has been done for you by the wonderful Casey McCormick and Natalie Aguirre at a blog called "Literary Rambles" at caseylmccormick.blogspot.com. It's one of Writer's Digest's top 101 sites for writers: a treasure trove of profiles of agents who rep YA (worth a check even if you don't write YA, since many agents rep a wide spectrum of genre).

Finally, don't take it personally if the "perfect" agent doesn't respond. We're in a brutal business. Go buy a lottery ticket. The odds will be more in your favor.

And there's always that Voodoo practitioner...

ANNE

HOW TO WRITE AN E-QUERY

THE IDEAL QUERY LETTER CONTAINS FOUR PARAGRAPHS:

1) Title, genre, and word count, plus a one-sentence lead into your hook. (No rhetorical questions. Agents hate them.)

2) A three or four sentence "hook." A hook is a very short synopsis. See the next chapter for a how-to on hooks, loglines, and pitches.

3) A one or two sentence bio with relevant awards and credits.

4) A nice thank you, mentioning why you chose to contact this particular agent.

If you're sending an e-mailed query, which almost all agents want these days, here are a few tips:

1) Never send an attachment, unless specifically requested. Requested writing samples should be pasted in the body of the email.

2) It's best to compose in Plain Text, to avoid formatting problems.

3) Always send a copy to yourself first to see how it's going to look when it lands in the agent's inbox.

4) Consider setting up a special email address for queries. Make sure it's professional and includes your actual name. Many spam guards delete addresses that don't match the sender's name. Also never use an auto-responder for queries.

The biggest mistake beginning novelists make is writing queries that sound as if they were written by, um, beginning novelists. I was cleaning out my files recently and found some seriously cringe-making queries I sent out a decade ago. I didn't make all of the following mistakes, but I have to admit to several.

Here are some surefire rejection-getters:

1) **Whining and/or Paranoia:** It's not a good idea to mention you've had over a thousand rejections and you're thinking of taking the Sylvia Plath way out. Writers tend to be suicidal. This is not news. And don't blabber about copyrights and pilfer-proofing your intellectual property. Remember there are no new ideas, just new ways of writing them.

2) **Getting Chummy:** It's a business letter. Don't cozy up with personal asides about the unfairness of the publishing

industry, the health care debate, or the coming Rapture.

3) **Verbosity:** A query should be one page—under 500 words. Some agents only want 250.

4) **Too Much Information:** Agents don't care about a novelist's hobbies or what we do for bucks—except stuff specifically related to the book. If your heroine works at a magazine edited by Beelzebub in Italian shoes, yes, do mention you've done time at *Vogue*, but keep to yourself how many years you've been a greeter at WalMart.

5) **Irrelevant Publishing Credits:** I see this complaint on lots of agent blogs. They don't want to know about your PhD dissertation on Quattrocento Tuscan pottery, or your Hint from Heloise on uses for dryer lint. When giving "publishing credits," cite only fiction or creative nonfiction, plus articles specifically related to the novel's subject matter—e.g. if your novel is about death by snack cake overdose, you can mention your paper for *The Lancet* on the toxic properties of Twinkies.

6) **Extraneous Kudos:** It's OK to say you were second runner-up for the "Best Paranormal-Chick Lit-Police Procedural" award at the RWA conference, but don't mention that a judge told you later over martinis that if they'd given an award for "best vampire-werewolf sex scene," you would have won.

7) **Omitting Vital Information:** Make sure you give the book's

title, genre and word count. It's amazing how many writers forget to do this.

8) **Gimmicks:** No matter what your marketing friends tell you, don't make your query into a jigsaw puzzle, include a pair of Barbie shoes with your SASE, or send the query by registered mail. Ditto printing your query with pink ink in the Curlz font or sending it in a black envelope shaped like a bat. This WILL get you noticed, but not in a good way.

9) **Call Yourself a Novelist if you Haven't Published:** Remember: pretentiousness invites ridicule.

10) **Call it a "Fiction Novel":** This sets off immediate nitwit-detector alarms. All novels are fiction.

11) **Query an Unfinished Project:** If you don't have an ending yet, you're at least a year away from thinking about representation. Don't send a query on a novel that isn't finished, critiqued, polished, edited, and proofread.

12) **Mass-Query Every Agent in the Business:** Nobody will read past a generic "Dear Agent," even if you've been smart enough to blind copy your mass mailing. Address each agent personally, and indicate why you've chosen her.

13) **Query More than One Book at a Time:** So you've got inventory. Most writers do. But don't present all twelve unpublished novels and ask an agent to choose. Pick one. It's OK to mention other titles in the final paragraph, especially if they're part of a series, but hold to one pitch.

ANNE

HOOKS, LOGLINES, AND PITCHES

WHEN YOU'RE GETTING READY TO SEND THAT MASTERPIECE OUT INTO the marketplace, you're going to run into words like "hook," "logline," and "pitch." The terms come from the film industry, but they're becoming standard in publishing as well.

So what do they mean? Are they just sexy terms for a synopsis?

Not exactly. The distinctions often blur, but here are the basics:

LOGLINE is a term that once applied only to screenplays, but has been creeping into the literary world. It consists of one or two sentences describing the story's premise, like a film description in *TV Guide*:

Here's the basic formula for a logline:

When_____happens to_____, he/she must_____or face_____.

"When Dorothy Gale gets tornadoed to Oz and accidentally squashes the head of state, she must find a wizard to help her get home to Kansas, or be killed by a nasty green witch bent on revenge."

A **HOOK** can be a little longer. Usually it's a paragraph or two giving the characters, premise, and conflict, like a book jacket cover blurb. (But skip the cover blurb accolades. Self-praise doesn't just sound narcissistic, it screams "clueless amateur.")

The hook should be the main component of a query letter to an agent, editor, or reviewer and is essential for your back copy or Amazon blurb.

"*The Wizard of Oz* is a middle-grade Fantasy novel set in a magical land where much of the population suffers from self-esteem issues. When Dorothy Gale, a Kansas farm girl, arrives via tornado, she accidentally kills the ruling witch. The witch's powerful sister wants Dorothy dead, but Dorothy only wants to get home, which she cannot do until she finds the right traveling shoes."

For help composing it, you can try the "Hook Me Up" hook formula of the late, great Miss Snark. (I suggest stating the setting first, especially for Fantasy or SciFi.)

X is the main guy; he wants to do_____.

Y is the bad guy; he wants to do_____.

They meet at Z and all L breaks loose.

If they don't resolve Q, then R starts and if they do it's L squared.

Don't take the "bad guy" reference to mean that novels must be portrayed with cartoony plots and Snidely Whiplash villains. The antagonist can be anything that keeps the protagonist from his goals, from a wicked witch to the hero's own addictions.

A **PITCH** can contain either or both of the above. You can make a pitch in writing or in person. It tells—in the shortest possible time—what your book is about and why somebody should buy it. This is what you memorize before you go to that Writers' Conference, hoping you'll get trapped in an elevator with Stephen Spielberg or an editor from Knopf.

When composing your pitch, you want to answer these questions: Who? Where? What's the conflict? What action does the protagonist take? What are the stakes?

There's actually an online "pitch generator" invented by comedy author Kathy Carmichael. You can find it at www.kathycarmichael.com/generator. It's fun and amazingly useful.

Here's her generator's pitch for the *Wizard of Oz*.

The *Wizard of Oz* is a (x) word Fantasy novel set in the magical land of Oz. Dorothy Gale is a Kansas farm girl who believes in loyalty and friendship. She wants to get home to Kansas to be with her Auntie Em. She is prevented from attaining this goal because her transportation vehicle is sitting on a dead witch, she's being attacked by flying monkeys, and her traveling companions are a little dim.

All three should be composed in the present tense, starting with title and genre.

None of the above should be confused with a formal **SYNOPSIS**, which is a detailed run-down of the complete plot. (But not too detailed: lots of submission guidelines ask for a one-page synopsis these days. More on that from Catherine in the next chapter.)

In all three, you also want to convey the tone of your book:

You can show genre with a humorous logline: "When the romantic adventures of a southern belle are interrupted by an icky war, plus her goody-two-shoes-BFF steals her boyfriend, Scarlett whips up a fabulous outfit in order to seduce Mr. Wrong, who in the end, doesn't give a damn."

Or punch up a coming of age story by emphasizing high-stakes conflict: "With his life in constant danger from the monstrous carnivore Snowbell, young Stuart must fight for his life, and prove once and for all whether he is a man or a mouse."

Or go for the thrills by emphasizing the most dangerous scene: "Marked for death along with his companions, a toy rabbit must learn to cry real tears in order to save himself from being tossed into the burning pit by the boy he loves."

Or try "When the adopted son of a Kansas farmer discovers he's a strange visitor from another planet, he tries to save the world—one clueless girl reporter at a time—in spite of opposition from an assortment of megalomaniacs armed with green rocks."

When you're composing, don't forget to weed out clichés. Here are some overused phrases to avoid:

- little did he know

- comes back to haunt her

- race against the clock

- web of deceit

- determined to unmask

- wants nothing more

- spins out of control

- torn apart by

- vows to expose

- world falls apart

- forced to confront

Whether you're writing a logline, a hook, or a pitch, remember that less is more. Keep it short. And keep working on it. These few words are as important as any you'll ever write.

CATHERINE

STILL MORE ABOUT PITCHES, PLUS WRITING THE DREADED SYNOPSIS

NOW THAT ANNE HAS SORTED OUT WHAT THE HOOK, PITCH AND logline mean and how to find the elements of them in your book, allow me to offer some advice about how to devise a pitch in a way that might help you ease into a good written synopsis. Think of hers as the "what to do" and mine as the "how to do it."

Yes, you will end up with an actual synopsis. You pretty much have to. All roads lead there. Except roads not taken by writers.

I would spare you this fate if I could.

I can't.

I'll start with some thoughts on developing the verbal pitch, also known as the elevator pitch. (And, by the way, I really did pitch my current agent in an elevator in a hotel tower during the La Jolla Writers Conference. It happens.) This is actually *a type of* synopsis. It's just spoken. And very short.

Then I'll move you on to the synopsis that came into your mind when I said the word synopsis. This is a written work of approximately one double-spaced page. If it's more, it had better not be much more, and it had better be a compelling read. The longer your synopsis and query letter, the greater the pressure to justify their length. Pass an unknowable threshold and you will not be under any pressure to justify them, because they will not be read. (Where is that threshold? Closer than you think.)

Now. I strongly suggest you start with your elevator pitch. I know Anne makes some mention of a memorized pitch. I'm not disagreeing so much as going into more specifics when I say the following: don't literally memorize it.

Two pitfalls await you if you do.

One, you may sound as though you are reciting a poem in grade school. In fact, because you're so nervous, you will probably sound as though you're reciting a poem poorly.

Two, you may experience the writer's version of the infamous actor's nightmare. You open your mouth and your mind goes blank. What was that first sentence again? Damn! You knew it so well! You will only be able to watch in horror as the floor numbers light up, one after the other.

Most of these chances do not come along twice.

The trick, in my opinion, is to sound as though you are simply talking about your book. Naturally. Easily. In reality, this will be the equivalent of spending three hours achieving "the natural look" with your makeup. You may never again work so hard to sound like there's no work involved. But the reality doesn't matter. What matters is the impression you've made by the time that little mechanical "ping" announces your floor.

Grab a writer friend, if possible. If not possible, grab a recording device. Talk about your book. If you're not sure what to say about it, go back to Anne's previous chapter for specifics.

Time yourself.

If you come in over a minute—and if you're human, I expect you will—decide on some aspects of your pitch that can go.

Practice this pitch dozens or even hundreds of times. Let it come out slightly different every time, but be sure the main points are always included.

Get very clear on your opening sentence. This is the one that should *almost* be memorized. Memorize the content but not necessarily the wording. But know your first thought, your log line, well. Freezing up is most likely when you first open your mouth. Once you've gotten the initial sentence out, the rest will be more likely to flow.

Got it short enough? And it comes out well almost every time?

Good. Turn it into a short synopsis (or hook) for your query letter.

This part is easy. Write the thoughts down, and polish them until they shine.

Now. I've played a little trick on you, but one I feel will be to your benefit. You were worried about boiling 104,000 words down to 250. Weren't you? Now you're not boiling down. Now you have a short synopsis...and you get to expand it! You've got some elbow room, now! Boy howdy! You get to fill up a whole damn page!

At this point, I have another trick I'd like to share with you.

Go to your home library (book shelf), public library, bookstore, or online bookseller. Here you will have access to jacket copy, also known as flap copy. Read examples of good flap copy. I don't mean two or three examples. I mean 20 or 30.

Then, with that style and punchiness fresh in your head, expand your short synopsis into a full one.

Notice how the examples you've read find the "hookiest" factor in the book and bring it up front? Notice how they quickly characterize the protagonist? How they briefly depict the brick wall facing said character? How they make it look really tall and impenetrable? Notice how the jacket copy examples left you feeling that the books had something important to say?

Right.

Do that.

In tone and readability, your synopsis should look like jacket copy. They are not exactly the same, though. Yours should be a tad more detailed in terms of plot development. (When you see how few words you get on a double-spaced page, you'll know why I say "a tad.") And it should reveal more about how you wrap things up. The flap copy withholds the ending, so you'll read the book. This tactic is unlikely to work on an agent. If you want her to read it, make sure she knows you have the talent to write a satisfying ending.

And, as Anne mentioned, none of the accolades. Just the facts, ma'am. Never say or do anything that invites an agent or editor to think, "I'll be the judge of that."

Part of me feels the following should go without saying, but experience tells me otherwise: when attempting to keep this down to one double-spaced page, *do not cheat*. I can't tell you how many times a student has handed me a synopsis in 1.5 spacing instead of double-spacing. I look at it and say, "This is 1.5." They inevitably say, "I didn't think you'd notice."

I notice.

And I spend less time looking at manuscripts than the average agent, or agent's reader.

Don't make the margins smaller. Or play with the spacing. Or go with a smaller font.

Do edit until every single word carries its weight. Until no sentence could be phrased any more simply and directly without changing its meaning.

Then follow the same process with your synopsis as you would with anything you write. Workshop it. Give it to your beta reader(s). Sleep on it, and give it yet another go. Proofread it tirelessly.

Treat it as though it's at least as important as the book itself. It is. It's the key to getting the book read. Make sure it's ready to turn some of the toughest locks in the world.

ANNE

DEALING WITH AGENTS #1—SHOULD YOU GIVE AN EXCLUSIVE READ?

SOMETIME DURING YOUR QUERY PROCESS, YOU'LL GET A REQUEST FOR A partial or full manuscript (yay!) that comes with a request for an exclusive read (not so yay).

It happened to me a couple of years ago. I really wanted to work with the agent, but it would have been impossible to grant her a truly exclusive read. Like most writers seriously seeking publication, I had a bunch of outstanding queries, as well as a couple of partials and fulls lingering on various agency desks.

I'd never been fond of the idea of exclusives. They've always looked pretty lose/lose to me. They take your work off the market—sometimes for years—without increasing your chances of being offered representation.

And it's even worse with mid-sized publishers, who often insist on exclusives for any unagented manuscript, but have an up-to-three-year reading time and a 99% rejection rate. (I sometimes suspect that's their passive-aggressive way of saying "get an agent".)

But what do you do if you're in my situation? This agent seemed enthusiastic about my work. And she was definitely my best bet. Those partials and fulls had been out for over six months, and the outstanding e-queries, although pretty fresh, might have been rejected already. In this "no response" era, we have no way of knowing.

One successful writer friend tells me you simply can't make it in this business unless you ignore "exclusive" and "no simultaneous submission" rules. Her advice is to send now and worry later—since few works get multiple offers. Another author says, "Send it without promising anything. Most agents are curious enough to peek."

But I hate lying, so I sent the agent the requested pages, along with a note disclosing that other agencies were looking. I offered a future exclusive on the full if the other agents gave me a pass.

But the "exclusive" agent replied—within minutes—that her time was too valuable to waste on anything that she could lose to somebody else. The snippy tone made me wonder if I'd done something wrong.

So I checked with other agent blogs to see if I should have handled it differently. Turns out I made a mistake—but not in sending the partial. I shouldn't have offered the exclusive at all.

Here's some advice from the pros:

From FinePrint agent Rachel Vater Coyne: "Exclusives are not good. Try to avoid [them] or specify a very short period of time. Two weeks maybe if you must."

BookEnds agent Jessica Faust said: "I HATE exclusives. I think they are unfair to the author and lazy on the part of the agent....If you can't compete, don't play the game… If an agent isn't aggressive enough to compete for your work with other agents, how aggressive will she be selling your work?"

The archives of Miss Snark offer the simple bit of wisdom: "Exclusives Stink!"

Ultra-nice agent Kristin Nelson said she would never ask for one, because "I never want a client to feel they have settled for my agency." But "if you're 100% sure" an exclusive-demanding agent is for you, she offered these rules:

1) If you grant an exclusive, honor it. Be sure to include a time limit.

2) If your manuscript is out with one agent and an "exclusive" request comes in from another, send the manuscript anyway with a note explaining the non-exclusive status. If she won't read it, "it's her loss."

3) Never allow an exclusive on a partial. "That's just silly."

4) If several agents have your full "and they've been nice enough to not request the evil exclusive," keep them posted about the manuscript's status with other agencies.

But what if you've already granted an exclusive, without stipulating a time limit, as I almost did? Don't despair. Rachel Vater Coyne suggested sending a note like this:

"I submitted TITLE at your request on DATE as an exclusive submission but forgot to ask for a time frame. If you haven't had a chance to read yet, could you give me an estimation of where it is on your reading list?"

If you don't hear back, Ms. Coyne said you can send an e-mail informing the agent you've had more requests, and will send manuscripts out next week "unless you'd like a little more time?"

In other words, be polite, but don't give away the store.

ANNE

DEALING WITH AGENTS # 2—SHOULD YOU DO REWRITES WITHOUT A CONTRACT?

IF YOU'RE A DILIGENT, TALENTED WRITER WHO'S DONE YOUR homework—and you have the good-luck fairy on speed-dial—sometime during your novel querying process your phone will ring and you'll hear the voice of an agent—a real, honest-to-goodness publishing industry professional—who's impressed enough to spend money and time ringing up little old you.

(You know she's the real thing because you researched her credentials before you sent off that query—didn't you?)

So you've hit the jackpot. Somebody out there likes you; she really likes you.

But after you scrape yourself off the ceiling and order the kids to turn that noise down right NOW, you hear the agent asking for a rewrite.

Uh-oh. Maybe she doesn't like you so much.

Not to worry. This is part of the process. Most agents make editorial suggestions before they sign a new client. That's right: BEFORE they offer a contract. You're asked to rewrite with no guarantee of representation.

Is it fair? No. But nothing in this industry is, so we get used to it.

Current rules dictate that you should NOT argue. You say, "Yes, sir/ma'am—O Great Publishing Industry Professional—you want the new manuscript when? Sure. I can skip my grandfather's funeral and write while the surgeon is doing my pesky little heart bypass, and I'll have it on your desk by Monday."

And then she's obligated to represent you, right?

Nope. The agent is likely to give you a pass anyway—or suggest further edits. One writer blogged about doing twenty-five requested rewrites for an agent who never did offer representation.

The first time an agent phoned me to ask for pre-contract changes, I was a newbie so clueless I didn't know I was being honored. She asked me to change the sexual orientation of a major character so the heroine could marry him. I said I was happy to make minor changes, but that big change felt like a betrayal of my values.

She hung up in a huff.

Did I screw up? I don't think so, but I sure broke the rules.

Several years later, when another agent finally called—also asking for rewrites—I knew better. I agreed to edit all three manuscripts that interested her. The changes to the first were fairly easy, but for the second, she wanted massive shifts of plot, tone and character.

I put in months of painful, heartbreaking work, but she sent the manuscripts back—along with a copy of a novel she'd just placed, to show me how it was done.

I found the model manuscript a boring, childish slog—

something I'd never choose to read.

Obviously she didn't sign me.

I eventually sold the novels without representation and my editor took out every one of the agent's "improvements."

I'm not suggesting these agents did anything wrong. Editorial suggestions are a gift. They're also subjective. Something in my work struck a chord, and they wanted to work with me.

They knew what they could sell and hoped I could produce that product. I couldn't. This is why we don't quit our day jobs.

So what should you do if you get that call?

I'd say give the edits a whirl—but stay in touch with your creative self (and save your original). If you have to hide the new version from your friends, and/or start to sob when you sit down at the keyboard, it's OK to say thanks but no thanks.

What you shouldn't do is procrastinate or send the original back with only a few changes. Miss Snark said of an author who wouldn't rewrite, "The author was really shocked when I said no, 'cause he believed my editorial comments meant an offer was a pretty sure thing. I said, look, you didn't make the changes I suggested…even if you did them now, I've got no confidence you'd be someone who can handle editorial direction."

An agency is like a retail shop: it sells a certain type of merchandise. You're being considered as a possible vendor. Don't go into business together if you can't supply the product.

It's good to keep in mind that if your rewrite is accepted, you'll be expected to write more of the same.

So if an agent asks you to rewrite your Western as a Romance, or your biting satire as Middle Grade Fantasy, agree to give it a try. But before you waste too much time, read some of the Romances or

Middle Grade Fantasy she's selling.

If you can't read them, you can't write them. Politely bow out and move on. There are other agents. And small presses. And self-publishing. Keep sending those queries.

ANNE

LITERARY AGENTS: ARE THEY AN ENDANGERED SPECIES?

PUBLISHING KEEPS ZOOMING INTO THE FUTURE.

Every day brings more reports of self-pubbed authors who are making good money without the help of agents or publishers.

Self-published ebook authors are being approached by foreign rights buyers and film companies (and making lucrative, 100% agent-free deals).

Brick-and-mortar chain bookstores seem to be heading for extinction faster than anybody predicted (although indie bookstores are still doing okay). This means the agent/big-corporate-publisher/big-corporate-store paradigm is also slouching off to dodoland.

The world's biggest online bookstore is also becoming a major publisher. Not only is Amazon's Kindle Direct the biggest retailer of ebooks, but they're now competing directly with traditional publishers. Amazon-the-publisher makes offers directly to its own top-selling self-pubbed ebook authors. No agent-gatekeeper required.

For a while now, the big publishing houses have been paying smaller and smaller advances for fewer and fewer titles. This is the era of the predatory multinational corporation and the international publishing conglomerates are not exceptions. Many no longer trust an agent's judgment as to whether a book is good or not—and don't care. Nothing matters but sales numbers.

So is the Literary Agent about to become extinct?

Some of us might do some secret gloating at the thought. If you've spent decades knocking on agents' doors, only to be told your work is too quirky/unremarkable, dark/light, similar/different, and "not right for us at this time," it's kind of nice to get your brain around this wonderful new fact: you don't need an agent to be a successful writer any more.

But most agents aren't leaving the profession. They're retrenching, redefining their roles, and trying out innovative concepts: some smart, some not so much.

Here are some of the new tactics:

1) Providing flat fee services for self-publishers:

- **Marketing**: Several top agencies offer themselves for hire to help you through all the steps of marketing your self-pubbed book. You get the expertise of a literary agent for a flat, upfront fee.

- **E-formatting:** Another side business some agents are providing is formatting ebooks for self-publishing in all the various platforms. At least one agent I know has her own formatting business on the side. It's nice to hire somebody in the business who knows how it all works.

Bottom line for authors? *Pretty Good.*

2) Only taking new clients with proven sales numbers:
There are several ways they're doing this:

a) Closing offices to queries. I recently read that only 1% of new books are by debut authors now, so some agents aren't bothering to plow through mountains of slush to find authors the big publishers won't look at anyway. They prefer new clients who are proven bestsellers.

b) Trolling the Kindle lists and offering representation to top-selling self-pubbers. This can pay off very well for both author and agent. A great example is Kristen Nelson, who approached indie bestseller Hugh Howey and then brokered a deal with Simon and Schuster for his print books only. Nelson managed to reserve Howey's ebook rights and sell only print. This is an ideal arrangement for a successful indie author who doesn't want to give up his lucrative self-publishing business.

c) Poaching other agents' clients. I've seen at least one agency that actually posts on their website they only want writers who already have representation. They suggest querying to get a better deal. Maybe 15 minutes could save you 15%, like with that insurance lizard on TV. At least they seem to have the lizard part right.

Bottom line for authors? *Mixed.*

3) Adding draconian clauses to contracts:

Here's the problem with some Kindle-list-trollers. Sometimes the contracts they offer the starry-eyed self-publisher are seriously predatory. Here's some of the stuff they're doing:

a) Demanding a percentage not just of your sales but of your COPYRIGHT. This means they will own part of your book for your entire lifetime—and, in the U.S., for 70 years after you die.

b) Making authors sign away rights to characters—so you can never write about those characters again without paying the agent a fee.

c) Adding "In perpetuity" riders: you must pay them even if you move to another agency (I guess this is supposed to be anti-lizard protection). This means you'll pay 30% in agent fees: 15% to this agency, and 15% to the agency that actually sells your books.

d) Making authors sign away a percentage of EVERYTHING THEY'VE EVER WRITTEN OR WILL EVER WRITE. I don't know if that gives them the right to ferret out your grade-school poems about "What Flag Day Means to Me" and publish them, but it probably does.

e) Adding "legacy" clauses that say you are bound to the agency even if your agent dies and her drug addled kid decides to run the business from prison. That kid has the right to sell every book you ever write to his cell mate for a pack of cigarettes and you can't do a thing about it.

f) Non-compete clauses. They try to keep you from self-publishing short fiction or other books even if they don't want them. They can also demand that you cease all your self-publishing operations immediately, even books they don't want to represent.

These days, it's always best to run a contract by a lawyer. Big, well-known agencies are just as guilty of these nasty deals as smaller, obscure ones, so do your research thoroughly before you accept a contract. If an agency won't negotiate on these clauses, walk away. If this agent wants you, a more ethical one will, too.

Bottom line for authors? *Seriously sucky.*

4) Becoming publishers and self-publishing facilitators:

There was much wringing of hands and gnashing of teeth when the Wylie agency began publishing ebooks of their clients' backlist instead of selling the e-rights to the Big Six at the beginning of the e-revolution. Many people in the industry have called this a conflict of interest and a predatory practice.

Kris Rusch of the Business Rusch Blog said: "If your agent has become an e-publisher, fire that agent now. That agent is not working in your best interest and never will again (if they ever did). Your agent has left the agenting business and has become a publisher, so your agent now has a conflict of interest."

And according to agent Meredith Barnes, some agencies have indeed charged too much for the service—especially when they pay themselves 15% to "represent" the client to themselves as "publishers" who get another hefty cut—often over 50%.

But the Association of Author's Agents has no problem with it, saying: *"There are certain activities that our code of conduct explicitly prohibits and the practice of agencies offering their authors a way to market their books directly to the reader is not one of them."*

The Andrea Brown Agency made headlines when they joined in the epublishing fray. But Catherine is repped by Andrea Brown and couldn't be happier. She has a number of titles that have not sold to U.S. publishers, although they sell well in the U.K. and other foreign markets. If the Big Five had their way, none of these books would ever be available to the majority of U.S. readers. Catherine will tell you all about her experience in an upcoming chapter.

And Amazon now has an exclusive "White Glove" program for agent-assisted self-publishing that offers a lot of advantages in visibility in exchange for an exclusive year-long contract with the 'Zon. So far, authors seem to have found this arrangement very satisfactory.

Bottom line for authors? *Mostly good. Depends on the ethics of the agency.*

***

Personally, would I like to have an agent? I've had six books published without one, but yes, I'd love to have one for the next step in my career. I think it's worth 15% of possible earnings to have a savvy advocate in my corner.

But are all agents savvy advocates these days? Nope. Especially the ones who are running scared or trying to cling to 20th century ways.

In the 21st century, writers have to screen agents as carefully as they screen us.

PART 6

TRADITIONAL OR SELF-PUBLISHING?

ANNE

THE WAY WE PUBLISH NOW

RECENTLY, I SAW A NEW ITEM AT OUR LOCAL DOLLAR STORE—hardcover books. Well, actually one hardcover book—hundreds of copies of it, dumped in a big bin. It's sad enough to see good books remaindered on the sale tables of Barnes and Noble, but these were being dumped for a buck apiece, along with off-brand detergent and dented cans of dog food.

What's worse, I recognized the title. That's because I saw the author interviewed by Stephen Colbert—just a few months earlier.

I felt a little sick.

Kind of like the way I felt when the only remaining indie bookstore in San Luis Obispo closed. And the *LA Times* killed off their book review section. And the Borders at the mall shut its doors.

What's going on? Have people stopped reading? Should we give up our dreams of becoming authors and take up hula-hoop decorating? Is the book dead?

Nope. It turns out the opposite is true. *The New York Times* recently reported that sales of books are going nowhere but up. Trade titles grew 5.8% in the past three years, juvenile books grew 6.6%, and adult fiction is up a hefty 8.8%—in the middle of a recession!

So the book business isn't really going to Hades in a handbasket. But it is on one wild ride—a ride that's moving so fast that even industry professionals can't keep up.

Here's a little recap—

Back in the dear, dead days of 2009 B.K. (Before Kindle), fiction authors had only three options:

Option #1: Go through the long, painful process of querying literary agents, hoping to find one who could sell your work to a big or biggish publishing corporation. From the mid-20th century until the early 2000's, if you wrote a book good enough to snag a reputable agent, you had an excellent chance of launching a professional writing career. But the agent-funneling-to-the-international-publishing-conglomerate paradigm had been developing flaws over the previous few years:

- Ever-shrinking advances.

- Marketing departments seizing creative control.

- Non-existent marketing budgets, except for superstars.

- Ever-more draconian contracts, demanding ownership of copyright and preventing writers from "competing" with their own books by publishing anything else, anywhere.

- "Creative" royalty-eating accounting.

- Rigid genre formulas.

- Fad-publishing and lemming-like overbuying: giving two or three genres dominance to the exclusion of all others, thus killing off those genres by oversaturating the market. Examples: Chick Lit and Vampire Romance.

- Dropping writers who didn't make the optimistic sales quotas established by the marketing department (as reported by the wildly inaccurate Bookscan.) Your career could be ended by an accounting mistake. The only way you'd ever be able to publish again involved changing your name and never, ever admitting you'd been published before.

Option #2: Submit to smaller, regional presses that read their own slush and don't require an agent-gatekeeper. This minor-league option sometimes led to the big leagues, but it had major drawbacks.

- Small or no advance.

- No standardized practices—hard to tell the good from the bad.

- Difficult distribution. Usually big chains wouldn't order from them, and many indie bookstores would order titles only as special orders.

- Tiny profit margins—with the high cost of materials and small mark-up on paper books, they often went belly-up, owing royalties to writers and back pay to staff (I'm speaking from experience here).

- No marketing budget.

- No reviews in the big publications like Kirkus, NYT, People, etc.

- Titles unlikely to get the notice of Hollywood.

Option #3: Self-publish

- Oh, pu-leez. You've all heard the stories. "I read a self-pubbed book by my hairdresser's son and it had no plot and typos on every page—and if I ever have to read another 50-page masturbation scene, I'm going to throw myself off a bridge."

- Unless you wrote something sappy and inspirational like *The Celestine Prophecy* or *The Shack*, you wouldn't even recoup costs.

- The only way you'd ever be able to publish again involved changing your name and never, ever admitting you'd been published before.

BUT A REVOLUTION STARTED LATE IN THE YEAR 2009 A.K.

You can read that as "After Kindle" or "After Konrath", since Mystery author J. A. Konrath sounded the first voice of the Kindle revolution on his blog *A Newbie's Guide to Publishing*.

The A.K. era has provided many new paths to publishing, and those paths go in remarkable new directions. Sometimes they even make U-turns.

Option #1 is still the same: query agents and hope for that Big Publishing contract. Some people will argue with me, but I think this is still the best path for a lot of writers. Especially the ones who have a shovel-ready, trending-right-now debut novel. If you're an accomplished writer and have a book that fits current trends—all edited, polished and ready to go—you just might be the next superstar. It still happens.

But be aware the traditional road is an even rockier path than before, because:

- The big bookstore chains who worked in partnership with the Big Five to create bestsellers are going belly-up. Borders is dead and the book shelf space in supermarkets and drugstores has shrunk drastically.

- The mass market paperback is disappearing. *Publishing Perspectives* recently gave it three years to live. Mass market publisher Dorchester went bankrupt and left a lot of authors unpaid.

- As the Big Five acquire fewer and fewer non-celebrity titles, agents are unable to sell books they adore, and being "on submission" can be an emotional Bataan Death March.

- Now less than 1% of books published by the Big Five are by debut authors.

- The Big Five have been pricing ebooks way too high, thwarting sales of even their bestselling authors.

- As marketing departments insist on "guaranteed sales numbers," agents are looking less at their own queries and more at the Kindle bestseller lists.

- Authors are getting tiny royalties on ebook sales from the Big Five, and paper books are being pulled from shelves within weeks of launch (and sent to the Dollar Store, apparently). The average advance is about $5000, and most authors never see any royalties. You have to write really, really fast just to make minimum wage.

Option #2: Small Presses. This is a much more appealing option than it used to be because technology has decreased overhead and Amazon and other online retailers have leveled the playing field. There are many, many niche e-publishers springing up all the time.

- Small companies, which have fewer cogs in their wheels, can move faster. Most are pricing their ebooks under $5.00. Many also provide paper books, using POD technology. That way they only print as many books as they have orders for. This drastically reduces overhead, so they're much more likely to stay in business than in the past.

- Because of low overhead, they often pay much higher royalties than the Big Five.

- With online retailers dominating the book market, distributors are no longer essential to sales numbers. Every book is available for browsing with a few clicks. A book from a tiny press has equal space with one from Random House on the big retail sites like Amazon and Barnes and Noble.

- Digital-only presses are mushrooming all over the 'Net. They are willing to take chances on new authors and innovative genre-bending because they have very little overhead. This also means they can afford to keep prices low. Some of them, like the Romance publisher Entangled have had huge success and are even partnering with the Big Five.

- Genre-specific publishers can service neglected niche markets and connect writers directly with fans looking for a particular type of fiction.

- Small presses offer professional book design, formatting, paper book distribution, and sometimes even more publicity than a big publisher.

- But you're still not likely to get that call from Stephen Spielberg.

Major drawback—small presses are usually extremely undercapitalized. They go belly-up with predictable regularity. So caveat emptor and research, research, research. Talk to their authors. Find out if any royalty checks have been bouncing.

Option #3 Self-Publish ebooks. Now anybody can join the wild-west gold-rush sparked by Amazon's Jeff Bezos and his little Kindle.

- This is no longer the "I've been rejected everywhere, so I guess I have to…" option that hairdresser's son took.

- Fortunes are being made, and even mid-listers are making a living (although most of them started by being traditionally published).

- Self-publishing an ebook costs next to nothing, especially if you can design your own cover and get a fellow writer to exchange editing/proofing duties with you.

- New companies like Smashwords, BookBaby and Direct 2

Digital provide assisted self-epublishing. Their services are very reasonable and they also supply helpful things like ISBNs. However, it's good to be aware that some facilitators like BookBaby have "incidental" charges that can add up. Every time you make a change it can cost 50% of the price of publishing the book in the first place.

- Agents, publishers and filmmakers are ignoring their own slush piles and trolling the Kindle self-published lists for new clients. (Yes, I mentioned this above, but my point is: although that's not so good for queriers, it's great for self-pubbers.)

- Big publishers are offering self-published stars the kind of huge advances usually reserved for literary superstars and members of the Rolling Stones. Self-pubbed Kindle stars like Amanda Hocking and Mark Edwards and Louise Voss have taken this U-turn route back to Option #1.

- You just might get that call from Hollywood. The film rights to Amanda Hocking's initially self-pubbed paranormal trilogy were sold for major bucks, and I'm hearing from indie writers who visit my blog that Hollywood has been knocking on their doors.

- But most self-pubbed books still sell under 150 copies.

Option #4 Query an agent who will help you self-publish ebooks

Agents like Catherine's are helping their clients self-publish to bypass the high cost of big publishing's ebooks. There's been a lot of noise about this being a conflict of interest, but the authors themselves aren't complaining. Agents know how to provide editing (which they've been doing for years), and hook you up with top-notch cover and book designers. They can also help with publicity, marketing and career management as well as handle film and foreign rights (a biggie).

Option #5 HIRE an agent who will help you self-publish ebooks.

Yes, hire. Some reputable agencies are forming separate branches that accept all comers and help them through the e-publishing process for either a percentage or a flat fee. Amazon's "White Glove" program makes this a very enticing deal because of increased visibility on Amazon's own site.

Option #6 Publish both ebooks and pbooks with Amazon's new paper book lines.

This is may be the new holy grail of publishing. Amazon is making changes almost daily, so stay tuned.

- The first of these was Amazon Encore. This doesn't provide a huge advance, but your book is printed on real dead trees and you get to sell to the 70% of readers who still don't have Kindles. Plus your royalties are way better than if you published with a big corporation.

- Then came Montlake Romance. Amazon lured some bestselling Romance writers from the traditional publishing to debut their new Romance line.

- Next was Mystery/Thriller line Thomas and Mercer. This is

where indie superstars Barry Eisler and Joe Konrath are now, having accepted reputedly huge advances and impressive royalties.

- Kindle Singles—Vetted short pieces published by Amazon as stand-alones have revived the short story, selling 2 million in their first year (more on that in my chapter on "Why You Should Be Writing More Short Fiction".

- There are now Kindle Serials (like Kindle singles, only serialized novels) and Kindle Worlds (fanfic). I'm sure more are coming—Amazon has its own gatekeepers and innovative ways to publish now.

- Other companies like Apple may follow Amazon's lead.

- Major drawback: these books will be sold mainly through Amazon. Amazon would like other retailers to carry them, but many bookstores are planning to boycott them, because Amazon is a rival bookseller.

These options aren't either/or, as some people seem to believe. Most of the corporate-published authors I know are releasing indie books as well. Some are also using small publishers for some of their books.

The "hybrid author," who works with an agent to both self-publish and publish with the big houses, is the future.

We have options that never existed before. For authors, it's all good.

The publishing world has changed irrevocably since the advent of the e-reader. The changes came about partly because of the e-revolution and partly because the old system was already in a state of decay. Some corner bookshops may be evaporating, but others are evolving. Who knows, they may soon become cool coffee house/wine bar/print-while-you wait media emporiums and community centers. And all in all, I think the good outweighs the bad—for both readers and authors.

The greatest thing to come from the ebook revolution may be the way it empowers writers.

We now have choices. Even authors who are still publishing only with international conglomerates know they can walk away if they want to. They can demand more equitable royalties. They can refuse to take orders on what to write and how many books to churn out per year. They can publish novellas and short stories and books outside a specified genre.

And for newbie authors—you've all got a chance to make the big time.

Catherine and I believe that in spite of all the publicity surrounding the self-publishers who have sold millions, every new writer benefits from the query process. Almost all writers are better off with a good agent to guide their careers (although not all of them are adjusting well to the new paradigm, so choose carefully). It's also worthwhile to query smaller publishers. Catherine and I were both first published by small presses.

CATHERINE

THE AGENT AS SELF-PUBLISHER'S HELPER

I ADORE MY AGENT, AND MY AGENCY, SO I WAS HAPPY TO LEARN THEY were willing to consider intelligent and well-executed self-publishing as part of our overall strategy for my career.

Under the circumstances, I was quick to agree.

It had been several years since we'd been able to make a sale to any adult publisher in the U.S. Sales figures on my last adult book weren't helping. I was still publishing young adult books with a major U.S. publisher, but end-user sales were slumpy there as well. We were selling my adult titles directly to the U.K., where I was much more popular, and they were doing quite well...but in the chaos that is modern U.S. publishing, this was not as helpful as you might think.

I felt I had nothing to lose.

Now, as Anne mentioned earlier, there has been a cry raised on this issue: the agent as publisher. Some call it a conflict of interest. I call it a complete misnomer and misinterpretation. In any case, I wasn't daunted or worried by that cry, for two reasons.

One, I know my agent and her agency. I know they wouldn't steer me wrong. Two, they are not my publishers. They are providing a service. The list of individual services an agent might offer include, but are not limited to:

- Hire the cover designer and formatter.

- Edit and proofread the book.

- Make sure it's compatible with all ebook platforms.

- Create promotional copy.

- Get it properly listed with online booksellers.

- Set it up as a print-on-demand paperback.

- Check and refine the finished product to be sure it's indistinguishable from a traditionally published book.

- Monitor and adjust the price for optimal sales.

- Create a (meta) tag list.

- Solve any listing or downloading problems.

- Adjust things like BISAC categories for optimal visibility.

What's a BISAC category? No idea. I not only don't know, I'm glad I don't have to know. That's why I'm happy to give up the small percentage.

My agent was careful to tell me up front that I could do all this myself. Yeah, I'm sure I could if I had to. I'm reasonably tech-savvy.

If I could learn to build my own website, I'm sure I could have learned this. But it's a huge job.

Do feel free to take it on yourself. Do not, please, underestimate how much work it really is.

We put two books out in late summer and fall of that year.

And there they sat.

This is certainly one common indie outcome.

I used my tried-and-true promotional muscle, such as the blog tour...to surprisingly little avail.

The agency had promotional ideas, and they were able to create some positive upswing in the numbers. Some.

Then we chose one of the ebooks, *When I Found You*, and put it on a 5-day free Amazon promotion. It took off. It hit #1 in Kindle Free, with over 81,000 copies downloaded. When the promotion ended, it climbed up to #12 in Kindle Paid. The combination of the free downloads and actual sales numbers created a "popularity" rating of #3 in the Kindle store as a whole, #5 on all of Amazon books. I was hovering between two Hunger Games books on the Kindle main page. I was selling almost 2,000 copies a day (for a few days).

The other title, *Second Hand Heart*, enjoyed some reflected glory and made it up to about #600, or over 100 copies a day.

As of this writing, the books are still inside #200 and #2,000 in sales rankings, respectively. As long as those numbers hold, I'm selling about 250 books a day, which singlehandedly covers my basic monthly expenses more than twice over.

This is another possible ebook experience.

I have to be honest and say I don't really know why a book takes off. But I'm not too ashamed of this ignorance, because I don't believe anyone else knows the whole story, either. There are many unknowable factors operating behind the scenes. Some of it has to do with Amazon algorithms, which are proprietary. Translation: they ain't talkin'.

I can't say for a fact whether I would have gotten the same result working entirely on my own. I'm sure it's possible, because writers are doing it. But I also know the agency put a lot of background work into that success.

My conclusion? My agency is as valuable here as in a traditional book contract. Because the service they provide more than recovers the commission. In both models.

And it is a service. As I said earlier, the agency is not my publisher. The difference is fairly simple: a publisher acquires rights to your work. I retain all the rights to my books in this deal.

The reason I feel there's no conflict of interest is because my agent continues to represent each book in the way we agree will be optimal for that title. She has no strong financial incentive to go one way or the other. Her greatest earnings rest in the best overall sales possible. Her win is my win. So we discuss each property and where we feel we can do the best with it.

This, of course, requires trust, and is probably best accomplished with a trusted agent. Then again, every deal made in the publishing world has possible pitfalls. Properly done, I still consider this a great example of how agents can remain completely relevant. As reflected in Anne's earlier chapter, some question whether the need for agency services will disappear. I think the answer is the same for agents as for traditional publishers. If they refuse to adapt, many could find their careers shrinking.

But I think there's a place at the modern publishing table for every smart, honest individual who provides a needed (or desired) service to the author, and who is willing to change with a changing industry.

CATHERINE

A "COMPARE & CONTRAST" ON THE TWO PUBLISHING MODELS

THREE POTENTIAL DISCLAIMERS TO START THIS CHAPTER:

First, I want to note that this information is voted most likely to date quickly. Both publishing models—traditional versus self-publishing in ebook and POD (print-on-demand) format—are rapidly changing. But I will share some thoughts on where they stand now.

I'm also aware that, while I'm breaking this compare-and-contrast down to two models, there are more. There are also small publishers, agencies, and other services who will do all the work of ebook and POD publishing. Some are publishers who acquire rights, some are flat-fee services, some take a (wildly varying) percentage. Anne speaks a good bit about this. It's new, it's hard to track in its newness, each deal is different, and the pros and cons rest almost entirely on the reliability of the person or company offering the deal. So I've purposely left it out of this chapter, because it's not one of those things you can pin down on a chart.

Third disclaimer: I confess that these thoughts represent a huge turn-around for me. Even a couple of years ago, I was down on self-publishing. I felt it stamped the book with one of two messages: either that every imaginable publisher had turned it down, or that the writer was simply unwilling or unable to weather the requisite rejections.

Not that this was the case with every self-published book, of course. Only that it was true of enough of them that I felt the stereotype conferred damage.

But, of course, things changed. Radically changed.

When mega best-selling Thriller author Barry Eisler walked away from a half-million dollar deal with St Martin's Press because he could do better on his own (he later signed with Amazon Publishing), it was the shot heard round the world. Authors who could easily enjoy publishing deals were quite voluntarily deciding against them.

Behold the new dawn.

And we don't even call it self-publishing anymore. We call it indie.

Yet indie is still not the best choice for every book at every phase of an author's career, in my opinion.

Let's take a look at the nuts and bolts of both.

1) **Advances:** Indie will require an initial outlay of money. You'll need to hire a cover designer, a formatter (or you can learn to do it yourself, but it's a big job), and a copy editor/proofreader. Yes, you can cut corners, but seldom with good results.

Traditional publishing will likely advance you money, though maybe not much.

Depending on your financial wherewithal, this could be a big point scored for traditional publishing.

2) **Royalties:** Online booksellers pay between 35% and 70% of the "cover" price for ebooks. Amazon pays 70% on most U.S. ebooks, though they have to fall within a limited price range to earn that big royalty. But it's a good price range for your indie book anyway, in my opinion.

   Traditional pays you 25% of net. That is, 25% of what's left after the online bookseller takes their cut. Then your agent takes another 15% of your 25% of net.

This, of course, is the biggest win for Indie.

3) **Control:** Well, this is simple. If you go with a traditional publisher, you have little. They will show you the cover (usually), but if you hate it you might get stuck with it anyway. They can change your title, slap you with a book-killing log line or description (in my case, calling *Electric God* "A modern retelling of the Book of Job"), and/or position it to exactly the wrong audience. They can (and do) charge as much for the ebook as for a print book, dampening sales. You can do nothing.

Score big for Indie.

4) **Rights:** Traditional, they hold 'em. Usually until the book has been out of print and unavailable for sale in any format for a period of time specified in your contract. Which, in the ebook revolution, may never come. You can't even use a longish excerpt from your own book without permission.

And they usually control sub-rights, too, such as audio and foreign. If they don't do anything with them, nothing gets done.

Indie wins! Full rights—and options—retained by the author.

5) **Accounting:** More bad news for traditional. Under-reporting of royalties is rampant. But it's hard to tell how pervasive it is, because royalty statements are opaque and nearly impossible to interpret. I've been told that audits are now so commonplace that publishers don't even take offense. Still, don't comfort yourself too much thinking you can always audit. The auditor takes 30% of any monies recovered.

   Online booksellers issue statements that are simple and clear. You moved this many units at this price, so you earned this amount.

Another huge win for indie.

6) **Paydays**: Sorry, traditional. What other business can get away with offering two paychecks a year for earning periods that closed six months earlier? Would anyone allow any other employer to hold a worker's money for six months to a year before paying it out? Online booksellers pay royalties on their indie books quarterly (and Amazon and Barnes and Noble pay monthly).

As I've yet to convince any of my creditors to bill me bi-yearly, this is a win for indie.

7) **Visibility:** Here we get into territory in which the traditional publisher can still earn points. Granted, they don't do nearly as much as they used to in book promotion. But they have catalogues in which your book will appear. They send out

review copies, which stand some chance of being reviewed because of the big publisher name. If you are a brand new author, this feels to me like a win. Not that you can't create visibility on your own. Not that the publisher will always do a bang-up job. But if your name is unknown, their name will help.

A win for traditional.

8) **Authority:** Yes, it puts a stamp of approval on your book if a Big Five publisher brings it out. Your indie book may be good, but many are not, so you will be required to prove it.

For the new author, this is a big plus for traditional.

9) **Shelf life:** A traditional publisher really only pays much attention to your book in its initial publishing season. Once they stop paying attention, sales usually slump. When they slump past a certain point, you will be remaindered and go out of print. I say "you" because if this is your first book, that might have been your career they just buried. Indie books don't go out of print. You lose nothing by keeping them up and available as long as you live. No warehousing of inventory. No outlay. When you die, be sure to leave a will, assigning your royalties to someone you love.

Another win for Indie.

Whichever route you choose, your core conundrum will be the same: how to get the book noticed so it can be purchased. The traditional publisher will help some, but gone are the days when they do it all for you.

There's plenty you can do to promote your indie book, but please don't fall into the trap of thinking this is anything less than a long, hard slog. Yes, people hit the jackpot on ebooks, which then sell themselves, making the authors rich. People win millions in the lottery, too. But that's a wish, not a game plan.

Do your best to choose wisely in publishing models, and have a good game plan for what comes next.

ANNE

WHY YOU SHOULD BE WRITING MORE SHORT FICTION

WHAT—SHORT STORIES? AREN'T THEY JUST FOR WRITING CLASSES? Why would I waste time on stuff that doesn't pay?

Because it does now.

In its first year, Amazon's Kindle Singles program sold over two million "Singles" ebooks. Yeah. 2 MILLION.

The short stories sell for between $. 99 and $1.99 and the authors keep a 70% royalty. Many of the top sellers are by big-name authors, like Lee Child, Stephen King, and Jodi Picoult. But others are by unknowns, according to Kindle Singles editor David Blum. (Only stories in the official Singles program get that rate. Other ebooks priced below $2.99 get a 35% royalty.)

This is where you should be doing a happy dance and shouting from the rooftops: THE SHORT STORY IS BACK! This is nothing but good news for authors, no matter where you are in your career.

After three or four decades of evaporating markets, the short story has found a new home in the ebook.

OK, we're not reliving the halcyon days of the mid-20th century when short fiction in weeklies like *The Saturday Evening Post* paid more than the average book advance does today. But short fiction fits the ADD-attention-span lifestyle of the E-age, and people are willing to pay for it. (This is yet another reason not to give away your fiction on your blog.)

I think it's time for all fiction writers to start re-thinking the short form. Personally, I know I haven't spent enough time on it. During the decade I spent writing and re-writing my "practice novel," I could have been building an inventory of short pieces that would be a gold mine now.

Unfortunately, most novice writers I know are still doing the same stuff I did. They're putting all their energy into book-length fiction or memoir and not bothering with short pieces, except maybe for a flash fiction contest or special event.

In fact, I visited a critique group not long ago where one writer complimented another with the misguided advice that he shouldn't "waste" his crisp little story—he should turn it into a novel.

In other words, she was telling the writer that instead of sending a 10,000 word short story to Amazon to sell for 99 cents, he should spend two years turning it into a 100,000 word novel, which he could sell on Amazon for...um, 99 cents. (OK, not all self-pubbed ebooks are priced that low, but even at $4.99, the bottom line news isn't good for the author. Especially if he puts money into editing and design.)

Of course, back in the Jurassic days when I started writing, that critiquer's advice would have been perfectly sound. In the 1990s, most magazines had stopped publishing fiction. Short stories had all but disappeared from the publishing world, and mega bookstores were in their heyday. Book-length fiction was happening.

So aspiring authors were told to keep eyes on the big prize and put energy into churning out novels in popular genres like Chick Lit, Glitz, and family sagas.

I've amassed quite a collection of half-finished books in those genres—all sadly out of fashion now. But if I had been writing short stories instead, I could be raking in the dough. (Not that any time spent writing is wasted. Everything we write improves our craft.)

But I didn't feel drawn to writing short stories. I like genre fiction. Back then, short stories were expected to be literary.

Yes, there were still some paying gigs for genre stories in super-competitive markets like *Asimov's, Women's World,* and *Ellery Queen.*

But mostly we were urged to write enigmatic tales of suburban angst and send them off to collect rejection slips from literary journals with a circulation of 26 and names like *Wine-Dark Snowflakes of the Soul,* or *The Southeastern Idaho Pocatello Community Colleges North Campus Literary Review.* All with the hopes we'd finally be rewarded with publication and payment of one free copy.

But ebooks have changed all that. Not just because of Kindle Singles. Short story anthologies are springing up all over. They don't all pay, but if you can get a story into an anthology with some well-known authors in your genre, you'll be paid in publicity that would be hard to buy at any price.

I've been offered a number of opportunities to publish fiction in anthologies that have really paid off. *The Saffina Desforges Coffee*

Collection where I have a short piece reached #1 on the anthology bestseller list as soon as it was released last December, and the *Indie Chicks Anthology* (which sends its profits to charity) has been a steady seller—and once it went free it sat at #1 in anthologies for weeks.

I'm not advising anybody to ditch that magnum opus—most novel writers get frustrated when limited by the short form. But I'm saying it makes sense to put an equal amount of energy into shorter pieces. Instead of putting every idea that illuminates your brain into your novel, give a few of them a spin in short stories first.

People like legendary Mystery writer Lawrence Block and bestselling SciFi writer Jeff Carlson have guest posted on my blog telling about the great success they've had self-publishing short stories and novellas their Big Five publishers didn't want.

But you don't have to be accepted at Kindle Singles or have a famous name to benefit from publishing short-form ebooks.

A bestselling author I know decided to put some of her old stories on Amazon. As an experiment, she didn't use her famous name. She made $500 in the first month. These were works she was told "had absolutely no commercial value." But she put them out there, "in case someone was interested." It seems they were—because "in spite of absolutely no promo or anything, people are finding them and buying them."

Indie writers are doing well with shorter pieces too. One indie writer wrote me recently with this advice: "unless you have a break-out success with a novel, [the short story] is probably more lucrative as a return on time invested. I can make as much per sale on a ten page short story as on a 120,000 word novel."

And I know many indies who use a short piece as a free

download to introduce readers to their work.

I heard from an author who self-published a short piece she wrote on a plane and "writing, formatting, cover, etc. took less than a day." It got 6500 free downloads in a few days—great advertising for her work.

So the magic formula for writers right now might be "less is more."

I do want to stress that the above writers are all successful, published novelists with hard-earned expertise in their craft.

PLEASE NOTE: I'm NOT advocating that new writers self-publish your fledgling short fiction.

A few self-pubbed singles by a brand new writer won't get anybody's attention—and may embarrass your future self. Wait until you have a body of work—either published short fiction you can re-issue as a collection, or a novel/memoir of book length.

To succeed in publishing—whether self- or traditional—you really need to put in those 10,000 Malcolm Gladwell hours.

But you can maximize your efforts by putting more of those hours writing short fiction. When it's time to make your professional debut, you're going to have some serious inventory.

If you're still unconvinced, consider that short fiction is much easier to adapt for the screen than novels. Some of our most enduring films have come from short stories. Classic films like *The Birds, Breakfast at Tiffany's, Don't Look Now, Double Indemnity, Flowers for Algernon*...and I'd need a whole post to list the stories of Stephen King and Philip K. Dick that have been made into great films. More recent Oscar contenders like *Brokeback Mountain* and *the Squid and the Whale* were originally short stories.

And until you get yourself established, you don't have to keep those stories in a drawer. One of the great things about short fiction is that it's re-usable. Most zines and journals only ask for first rights (and be very careful with the ones who want more).

Gone are the days when obscure college literary journals were the only game in town. New zines are springing up all the time, and there are contests everywhere online—some even have cash prizes. I suggest subscribing to C. Hope Clark's newsletter, Funds for Writers, for vetted info on contests.

Contest wins and credits for a few stories published in some good online zines look very nice in a query letter or bio, too.

So forget the so-last-millennium advice to concentrate on novels. Polish those short pieces and prepare yourself for a 21st century audience.

If, like me, you can't kick your book-writing habit, try writing a short piece about a secondary character in your WIP. It's a great exercise for exploring your character's backstory, and once your novel is published, it can benefit you in lots of ways:

1) It could make you a nice chunk of change as an e-single.

2) It might go into an anthology where it could get you new readers.

3) You can offer it as a free download for some inexpensive publicity.

4) It might work as a film.

Even if you're unpublished and have a long way to go before you publish your first novel, I suggest taking time to work up some stories and build your inventory.

And I recommend you enter a few contests and submit to those zines. You might just win something.

"Award-winning writer" has a nicer sound than "unpublished novelist," doesn't it?

ANNE

THREE THINGS TO CONSIDER BEFORE JUMPING ON THE SELF E-PUBLISHING BANDWAGON

THERE'S NO DOUBT ABOUT IT: WE'RE IN THE MIDST OF SEISMIC CHANGES in the publishing world, with new quakes altering the landscape on a daily basis. The pulp paperback is in its death throes, as mass market houses like Dorchester slink into ignominious bankruptcy. Kindle and the Amazon $2.99 ebook/70% royalty paradigm have changed an entire industry in the matter of a few years.

Hocking, Howey, and Eisler have become household names with their runaway indie publishing success. Joe Konrath and his disciples prove daily that some midlist fiction writers can make more self-publishing cheap ebooks than by going the traditional route. Trusted voices in the publishing industry—even many agents—who once scorned self-publishing are now singing its praises.

This means writers have the option of starting our careers right now. Not three or four or ten years down the road after an excruciating query/submission/editing process, but now. TODAY. And there's a possibility we'll make real money. Konrath regularly posts hot financial statistics that are pure writer porn. We all want to join in the orgy.

But there's a dark side to self-publishing that should give some of us pause.

Things can get very messy when indie authors come to cyberblows with indie book bloggers. New authors can have very childish meltdowns. Then the entire blogosphere likes to follow suit. Vicious bullying can happen. We all have inner children who are prone to temper tantrums on occasion, and the anonymity of the Interwebz can make people just plain mean.

Isaac Asimov once observed that writers fall into two groups: "those who bleed copiously and visibly at any bad review, and those who bleed copiously and secretly at any bad review."

But in these days of social media we have no "secretly" any more. Everything is visible—on a global scale.

When writers haven't developed the soul-calluses that are required of a professional author, they can lash out with personal attacks on reviewers, which always end badly.

There are some unspoken benefits to the old "query-fail-query-fail-submission-fail-editorial meeting-fail, fail, fail" system. It not only gives us numerous readers to help hone that book to perfection—it also teaches us to deal with rejection, failure and bad reviews.

And these days, many books get one-star reviews simply because of bad formatting. One huge sorry battle was sparked by the question of whether the reviewer had read a first or repaired version of a book.

So anybody thinking of simply uploading a Word.doc into Amazon's form to convert to Kindle should think again. Some people say it's pretty easy, but "easy" is a relative term. If you don't know what you're doing, apostrophes become incomprehensible lines of code, bullet points turn into weird characters, and page and line breaks appear in nonsensical places.

If you choose to self-publish because you can't handle the rejection of the query process, you're setting yourself up for worse pain later on. If those form rejections in your email sting, think of how you'll feel when they're broadcast all over the blogosphere.

So when you hear all the stories of self-publishing "instant millionaires," consider that Amanda Hocking had eight books in the hopper before she self-published. Eight. She was also professional enough to hire an editor and a book designer. She was ready to treat her writing as a full time job.

So here are three questions to ask yourself before you take the self-pub plunge:

1) Can you afford to present a professional book in a professional way? This means hiring an editor, book formatter, and cover designer, plus putting together a marketing plan and making the time to implement it. Just throwing it up on Amazon to see what happens could backfire. Big time.

2) Are you emotionally ready for your close-up? Every successful author gets nasty reviews. Every. Single. One. If you want proof, go read the one-star reviews of literary classics on Amazon.

Learning how to deal with crushing criticism needs to be part of your skill set. Make sure you keep in touch with the part of you that has nothing to do with your books—the one that goes outside to hear real birds twitter and gets face to face with actual friends. Understand that after a nasty review, you need to STEP AWAY FROM THE COMPUTER. Hide all electronic communication devices and bring in chocolate, wine, DVDs, and/or your BFF, and hibernate.

Catherine suggests you allow yourself to mourn for at least three days after a bad review. I think that sounds about right.

3) Is your book really, truly ready? Not just for friendly readers, but unfriendly ones. I advise finding some not-so-tame beta readers and asking them to do their worst. Find the book's vulnerable spots. Then imagine seeing their harshest words in a review. Can you see how a reader might accept them as valid? If so, hold off and do some more editing. Better yet, write another book. Then edit the first one again.

You owe it to your characters to present them in the best possible way—and you owe it to yourself to start your career with your very best work.

ANNE

IS THE EBOOK THE NEW QUERY?

WELL-RESPECTED AGENT JENNY BENT SURPRISED A LOT OF WRITERS when she announced on her blog:

"Unpublished authors, do you have a great book but can't find an agent? There's no excuse not to get that book out there independently and prove to yourself and to the world that there is an audience for your writing."

It seems the self-published ebook is fast becoming the query of choice for many New York literary agencies. Rather than slog through mountains of slush, agents are closing their offices to queries and shopping for new clients in the Kindle bestseller lists.

Why not? That's where they'll find unrepresented authors with proven sales numbers, which is what more and more publishers require.

Successful indie authors know how to write what sells, plus

they're savvy marketers—a win/win for agents and editors alike.

Big name, prestigious agencies have taken to Kindle-trolling. Agent Noah Lukeman (author of *The First Five Pages*) has been making deals for a number of formerly self-pubbed first-time authors although he's been closed to queries for some time. And über-agency Trident Media Group has been signing indies like mad.

These agencies seem especially interested in the international bestseller lists—probably hoping to reel in the next Steig Larsson or J. K. Rowling.

So it's a heady time for successful indie authors.

Imagine: here's you, first-time author, who self-pubbed after years of rejection—having a nice cuppa at home in Claxby Pluckacre, Firozabad, or here in San Luis Obispo, CA—when the phone rings and it's someone from NEW YORK. It's that call: the offer of a contract and soon-to-come book deal (with maybe a tantalizing hint of a film option). Opportunity has knocked: fame and fortune and glory to follow. Your dream has come true.

But beware: you may be running into a 21st century version of one of the old agent scams I warned you about in my chapter on "Bogus Literary Agents."

Just the way agents see gold in them thar Kindle hills, so do the scammers. I've heard some horror stories. So educate yourself.

The words "I'm calling from New York" are dazzling, and most international writers don't know the difference between a prestigious agency in Manhattan or some con-person calling from the 24-hour Denny's in Rochester (New York is a big state). And even a lot of Americans can be temporarily blinded by the idea of a New York agent.

So beware. There's a big chance this call will never lead to seeing that dreamed-of print book sitting in your local bookstore window.

It might be best to go back and finish your tea before making any decisions.

Here are some tips to keep yourself grounded if/when you get that call:

1) Be skeptical if your Amazon sales are not huge. Real agents are looking for superstars, but scammers are just going down the list looking for pigeons.

2) Ask what they like about the book. Agents read books before they make offers. A scammer will only quote blurb copy.

3) Ask where they plan to submit your work. If they are unable to name names and particular imprints, be wary. They may not be crooks, but they're also not likely to be good agents. An effective agent will personally know editors and the imprints that are looking for your type of book.

4) Find out how long they've been in the business. Nothing wrong with new agents—in fact they're often the best—because they need clients and they're hungry. But you want to make sure they're well-connected. If they never interned or worked at an established agency or publishing house, they probably aren't going to be able to sell your book.

5) NEVER agree to pay up-front fees—even if these fees are just for "copying and mailing." (I'm hammering a few of these tips that should be familiar from my chapter on Bogus Literary Agents, but it's good to be aware some recycled scams live on in the e-age).

6) Be wary of agency websites with "testimonials" from happy clients. This isn't done in the publishing business. A good agency's "testimonials" are their sales record.

7) Note if there are grammatical mistakes on the website. If you see any, run. Some bogus agencies seem to use bad grammar on purpose, maybe to weed out the savvier writers.

8) Check client lists. If there's no client page on their site, you know you're in scammer-land.

9) Check recent sales. If they haven't made a sale in the past few years, they won't have the contacts to sell your book today. There's a fast turn-over in editorial departments.

10) Pay attention to where their clients have been published. If they're all at the same handful of presses—none of which you've ever heard of—this is very likely a vanity publishing outfit. This is a common publishing scam these days: the agent "sells" your book to one of several "imprints" of a publishing company—which he owns—charging an agent's cut of 15%. Then (his) press will charge you to print the book, or require you to buy a certain number of copies at inflated prices.

11) Check them out with respected writers' watchdog groups like Writer Beware and QueryTracker.

However, as I said above, some agents who contact successful indies will indeed be big-time, big-name literary superstars.

So you can put down the tea and pop open the champagne, right? Uh, maybe not.

A lot of agents are asking that indie e-publishers take their books down from Amazon as soon as they sign. That's ALL of your books, not just the one the agent wants to rep.

This means you have to give up your income and remove your briskly-selling, successful books from the marketplace while the agent shops your new manuscript around.

And that may take years.

If you've ever talked to an author whose work is on submission, you'll know this can be a soul-crushingly long, slow, and miserable process, with no guarantees. I've been through it with three different agents. And not one of them made a sale.

Meanwhile, you've lost all your sales momentum and brand recognition. If you finally do get a contract with a Big Five publisher, your marketing plan will have to start over at square one when your book comes out—three or four years from now. The world of traditional publishing still moves at a horse-and buggy pace. Plus you'll have a much more expensive product to sell.

The marketing thing is no big deal for the agent or publisher: writers are expected to do all our own marketing these days—or so they keep telling us.

But it's going to be a big deal for you.

So even if an agent is for real, I strongly suggest you resist any requests to remove all your inventory from the marketplace. Maybe some agents can make a hiatus in your career worthwhile, but be aware they're asking you to take a huge gamble.

Most of us are stuck in the old paradigm of, "I need an agent to be a REAL writer." But this is a whole new publishing universe, and agents are still trying to figure out how they fit into it. So if you're an indie author with good sales, you might be fine where you are. As exciting as it feels to be wooed by the people who once spurned you, don't welcome all comers with hugs and kisses.

On the other hand, the big name self-publishers like Konrath and Eisler and Howey have agents, and a professional, savvy agent can do wonders for your career.

So should all writers be learning to design covers and format ebooks instead of researching more agents and rewriting that query for the 100th time?

I don't think so.

For one thing, a rejected manuscript can be tweaked and re-queried ad infinitum. But a bumbling beginner's ebook that has only sold three downloads, all to his Mom, is not going to attract any agents. And a bunch of negative reviews about a writer's lack of skills could pretty much put the kibosh on a career.

DO consider self-publishing if you've been writing for many years, have several super-polished, critiqued and edited books in the hopper—plus a marketing plan—and love social media. It helps if you write in a genre that's doing well in the Kindleverse, which seems to be a great place for gritty crime stories and Thrillers (especially those that appeal to men: the tech has made reading fiction macho again) plus Paranormal Romance, Erotica, and Fantasy/SciFi.

Children's ebooks have not yet taken off the way adult books have, so if you write for children, check what's selling before you decide.

DON'T consider self-publishing if you don't have a large online network in your genre and don't have time to blog or tweet. As former *Writers Digest* editor Jane Friedman says: If "it's your first manuscript and you don't want to see all that work go to waste...wait until you've written book #2 or #3 or #4 before you decide to release that first one." And pay attention to what's selling and where. Some genres that seem to do better with traditional publishers are YA and Middle Grade, adult literary novels, cerebral mysteries, memoirs, and women's fiction.

The old order changeth. But it ain't dead yet. As of this writing, 70% of book sales are still for print books.

Also, if you read *Publisher's Lunch*, you'll see traditional deals being made every day. Big ones. Some for debut novelists. Even ones who aren't stars of reality TV shows. So some agents must still be reading slush. And at least a few editors must be taking their calls.

Remember not all publishers are unwilling to take chances on newbies. There are thousands of small and medium-sized independent presses out there, and many are thriving.

Bottom line: do I recommend first novelists self-publish as a way to get the attention of an agent? No. Wait until you have several books written. Then, if you're a savvy marketer in the right genre, and you have fantastic sales, you may get the added perk of an agent like Jenny Bent calling to query YOU.

ANNE

12 SIGNS YOUR BOOK ISN'T READY TO PUBLISH

FOR WRITERS CONSIDERING SELF-PUBLISHING, LET ME SUGGEST YOU repeat this mantra: KINDLE NO BOOK BEFORE ITS TIME! Don't throw your fledgling book out into the marketplace without some serious thought.

Of course you feel pressure to join the ebook revolution. Stories of Kindle millionaires are everywhere. The ebook provides a magnificent way for established writers to monetize their backlist— or even their frontlist—and has worked magic for some new novelists, too.

But it's important to keep in mind the successful indies were all seasoned writers before they self-published. They had inventory. They knew how to build platform and make sales.

So don't expect their results until you're a seasoned writer, too. Even if you don't get pounded with bad reviews, you could be sabotaging your future career. If a reader finds bad grammar, misused words, and no plot—even in a 99 cent ebook—they're not going to want to read that author again. Maybe only a handful of people will buy it, but if you become a literary darling someday, that bad book will always be lurking somewhere on somebody's Kindle, waiting to destroy your reputation.

Writing has a learning curve like any other skill. You don't get to play Carnegie Hall after a few piano lessons. You don't play Wimbledon after a couple of afternoons on batting the ball over the net.

Learning to write takes time. Way more time than you think. All beginners make mistakes. Falling down and making a mess is part of any learning process. But you don't have to display the mess to the world.

Here are some tell-tale signs that a writer is still in the learning phase of his/her career:

1) Lots of writerly prose. Those long, gorgeous descriptions that got so much praise from your high school English teacher and your college girlfriend are a huge turn-off for the paying customer who's searching for some kind of story in there.

2) English-major showing off. It may feel incredibly clever to start every chapter with an epigraph from *Finnegan's Wake*. But unless it's really important to the plot, this will probably annoy rather than impress readers. Ditto oblique references to the Cavalier poets or anything by Thomas Mann. People want to be entertained, not worship at your self-erected literary altar.

3) Episodic storytelling. I admit my own guilt on this one. I could never end my first novel, because it didn't actually have a plot. It was a series of related episodes—like a TV series. Critique groups often don't catch this problem, if each episode has a dramatic arc of its own.

4) Hackneyed openings. (See the following chapter on "Introducing the Protagonist.") The worst is the "alarm clock" opening—your protagonist waking up—the favorite cliché of all beginning storytellers. I've heard that 78 % of all student films start with an alarm clock going off. I think student novels are probably about the same.

5) Thinly disguised oh-poor-me memoirs and revenge fantasies. Having a terrible childhood does not make a great story. Neither does surviving a life-threatening disease. That kind of experience needs a lot of processing before it can be worked into entertaining fiction. Also, readers probably won't be enthralled by a 200,000 word description of a guy just like your toxic ex, even if he gets hacked up by his ax-murdering second wife in the final scene. (Yes, I know that was fun to write.)

6) Semi-fictionalized religious/political screeds. You have to be really, really good (or Ayn Rand) to get away with political fiction. Carl Hiaasen manages to throw quite a bit of his green politics into his comic mysteries, and Chris Moore gets in some digs in his hilarious horror tales. But if you aren't as funny as those guys, save it for a letter to the editor.

And if you've written a novel just so you can send everybody who isn't exactly like you to Hell, your reader will want to send you there, too.

7) Dialogue info-dumps and desultory conversation. Another of my personal pitfalls. After 25 years in the theater, my brain's natural habitat was the script. It took me years to learn characters don't have to say all that stuff out loud. And "hello how are you fine and you nice weather" dialogue may be realistic, but it's snoozifying. Readers don't care about "authenticity" if it doesn't further the plot.

8) Tom Swifties. The writer who strains to avoid the word "said" can rapidly slip into bad pun territory, as in the archetypal example: "'We must hurry,' exclaimed Tom Swiftly." Bad dialogue tags may have crept into your consciousness at an early age from Nancy Drew and Hardy Boys books. They're great fun, but they were written by a stable of underpaid hacks and although the stories are classic, the prose is not.

9) Mary Sues. A Mary Sue is a character who's a stand-in for the writer's idealized self—an ordinary person who always saves the day and is inexplicably the object of everyone's affection. She's beautiful. Everybody loves her. She has no faults. Except she's boring and completely unbelievable.

10) Imprecise word usage. This is what snagged the infamous unhappily-reviewed indie author I mentioned in the last chapter. If you don't know the difference between lie and lay, aesthetic and ascetic, or electrical and electoral (unless you're Yogi Berra), you'll get two-star reviews, too.

11) Incorrect spelling and grammar. The buying public isn't your third grade teacher; they won't give you a gold star just to boost your self-esteem. Spelling and grammar count. Words are your tools.

Would you try out for professional baseball if you didn't know how to hold a bat? Electronic grammar checks can only do so much. And they're often wrong. Buy a grammar book. Take a course. Seriously. Even a good editor can't do everything.

12) Wordiness. There's a reason agents are wary of long books. New writers tend to take 100 words to say what seasoned writers can say in 10. If your prose is weighty with adjectives and adverbs, or clogged with details and repetitive scenes, you'll scare off readers as well.

***

If you're still doing any of these things, RELAX! Enjoy writing for its own sake a while longer. Read more books on craft. Build inventory. You really do need at least two polished manuscripts in the hopper before you launch your career. Meanwhile, learn some tricks of self-editing in our next chapter.

PART 7

EDITING: THE KEY TO GOOD WRITING

ANNE

INTRODUCING THE PROTAGONIST—14 DOS AND DON'TS

INTRODUCING YOUR MAIN CHARACTER TO YOUR READER MAY BE THE single trickiest job for a novelist. You have to introduce the reader to a character in a very short time and entice us go on a journey with her into a brand new world. If you tell us too much, we're bored, but if you tell us too little, we're in the dark.

Important note before you read on: these are rules for your final draft ONLY.

When you're first diving into a novel, you're not introducing your characters to a reader; you're introducing them to yourself.

All kinds of information about your MC will come up while you're writing your first draft. Maybe she lives in a noisy apartment building. Or her mom is a gung-ho Amway seller. Or her next door neighbor is recuperating from a terrible accident. Or she feels a deep hatred for Smurfs. This stuff will spill out in your first chapters. Let it. That's the fun part.

But be aware you'll want to cut most of the information or move it to another part of the book when you edit.

It helps to remember this formula—FIRST DRAFTS ARE FOR THE WRITER; FINAL DRAFTS ARE FOR THE READER.

Here are some dos and don'ts that should help in the revision process.

1) DON'T start with a Robinson Crusoe opening. That's when your character is alone and musing. Robinson Crusoe is boring until Friday shows up. So don't snoozify the reader with a character:

- driving alone in a car
- sitting on an airplane
- waking up and getting ready for the day
- out on her morning jog
- looking in the mirror

Especially looking in the mirror. It's not wrong, but it's a seriously overdone cliché.

2) DO open with the protagonist in a scene with other characters—showing how he interacts with the world. Two or three is ideal: not too many or the reader will be overwhelmed.

Here's the opening of my Romantic Comedy/Mystery, *The Best Revenge*:

"Camilla fought her rising panic by clutching Plantagenet's strong, Armani-clad arm as the Mâitre d' led them to their usual table at Votre Maison.

She had no idea how any debutante survived without a gay best friend.

Plant seemed to read her mind, as always. "Stop worrying, darling. You look beautiful. Heartbreakingly beautiful."

We can see our protagonist is full of anxiety about something, and her relationship with Plantagenet is warm and supportive—without anybody speaking a word. The Maitre d' is present, and we know we're in a restaurant full of people, but none of them has to speak or be introduced for us to be fully immersed in the scene.

3) DON'T give a lot of physical description, especially of the police report variety. We don't need to know eye color/height/weight. Give a general impression in a few broad strokes and the reader's imagination fills in the blanks.

In the above scene, we know Camilla is a debutante and "heartbreakingly beautiful." Most people have a picture of a pretty young rich girl in their heads they can plug into this scene. We don't all need to see the same picture. It's up to the readers how they visualize the details of Camilla's appearance.

4) DO give us a few strong physical markers that indicate personality. Unusual characteristics like curvy hips or striking hair or an unusual way of dressing will tell us something about who a character is and make her memorable. But if all you say is she has green eyes and curly red hair—you've only told us she's identical to the MCs of 90% of all YA Romance novels, according to one agent. We don't need to know the hair/eye thing unless the characteristic is important to the story—like Anne of Green Gables hating her hair and dying it green.

In the above scene, we know from a few words that Plantagenet is a fit, extremely well-dressed gay man. The next time he appears, we're likely to remember him.

5) DON'T present your MC as a flawless Mary Sue. I talked about Mary Sues in the previous chapter. A Mary Sue will make your whole story phony, because a too-perfect character isn't believable (and is seriously annoying).

6) DO give your MC strong emotions we can identify with in the opening scene. We don't have to identify with the situation, but with the emotion: if the character is furious because her roommate keeps watching that DVD of the Smurfs—even if you've never heard of a Smurf—you'll identify with the anger because everybody's had their buttons pushed by somebody's repetitive or insensitive behavior.

When we see Camilla entering a restaurant feeling panic about what she's going to encounter, we can identify, because we've all felt anxiety, even if we've never been heartbreakingly beautiful debutantes.

7) DON'T start with a POV character about to be killed or otherwise eliminated from the storyline (ditto dreams, or putting the MC in a play or videogame). If you get us intrigued and then say "never mind," the reader will feel her time and sympathy have been wasted.

8) DO introduce the MC as close to page one as possible. Don't waste time on weather reports or long descriptions of setting. That doesn't mean you have to neglect setting, but make sure you're doing something emotional and original with it. Remember that modern readers want to jump into the story and get emotionally involved. Also, a modern reader doesn't need the kind of long descriptions of far-off lands that Victorians loved. Even if we've never been there, we all know what London, or the Alps, or rain forests look like because we've seen them in films and on TV.

Here's the opening of my Mystery, *Ghostwriters in the Sky*:

"The subway car was so crowded I couldn't tell which one of the sweaty men pressing against me was attached to the hand now creeping up my thigh. I should have known better than to wear a dress on a day I had to take the subway, but in the middle of a New York heat wave, I couldn't face another day in a pants suit."

You're on a New York subway. You don't need a long description of the smell of the sweat or the stickiness of the bodies pressed against each other. You already want to get off at the next stop. You also know the protagonist is a young professional woman who's almost pathologically polite and concerned with decorum. All it took was 66 words. (No. That opening didn't come easily. And I wrote it almost two years after I thought the book was finished.)

9) DON'T start with a prologue. Sigh. I know a lot of you love them. But here are some reasons why prologues aren't such a great idea.

a) People skip them. The reader has to start the story twice. Just as she's getting into the story, she's hurled to another time or place, often with a whole new set of characters. This is annoying. Annoy a reader at your peril.

b) When an agent or editor asks for the first chapter—or you have a preview of the book on Amazon—you've got a major dilemma. Do you send the actual chapter one—where the plot starts—or that poetic prologue?

c) Agents hate them. Here's what some agents have said about them:

From former agent Colleen Lindsay:

"In pages that accompany queries, I have only once found an attached prologue to be necessary to the story."

From agent Jenny Bent:

"At least 50% of prologues that I see in sample material don't work and aren't necessary. Make sure there's a real reason to use one."

From agent Ginger Clark:

"Prologues: I am, personally, not a fan. I think they either give away too much, or ramp up tension in a kind of 'cheating' manner."

From agent Andrea Brown:

"Most agents hate prologues. Just make the first chapter relevant and well written."

From agent Laurie McLean:

"Prologues are usually a lazy way to give backstory chunks to the reader and can be handled with more finesse throughout the story. Damn the prologue, full speed ahead!"

Even usually ultra-tactful publishing guru Nathan Bransford says:

"A prologue is 3-5 pages of introductory material that is written while the author is procrastinating from writing a more difficult section of the book."

I know you're all wailing. But try removing the prologue. Read chapter one. Does it make sense? Could you dribble in that backstory from the prologue into the story later—while the actual plot is going on? A prologue is like a first draft—usually it's for the writer, not the reader. It isn't the overture: it's the tuning-up. Like a character sketch, a prologue usually belongs in your book journal—not the finished project. Go ahead and write one to get your writing juices flowing. Use it to get to know your book's basic elements. It can be mined later for character sketches, backstory and world building, but try to cut it in your final revision.

10) DO put the MC in a place and time right away. If the MC is thinking or talking to someone—where is she? As I said, we don't want a long description of the scenery or the weather, but let us know what planet we're on. Sometimes the best way to handle it is a simple declaration of the date.

This is how I introduced my Comic Historical Mystery *The Gatsby Game:*

"Some people still think I'm a terrible person because I didn't call the police right away. If I had, we might have avoided one of Hollywood's most notorious sex scandals, and I wouldn't have spent a lifetime living down the whole 'killer nanny' thing.

But seriously, when I saw Alistair lying on the floor of Delia Kent's motel room that night in 1973, I had no clue I was looking at a corpse. The room was dark, and I didn't see any blood on that brown shag carpet. I thought Alistair was sleeping off the Mandrax he'd stolen from Delia's medicine cabinet."

If you were alive in 1973, the brown shag carpet and mention of the drug Mandrax may trigger memories, but you don't need to be that old to know where you are. That's because I told you: We're in a cheap motel room on a night in 1973. Sometimes it is actually better to tell than show.

11) DON'T start with dialogue. Readers want to know who's speaking before they'll pay much attention to what they say. It's just like real life: if strangers are shouting in the hallway, it's noise. If you recognize the shouters as your boss and the hooker from 12B—you're all ears.

In the opening from *The Best Revenge* above, it helps to identify with Camilla and her anxiety before Plantagenet tells her she's beautiful. His line might make us dislike her if we thought she was secure and self-satisfied.

12) DO dribble in your MC's backstory in thoughts, conversations and mini-flashbacks—AFTER you've got us hooked by your MC and her story.

13) DON'T plunge into action before introducing the characters. The introductions can be minimal, but they have to make us feel connected enough to these people to care. If you hear some stranger got hit by a car—it's sad, but you don't have much curiosity about it. If you hear your neighbor got hit by a car, you want to know when, where, how badly she's injured, etc.

14) DO give your MC a goal. All characters need goals in each scene. But the protagonist needs a compelling, over-arching goal for the whole book and you need to tell us pretty close to the opening. She can't be easily satisfied. She must need something very badly. A novel needs to be about one big thing, and the character has to have one big goal. Too many goals? You may have a series. That's good, too.

Here's the opening of my comic Thriller, *Food of Love*:

"Her Royal Highness Regina Saxi-Cadenti, Princess of San Montinaro, backed out of the bathroom stall on her knees, pulling the scrub bucket.

She felt her backside collide with something.

Or someone.

She froze. So the assassins had found her, even here at the recovery clinic, half a world away from the palace and its intrigues. They were back to finish last night's botched job."

We know our heroine is in jeopardy from the get-go. Someone—presumably from "the palace" is trying to kill her. Her goal in this book is going to be to figure out who "they" are, and keep from being killed.

***

I know. None of this is easy, and PLEASE don't agonize over the opening until your book is finished. If you're like me, you may write that opening scene fifty times. That's part of what we do, so don't feel you're doing something wrong if it takes a while to get it right.

CATHERINE

TRICKS OF SELF-EDITING

I'LL OPEN WITH THE WORDS OF CARTOONIST JOE MARTIN, CREATOR OF the Mr. Boffo comics:

"Pay attention to detail: the five most important words in business."

If you're wondering why that's funny, you need some tips on finding flaws in your own manuscript. And you probably need someone else to double-check your work. But don't feel bad, because we pretty much all do.

Years ago I was rereading a short story of mine, which contained the following line:

"In the morning she photographed Vincent making coffee in his boxer shorts."

Now, I had already read that line dozens of times. And nothing had struck me as out of place. But on that last reading, something broke through. It was...laughter. I began to laugh uncontrollably. Real hurt-your-ribs kind of stuff. And I said, out loud (when able), "Why doesn't Vincent just use a paper filter like everybody else?"

"In the morning she photographed Vincent in his boxer shorts, making coffee."

That's what I had meant to say.

Unfortunately, you are the author. And you know what you meant to say. Ergo, you are the least qualified person on the planet to judge whether you are saying what you meant to say.

I have no magic bullet to remedy this special form of blindness. If I did, I'd be a rich author, indeed. But here are a few helpful hints:

1) Always use spellcheck but never rely on it. Do an editing run-through dedicated to the errors spell-check won't catch. Look at every "through" and "though," and pay special attention to "it's" and its," and...well...I could go on, but you get the idea.

2) Try the proofreader's trick of reading one sentence at a time, starting with the last one at the end of the page and working backwards. It helps you not to get caught up in content when you mean to study form.

3) Create your own "search list." Pay close attention to the errors that are pointed out in your critique group, or by your beta readers. If they note that you've misused a semi-colon or put your punctuation on the wrong side of the quote marks, make a list of these shaky areas. Then open the manuscript file and do a series of computer searches. Enter a semi-colon in the search field. It will stop at each semi-colon, one at a time, allowing you to check its usage. Then move on to search a quote mark followed by a comma or a period. I guarantee you, your eye will miss instances of the error. I guarantee you, the computer will not.

4) **Read your work out loud, slowly, to a friend.** Better yet, have them read it to you. No friends, or friends out of patience? I know. I empathize. You're a writer. It comes with the territory. Read it into a recording device. Read slowly, and read it exactly as it appears on the page, pausing where there is a comma, not pausing where there is not. See if it comes out the way you thought it would.

5) **Give up and seek help**. No one ever said writing could be accomplished as a solo flight. A helpful member of your critique group can be quietly enlisted. You can arrange a trade. You will do a great job editing his or her manuscript for obvious errors, and he or she will do a bang-up job on yours. It's just one of the many unwelcome truths in the life of an author: it really helps when the page is not fully memorized.

One of the best self-editing strategies you can develop is more an attitude than an actual technique. Take pride in the cleanliness and correctness of your manuscript. Imagine that you are preparing for a job interview, and that you want this job more than you've ever wanted a job in your life. Prepare your manuscript the way you'd prepare yourself for that interview.

The sneakers with the holes in the toes won't do.

Maybe that seems unfair to you. After all, it should be about whether or not you can do the job. You're qualified. So why should your sneakers matter?

What if 200 fully qualified applicants show up to apply for one opening? Then the choices boil down to more subjective factors. And the applicant in the clean, un-holey shoes is showing better judgment, more desire for the job, and a good overall personal ethic.

But it's up to you. Just ask yourself how much you want this job and go from there.

ANNE

DO YOU NEED TO HIRE A PROFESSIONAL EDITOR?

AS I'VE SAID BEFORE: LEARNING TO WRITE BOOKS IS HARD; EARNING money from books is even harder.

So questions keep coming up:

1) How much money should you put into polishing a novel?

2) How much can you reasonably expect to recoup?

3) Should you hire an editor if you hope to get traditionally published?

4) When should you hire an editor if you plan to self-publish?

Self-publishing has been a great boon to freelance book editors. But an awful lot of writers aren't totally clear about their function.

When I was doing freelance editing, I was amazed by the people who came to me with over-inflated ideas of what an editor can do. They'd arrive with collections of raw taped interviews, notebooks full of verses and random jottings, or old letters they wanted me to make into a salable book.

There are people who do these things. They're called ghostwriters. They're going to cost a lot of money. And unless you're Justin Bieber, you'll never make back the money you put into them.

(That doesn't mean you shouldn't publish them for yourself. Sometimes a personal or family history can be a fantastic gift to your children and grandchildren—for more see the chapter on writing memoir.)

The term "editor" has several meanings in the book business. The "in-house" editors at publishing companies—the ones who decide what manuscripts to publish—don't do a lot of literal "editing" these days. According to Jenny Bent, the amount of hands-on work they do "varies wildly from editor to editor…because many editors simply don't have the time or desire to actually edit." You'll probably get more editing from some smaller and midsized presses than you do from the Big Five. I'm lucky to have had great editors at all three small presses who have published me.

But no matter what the size of the publishing house, by the time a manuscript lands on an editor's desk, it needs to be pretty close to print-ready. Agents can help you polish, but they don't have much time for nitty-gritty text-honing either, so most won't look at manuscripts that aren't carefully proofed and edited.

The truth is the majority of professional writers learn to edit themselves, with the help of a beta reader or two.

Too many newbies hire editors when what they really need is a few basic writing classes and some knowledge of the industry.

A lot of new writers are getting caught up in premature marketing frenzies and failing to learn basic craft. It's not their fault. Some very successful self-publishers are telling writers "every day your book isn't for sale you're losing money." This is pretty good advice for an established author with an out-of-print backlist, but it's very bad advice for a fledgling writer who's just finished a first novel.

When she was well into her career, successful YA author Natalie Whipple wrote a list of things she wished she'd done differently. Here's #4: "I wish I'd spent more time studying the craft. I used to think my natural talent would get me through the gate. I would write stories without much thought to if the plot worked or not, if the characters were real or not, if the world made sense or not. I feel like I squandered my talent for a long time because I relied solely on talent instead of pushing myself to get better."

And social media guru Kristen Lamb advises her students to hone their writing skills before they publish. "We aren't born knowing three-act structure or how to layer complex characters or how to infuse theme and symbol into a work spanning 60-100,000 words. All of that is learned through struggle." (Yes. Struggle. She didn't say "hiring somebody to do the hard work for us.")

Agents have been saying the same thing for years: the number one mistake new writers make is trying to publish too early. With the self-publishing revolution, the problem has become much worse.

No amount of editing can fix a book that is seriously flawed or amateurish. I see many self-published writers who blame bad reviews on a hired editor. But the problem often lies with the writing, not the editing.

Of course, if price is no object, you can hire an editor to be your personal writing teacher. Some editors offer "writing coaching" services.

But most professional writers didn't start out wealthy, so they learned their craft through workshops, extensive reading, critique groups, and years of trial and error.

The people who benefit most from a freelance editor's work are:

Self-publishers. If you're not working with a publisher, you do need to hire an independent editor before going to press.

Experts whose primary field is not the written word. This includes self-help books by psychologists or medical professionals, specialty cookbooks, local history, etc.

Memoirists who have a unique, marketable tale to tell, but are not planning a career in writing.

Writers who have been requested by an interested agent or publisher to give the book a polish. Many agents will ask a writer to hire an independent editor at this stage.

Novelists who have polished their work in workshops and critique groups, but after many rejections, can't pinpoint what is keeping them in the slush pile.

If you decide to hire an editor, do some research and be clear in your goals. You don't want just any out-of-work English major. If the editor doesn't have a good knowledge of the publishing industry, your money will be wasted.

I've seen "professionally edited" manuscripts that are ridiculously long or too short to be considered by a contemporary publisher, or contain song lyrics (prohibitively expensive) or copyrighted characters. You want an editor who knows the business. Preferably somebody who knows what's selling now and how to write for the marketplace.

NOTE: About those song lyrics. Most beginning writers are tempted to use songs to create mood or evoke a time period, but unless that period is more than 100 years ago, don't go there. Authors who have quoted a single phrase from a copyrighted song have been presented with bills for thousands of dollars from the owners of the copyright (often not the songwriter or even his heirs).

Using even three or four words of a song is copyright infringement—it's not like prose where you're allowed a few lines. I made that mistake in one of my own books—thinking a 90-year old song was out of copyright, but copyrights can be renewed for 75 years after the author's death. Thank goodness my editor caught it before the book went into print.

The best way to find a good editor is by referral from satisfied clients. A lot of self-published authors will sing the praises of their editors, so visit their blogs. Or ask a favorite indie author for a recommendation.

The standard pay scale for editorial services is posted by the Editorial and Freelancers Association (in the U.S.). In the U.K., check the Society of Freelance Editors and Proofreaders; in Australia, the Institute of Professional Editors, and in Canada, the Editors' Association of Canada.

Membership in these organizations isn't essential to a good editor, but it is indicative of professionalism. Plan to spend from five hundred to several thousand dollars for a book-length manuscript.

Unfortunately, there are also a lot of scammers out there who just run your book through spellcheck or give you bogus advice.

Check Writer Beware for in-depth advice: The Edit Ink scam of the late '90s bilked thousands. Here are seven warning signs:

1) Extravagant praise and promises. Anybody who guarantees you a place on the best-seller list is either crooked or delusional.

2) Claims that all publishers require a professionally edited manuscript. Not true. It's also not true that an edit will get you a read. In fact, do not say in a query that your work has been "professionally edited." Agents don't care who you've hired. They care how well YOU can write.

3) An agent or publisher who recommends their own editing services or gives a specific referral. Beware conflicts of interest. Edit Ink scammed writers by giving agents kickbacks for referrals and even setting up fake agencies to tell all queriers they'd get representation if they used Edit Ink's expensive, useless services.

4) One-size-fits-all. You need somebody who's familiar with your genre. I can't picture sex with elves without laughing, and torture scenes make me retch. You do NOT want my help with your paranormal erotica or horror novel. Conventions that are required in one genre, like Romance, can be poison in another.

5) Direct solicitation. Scam editors purchase mailing lists from writing magazine subscriber lists. Beware.

6) Sales pressure. "Limited time offers" are rarely good deals.

7) No client list on their website. You should be able to get a list of clients and a sample of the editor's work. Some editors often will offer a sample edit of a few pages before any money changes hands.

There are many kinds of edits, priced differently, so be aware of what you need.

Manuscript evaluation: A broad overall assessment of the book.

Developmental editing: In depth work on story arc, character development, POV, voice, description, etc. Get the basic elements of a great story nailed before you spend months perfecting each chapter.

Line editing: Reworking text at the sentence level.

Copy editing: Attention to grammar, spelling, punctuation and continuity.

Proofreading: Checking for typos and other minor problems.

A good editor can make the difference between a successful book and a dud. Just choose your editor carefully and wait until you have a marketable project.

And most of all, don't hire an editor too soon. Editing is polishing, not re-writing. First you have to put in those 10,000 hours that Malcolm Gladwell says are necessary to learn a craft. That's a lot of hours. Go write.

CATHERINE

I'M AN EDITOR. IMPRESS ME.

I HAVE BEEN AN EDITOR, ACTUALLY. ALBEIT BRIEFLY. I THINK I mentioned two stints reading short fiction for small periodicals.

Let me put that hat back on for a moment and tell you what I think.

From my perspective, I feel I'm not asking much. Two things I want you to do to impress me, and I feel quite justified in asking for both:

1) Send me a well-written version of a damn good story.

2) Don't waste my time.

One way you can waste my time is by sending a story that isn't well-written, isn't ready, or isn't in any way unique or worth reading.

But there are others.

Oh, there are others.

Are you troubled by the nitty-gritty work of making sure your punctuation, grammar and formatting are correct? I empathize with you. Most of us went to school, but not yesterday. Like math, the finer points of English fade. What you don't use, you lose. I can balance my checkbook just fine, but I can't do geometry, though I could at one time.

Sure, I get it. Some punctuation is tricky.

Once your story/novel ends up on my desk rife with punctuation errors, you will have hit and exceeded the boundaries of my empathy.

Yes, it's a problem. Solve it before I see your work.

Editors (and agents) get tired of seeing the same punctuation errors over and over again. They become red flags. We become bulls.

We get right ticked.

Now. You don't want me getting right ticked while I'm reading your manuscript, do you? Didn't think so.

The following is a brief list of errors that will make me see red. It is not meant to be comprehensive. There are others. But these are my pet peeves. Check your manuscript and see if you are guilty of any of them.

- There's a difference between an em-dash and a hyphen. Please know it.

- Do not use a semi-colon unless prepared to use it correctly. (Plus, if you use a weird amount of them, I'll start counting. You don't want me counting. You want me reading.)

- Know the difference between it's and its; their, they're and there; your and you're. And even if you do know, make sure nothing slipped by you. You may miss some. Your search function will not. (Though, of course, it can't judge for you. It can only stop at each usage, to allow you to check.)

- "Look at that, Bob!" means you want Bob to look at something. "Look at that Bob" means you want somebody to look at Bob. That one. That Bob.

- Know how to paragraph and punctuate dialogue.

Too many typos will make me stop reading. Know why? Because it was your job to find and correct them. And it makes me mad if you didn't do your job, but you still want me to do mine. This is your manuscript, and you are the one who wants it to succeed. If you cut corners, I'll start asking myself why I should give it more quality time and attention than you did.

I know there are those who will argue that the heart, the plot, the meaning of the work is important, and punctuation is…less so.

This reminds me of the old story about the school principal who felt that same way. He listened in on an English teacher's lecture regarding the importance of punctuation. Thinking this silly, he walked to the board and wrote "THE PRINCIPAL SAYS THE TEACHER IS WRONG." The teacher then took the chalk and added two commas, causing it to read "THE PRINCIPAL, SAYS THE TEACHER, IS WRONG."

Is the meaning of a sentence important?

Then punctuation is key.

I'm also rather fond of the tee-shirt that says:

"LET'S EAT GRANDPA
LET'S EAT, GRANDPA
Commas. They save lives."

But let's say it's not life-and-death. Let's say all I have to do is send your manuscript off to copy-editing and all those problems disappear.

Because I can.

And they will.

Psychology and self-help author John Bradshaw says, "What we pay attention to is what we love."

Do you love your manuscript? Prove it. Pay attention to it. To all of its details. Story. Gross editing. Copyediting. Proofreading. Formatting.

If your presentation shows no love and commitment, don't be surprised if I don't fall in love with it, and don't be surprised if I won't commit to it.

And, by the way, if your goal is to self-publish, then please retitle this chapter in your own head. Call it, I'M YOUR END READER. IMPRESS ME. And then read it all over again.

There's always somebody a writer must impress.

CATHERINE

BEWARE TOTOS!

THE TOTO IS MY OWN EXPRESSION, THOUGH WHETHER I SHOULD BE proud or ashamed of its coinage is unclear.

It started like this: You remember *The Wizard of Oz*. Right? Sure, we all do. I hope. Or this falls flat.

Remember the scene when they're all quaking before the great and powerful Oz? The Tin Man's knees are knocking, audibly. The lion is about to wet himself. Hey. The Wizard is a scary dude, all puffs of smoke and bellowing.

Remember what Toto does? He pulls back the curtain.

Behind it is a little old man. Pulling levers. He's not scary. He'll never be scary again.

A Toto, then, in writing, is anything that reminds your reader that there's an author behind the curtain, pulling levers. Ideally your readers should have forgotten they are reading. Once you remind them, you've broken the spell. You've lost everything.

A huge variety of small mistakes can serve as Totos—something as small as a nagging word repetition, or a tendency to put too many adverbs in your dialogue attributions.

Factual errors will bump a reader out of the story every time. I remember hearing a story once in a workshop. In it, a character was stuck in a small town day after day, waiting for the local mechanic to rebuild her alternator.

Wrong.

Apparently the author had heard the expression "rebuilt alternator," and made up the rest from there. But alternators are rebuilt by auto parts manufacturers, in big factories. Old alternators are sent back, and the outer metal casing is reused, while the coils inside are replaced. The small-town mechanic might order a new alternator, or he might order a rebuilt one, but he won't take yours apart and put it back together.

So mind your details carefully, particularly when it comes to places and professions. If you don't know, it will show.

Even pushing too hard for literary brilliance can be a Toto if overdone. It may be a complex and stunning sentence, but when people are paying attention to style rather than story, it's only getting in the way.

At the level of the agent search, typos and grammar mistakes are as bad as Totos get. You want to bump an agent out of your story? It's easy. Use hyphens in place of em-dashes, and use lots of semi-colons, but not correctly. That'll work every time. Trouble is, the answer to that question was supposed to be no. You don't want to bump an agent out of your story.

The trouble with Totos is that you are not equipped to find them.

There may be an error, but it didn't bump you out of the story, which is why it's still there.

Another great reason (as if we needed more) not to write in a vacuum. Another reason your critique group or beta reader is indispensible. If you're using a read-and-critique group, their feedback won't be all you need. Someone will also need to read it through on the page.

First proofread your own work until you're blind, then accept that you are the least qualified person on the planet to do so, and get some help. There is no such thing as too much proofreading. Revision, maybe. Editing, maybe. Proofreading, no.

PART 8

THE WRITING LIFE

ANNE

DOES DEPRESSION HAVE TO BE PART OF THE WRITING LIFE?

THERE'S NO GETTING AROUND IT: GREAT WRITERS TEND TO BE depressives. From Plato, who was reported to suffer from "melancholic disease," to the 2008 suicide of David Foster Wallace, writing and depression seem inexorably linked. In Nancy Andreasen's famous study at the Iowa Writers' Workshop, 80% of writers surveyed met the formal diagnostic criteria for depression.

Until recently, nobody knew the reason for this. But new research is giving us fresh data on the anatomy and purpose of depression. An article in the *New York Times Magazine* in 2010 gave a fascinating overview of the new information concerning what some call the "common cold" of mental illness—and suggests depression could even be good for you.

It reported that brain function researchers have discovered the part of the brain active in depressive episodes is the same area we use for complex thought.

This is huge: CREATIVE THOUGHT IS ANATOMICALLY IDENTICAL TO DEPRESSION.

As a result of the new research, some evolutionary psychologists are hypothesizing that humans developed depression—with its accompanying rumination and lack of interest in normal activities—as a mechanism for focusing on problem-solving.

In other words, when Gog's bestie got smoked trying to spear that saber-toothed tiger, Gog got sad, mooned around not eating, sleeping, or making little Gogs, and…invented a longer spear.

These studies show depressed people have enhanced reasoning power. The article quoted one researcher who said, "the results were clear: [depression] made people think better."

Another researcher said this was especially true for writers. He said, "sadness correlates with clearer and more compelling sentences." And concluded, "because we're more critical of what we're writing, we produce more refined prose, the sentences polished by our angst."

As somebody who sometimes suffers from that "angst" myself, I can't buy into the idea that it's "good for me." But it helps to know there may be a correlation between the symptoms and writing that's not altogether a bad thing.

Whether or not you buy the evolutionary cause-and-effect, this research gives us tools for understanding—and perhaps managing—the depression that overwhelms so many writers. If we accept that depressive episodes are going to come with long periods of building complex worlds in our heads, maybe we can cope by making sure we take frequent breaks for physical activity, social interaction or non-cerebral tasks. (Who knew that boring day job was saving you from mental illness?)

What we should not do is fear the darkness that seems to be inherent in the creative process. If we can see the pain is sometimes part of the creative package instead of a disease, maybe we can work with it instead of labeling ourselves or diving immediately for the pharmaceuticals.

In her blog "This is Madness," Chicago professor Dr. Jeanne Petrolle has blogged that the pharmaceutical industry is raking in stupendous profits by pathologizing normal emotional processing. I know from my own experience that antidepressants slow down or eliminate my creative activity—as well as lighten my wallet and make me fat(ter) .

This research shows that anybody can fall into depression if they spend too much time in that "zone" where creative thought happens. So this emphasizes the need for taking breaks and being zealous with self-care.

Ultimately I think this research brings good news for a lot of us: we're not nuts; we're writers!

CATHERINE

IS WRITER'S BLOCK TRYING TO TELL YOU SOMETHING?

CALL ME CRAZY, BUT I THINK IT IS. AT LEAST, I KNOW IT'S TRYING TO tell *me* something when it happens to me. Every time.

Philosophically, I tend to fall somewhere in between writers frozen in the dreaded block and those who laugh and claim there is no such animal. Hard to deny the existence of something so many people are experiencing, yet I see the point of the deniers to some degree. The more you see something as existing, the more you lend credence to it. The more you believe in it, the more you fear it, the more likely it is to appear in your life, and the more havoc it will wreak.

And yet there's no denying that at some point in most of our projects, forward momentum halts.

The newer writer (and believe me, I remember this, from when I was newer) panics, thinking the muse has left forever and is never coming back. Kind of like your dog the first few times you leave the poor guy alone. You say, "Trust me. I'm coming back." But still he panics. And nibbles on the sofa. And pees in the hall.

Trust me. It's coming back.

The only way creativity will leave you and never return, as far as I can tell through my own experience, is if you give up and move away. So even in that case it will return, but you will have unwisely chosen not to be there to greet it.

But you won't do that. Right?

Now. What is this dreaded lack of motion trying to tell you?

I can only share my own experience with lack of forward motion. I refuse to call it the nasty "WB" words, partly because it gives it too much power, partly because it reminds me of a movie studio that Hollywood-ized one of my books. But that's another story for another piece.

In its mildest form, an inability to write the next scene probably only means the next scene is not ready to write. An inner voice is telling me there's some rich detail or two missing. Or that a plot junction I might not even have anticipated is coming up, and if I write past it, I might miss it forever. So I do more internal work. This is the part of the creative process that always reminds me of a rain cloud. The way a cloud takes on more and more moisture, gets darker and darker. And yet it doesn't rain. Yet. Not until the exact moment it does. And then, by God, you'd better get yourself indoors.

So it may only mean you have a bit more imagineering to do.

Would that they were all so quick and easy.

Now let's say the work has seriously stalled.

Right. Been there.

You try to write through it, but what you write is trash, and you know it's trash even as you write it.

Here I part ways from those who say "Crank out X pages every day." If that works for you, fine. Whatever gets words on the page. But I don't do it that way, and I don't advise it. How many pages do you want to later dump? If you think you're on the wrong road, how far do you want to travel in the wrong direction before you turn around? And aren't you just getting yourself more and more lost?

At this point, I assume the blockage is telling me I'm on the wrong road.

Now. Can we stop for a moment and honor our blockage? Thank it for its good work? Because when I first started writing, I finished everything, no problem. Even though I had taken a wrong turn one-third of the way in. I just trudged to the end of the wrong road and ended up with a finished novel. One that didn't work. I'd rather have an internal guidance system that stops me and says, "Wait. I don't recognize any of this scenery. Are you sure it isn't time to ask directions?"

So a wrong turn message is relatively easy to swallow. You were on a great road, but you missed your cutoff.

What to do? If you have the luxury of time, put it down. Do something else. Get outdoors. Do all those jobs you let slide because the work was on a roll. Work on a different writing project. Then come back to the stalled project, read it over from the beginning. See if you can pinpoint the moment you slipped off track.

Now for the painful part. When you find that moment, toss out everything after it. Well, toss it into another file. Never really throw away anything. You'll find yourself going in for scraps that did work, rather than rewriting them from scratch.

I create a file called "Scraps" for just that purpose. Even if the scraps are 125 pages long.

Hurts. I know. But you want it right, not just done. Well, let's take it a step further and say it's not done until it's done right. So you're actually speeding things up.

Now for the toughest message of all. The one no one wants to hear. Maybe the blockage is telling you that your whole novel is one big wrong road. Maybe the work is just…not…working.

Been there, too.

The only way you're going to sit at your computer for hundreds or thousands of hours, doing the gritty work of creating a good novel, is if it's a good novel. If it's a good novel, it's a joyous thing to work on. It's interesting. It's fun. And if it's fun for you to write, it's probably going to be fun for readers to read.

So…if you really can't bring yourself to work on it in the long haul, it could be—stress, *could be*—a bad sign.

Could be some other things, too, like fear of failure, fear of success, fear of both, or other negative messages that aren't about the work. But, not being a psychologist, I'd better stick to the ones that are.

How do you know one message from another? Now there's a hard question to answer. My best advice is a combination of the luxury of distance and the help of fresh eyes. Being a writer always reminds me of the old joke about being a painter on a scaffold. The problem is you can't step back and get any perspective on your work.

Here's what I *can* tell you. I can advise you what to do in a case of a complete block. One that seems to suggest that the novel is not working.

Give yourself permission not to finish it. Period.

Some readers feel they have to read a book to the end because they started it. I am not that reader. Most writers think it's a type of failure to start a novel and not finish it. I think it's more successful than finishing something only to find it wasn't worth your time.

Again, don't throw it away. Don't throw anything away. File it as a partial, make a backup of it. Then start something exciting and new, something you think is worth the time and effort. Later (maybe months later, maybe years), go back and read over your abandoned partial. Maybe it just needs a new approach. A different character viewpoint, a new plot twist. A character complexity that adds weight to everything that happens. Or maybe it still just...doesn't work. In which case I tend to cannibalize it, drawing out whatever small bits are worth keeping, usually for a short story, sometimes as a character or subplot for a newer novel.

Bottom line, you can fight blockage all you want, but your resistance seems to make it stronger. Try listening instead. If you really are deeply stalled, I submit you have very little to lose by working with the dreaded block instead of against it.

ANNE

WHY YOU SHOULDN'T BULLY YOUR MUSE

SOME PROFESSIONAL WRITERS CLAIM WRITER'S BLOCK DOESN'T EXIST. They'll tell you they never have any trouble banging out their daily pages—and laugh at people who do. William Faulkner said, "I only write when I am inspired. Fortunately I am inspired at 9 o'clock every morning."

Terry Pratchett—not earning himself any fans in my home state—said, "there's no such thing as writer's block. That was invented by people in California who couldn't write."

And comic Steve Martin was even harsher. He said, "writer's block is a fancy term made up by whiners so they can have an excuse to drink alcohol."

But, um, dudes—if there's no such thing as writer's block, what is that thing that happens when you sit down to write and your body gets the fidgets, your brain grows fuzz, or you suddenly develop a bad case of narcolepsy?

It's an experience a lot of us have been through.

We have days when the never-used wedding silver screams to be polished, books and DVDs must be alphabetized immediately, and we're seized by an uncontrollable desire to make hand-dipped truffles instead of mix brownies for the meeting on Friday. Or we bravely apply derrière to chair, fingers to keyboard, and force ourselves to work through the prescribed hours—only to produce pages of literary manure.

Mystery author Clarissa Draper says it's not "writer's block," but "writer's boredom." If you're bored with your own work, she points out, your audience will be too.

But boredom can also be a sign of something else: depression. Because of the prevalence of depression in writers, I think it's important to pay attention to episodes of writer's block/boredom that can't be fixed by cutting a few scenes, upping the plot stakes, or changing point of view as Clarissa suggests.

In the famous study of the Iowa Writers' Workshop, 80% of writers surveyed met the formal diagnostic criteria for depression. And as I mentioned previously, recent research shows the part of the brain used for complex thought is also active in the brains of the clinically depressed. Researchers found evidence that if you spend too much time engaged in intense thinking, your brain can get stuck in thinking/depression mode.

So it's quite possible that "writer's block" is the brain's way of protecting itself from a depressive episode.

Unfortunately, we live in a society that increasingly expects us to push ourselves to the point of exhaustion. More and more is expected of fewer and fewer workers. Many of us are forced to take several jobs, work ridiculously long hours, and tough out illnesses without a break (ignoring the fact we're infecting everybody around us).

A quick Google will turn up a "boot camp" for everything from food bloggers to hip-hop street dancers. Everybody's expected to blog, tweet, and Facebook as well as work on our creative projects. We live in a 24/7 age of more-is-better, feel-the-burn, and sleep-when-you're-dead. We're all bullying ourselves with starvation diets, daily gym workouts, and endless pressure to be Martha Stewart/Mary Poppins at home, Bill Gates at work, and Stephen King when we hit the keyboard.

But can you bully your muse?

In my experience, no.

You can't bully the creative process. Your muse will simply disappear. And—whether you call that disappearance writer's block, boredom, or being an untalented, drunken Californian—if those researchers are right, it's not such a bad thing.

So instead of worrying about being "blocked," why not embrace the experience? Send your muse on vacation. Decide not to write for a week. Writing uninspired dreck is not going to help you meet that deadline, so unless you've got an editor who needs that piece last week, why not forget about writing for a few days?

I remember a great expression from Plato: "*eu a-mousoi*" literally "happily without muses." Socrates used it as derogatory term to mean an unphilosophical lout who lives only in the here and now.

But I think a visit to the here and now can be pretty healthy for those of us who spend most of our time in imaginary worlds.

Allowing yourself to be muse-free for a few days might be what your brain needs to fight off that looming depression. Let your creativity re-charge its batteries. Creativity guru Julia Cameron called it "filling the well."

Here are nine things you can do when your muse needs to take a break:

1) **Take your characters out for some retail therapy.** I love to shop for my characters. Sometimes I look for stuff in real stores. Or I use magazines, catalogues, or surf around online. And it doesn't cost a thing. Choosing my characters' cars is one of my most important rituals when I'm working on a new novel. I usually find a photo and keep it in a folder.

2) **Read, read, read.** Stephen King says writers should spend as much time reading as writing. If the book is great, maybe you'll get inspired, and if it's bad, you'll love that "I can do better" feeling.

3) **Go ahead—polish the silverware and dip those truffles.** Repetitive, mindless tasks can be good for the soul. At least all those monks seem to think so.

4) **Garden.** Play in the dirt. Literally get yourself grounded.

5) **Get a massage.** Aromatherapize your mind and get in touch with your body.

6) **Try another medium.** I had a "blocked writer" friend who got so frustrated, she went out and took a painting class. She turned out to be a much better painter than writer—and started selling her work after only a year. Try to do that after taking one writing class!

7) **Change the scenery.** Go for a walk, sit in a café—or hop on a

bus. Busses are packed with fiction-fuel.

8) Music. Go listen to some. Preferably live. Not as background for chatter, but really listen. Or make some yourself.

9) Move. Walk, run, dance, bike. Do the hokey-pokey. Or the hanky-panky—sex is good too. Lie on a beach—or climb a mountain, sail, ski, or whatever.

10) Literally take a vacation. If your muse can do it, you can too.

ANNE

CAREFUL, OR YOU'LL END UP IN MY NOVEL

THAT'S THE MESSAGE ON A TEE-SHIRT I SEE AT WRITERS' conferences A lot. Apparently it's been a popular item in the *Signals* catalogue for years.

It's interesting that most writers I've met who wear them say the shirt was a gift from a friend or family member. I can't help wondering if those gift-givers weren't expressing their own anxiety. A lot of people presume all novels are thinly disguised autobiography that's based on factual experience.

But the truth is, most fiction writers don't like to write about real stuff. If we did, we'd be writing nonfiction, which pays better.

OK, I have to admit I've tried to skewer a few real people in my fiction, but it never works. The character always takes over and makes herself sympathetic, and/or entirely different from the person on whom I tried to perpetrate my literary revenge.

That's because novelists can't help making things up. It's what we do.

As John Steinbeck said— "I have tried to keep diaries, but they didn't work out because of the necessity to be honest."

But a lot of non-writers don't seem to get this.

I discovered that with my very first published fiction piece—a story I wrote for the newspaper of a new high school. It was a silly story about how a football team lost when a school was divided by squabbles between the team and the pep squad. The satire was so ham-handed, I called the protagonists Joe Jock and Cherry Cheerleader.

I'd been at the school such a short time, I didn't even know there was a cheerleader named Sherry dating/squabbling with a football player named Joe.

After my story came out, Sherry accosted me in homeroom and said—

"I hope you're happy. Joey and me broke up."

I sat in stunned silence. No cheerleader had ever even spoken to me—and I had no idea what she was talking about.

She went on to accuse me of listening in on her private conversations. Then, as she flounced away, she said—"Anyway, I'm nothing like the girl in that story. I am not blonde, I'd never hold a bake sale, and I don't have freckles."

She was accusing me of both writing about her and NOT writing about her.

Things like this have continued to happen throughout my writing career. Like the time I ran into a friend I hadn't seen in 20 years. She asked me about my writing and I sent her my latest manuscript. When she finished it, she phoned me in tears.

"You've written my whole life here," she said. "I work at a place just like this. My husband left me in the same horrible way. He said the exact same things. How did you know?"

I didn't, of course. I'd made it all up—pure fiction.

It happened again in a critique meeting this week. I read a scene that revealed the antagonist's abusive childhood. One member said, when he finished his critique:

"You pretty much described my own childhood there."

He wasn't angry. As a fellow fiction writer, he was praising me for tapping into an archetypal human experience and expressing it in a way that related to his own.

In fact, nobody except Sherry the Cheerleader has ever expressed anger after "recognizing" themselves in my fiction (and you'll be happy to know she and Joe got back together). Most people understand the similarities are coincidental—and they come from the collective unconscious that all writers tap into when we create.

But what if it's not coincidence? What if something a friend has told you about his past wanders into your fiction? Or a character resembles someone you know?

"That awful mother is supposed to be me, is it?" says your mom, looking teary.

"Of course not," you say. "It's fiction."

Although maybe, now that you think of it, the bad mom is a little like your mother when she first started getting those hot flashes…but no, Bad Mom is more like your childhood friend's mean Aunt Harriet. Yes, definitely there's some Harriet in there. Funny, you never thought about her when you were writing the novel, but there she is, saying those mean Aunt Harriet things.

Do you owe Aunt Harriet an apology? Should you find out if

she's still alive and ask permission to put her nasty remarks in your novel?

I don't think so. We can't be expected to keep our memories out of our fiction. As Isabel Allende says, "writing is a journey into memory." What does your imagination draw on but what's in your memory banks?

What a fiction or poetry writer does is take tiny fragments of memory and make an original mosaic that is "the lie that tells the truth."

But not everybody understands this. Catherine has recently been attacked for "stealing the life" of an estranged relative in a novel—as well as "getting it all wrong." Just the way I did with Cherry Cheerleader.

And I've been cyberstalked recently after an offhand comment on an agent's blog about an unfortunate man who thinks a line of poetry by a famous poet "proves" said poet has participated in animal cruelty.

This guy also "proves" on his website that I am an evil person because I advise writers to "activate your inner sadist. Never let your characters get what they need. Throw as many obstacles into their path as possible. Hurt them. Maim them. Give them cruel parents and girlfriends who are preparing to kill them for alien lizard food."

Yeah, if I was talking about doing those things to real people, I'd be pretty rotten. Especially about feeding them to alien lizards.

These two incidents have reminded me that some people really do take every written word to be a solid, concrete fact. Irony, fantasy, metaphor, hyperbole, whimsy, and humor are incomprehensible to them.

It's not their fault, and I shouldn't have scoffed at the

unfortunate man.

Instead I should have directed him to the works of the brain-chemistry pioneer Dr. Temple Grandin, who explains to the rest of us how autistic minds work, and why they are essential to our survival as a species. People with this kind of brain can't "read" people or understand non-literal communication. They need to stay far, far away from poetry and fiction. Not that they miss it. Dr. Grandin says anything about nuances of emotion bores her silly.

So, for the people who don't understand the nature of fiction, I'm wondering if maybe writers shouldn't Mirandize everybody we meet. Shake hands and say—

"I'm a novelist. Anything you say can be taken down and used against you in a work of fiction."

And we should probably stock up on those tee-shirts.

ANNE

NANOWRIMO—SHOULD YOU JOIN IN THE SILLINESS?

FOR THE UNINITIATED: NaNoWriMo IS THE NATIONAL NOVEL Writing Month project. Started over a decade ago by a young San Franciscan named Chris Baty—and 21 of his verbally ambitious friends—it challenges you to write a complete novel in a month. That month is November.

Entering the contest—now run by Mr. Baty's non-profit outfit, the Office of Letters and Light—is free. Anybody who finishes 50,000 words by midnight November 30th is a winner. No prizes that I know of: completion of your novel is its own reward.

To become eligible for the honor—and an official "Wrimo"—you register at www.nanowrimo.org so you can have your word count verified at the end of the month, and on November 1, start writing.

Crazy? Absolutely. But all fiction writing is crazy.

But…don't they write a lot of crapola?

Yup. And that's the point.

It's all about creating that sucky first draft. (See Part 1.)

As Anne LaMott wrote in her classic book for writers, *Bird by Bird*, "The only way I can get anything written at all is to write really, really, really shitty first drafts."

NaNo forces you to get that dung onto the page.

Here are some benefits:

1) No time to agonize over your first chapter. You've read endless carping on blogs like mine about how the first chapter has to hook the reader, introduce all the major themes and plot elements, begin with the world's most exciting sentence, etc. But when you're writing your first draft, none of that matters. You're introducing yourself to your characters and their world. You can worry about your reader when you start editing next January.

2) No frittering away time on excessive research. If you're one of those writers who has procrastinated for years, piling up reams of historical and biographical detail, this is your chance to actually write the book. The truth is, most of those details would bore the reader silly if you actually put them in your novel, anyway. You're better off writing the book first and figuring out later whether your reader needs to know what they used for toilet paper in 13th century Scotland or what kind of underpants Genghis Khan wore.

3) No time to censor yourself. You can't afford to agonize over whether your brother–in-law/former teacher/ex-girlfriend will recognize him/herself. Or if your mom will find out you weren't really at band camp that summer when you and your buddies took the road trip to Cabo. Besides, you'll be amazed how characters/situations inspired by real life take off on their own and create an alternate reality.

4) You won't be tempted to save your best ideas for later. New writers are often terrified they'll run out of ideas. But it's amazing how many more will show up once you're in the zone.

5) You'll give up trying to control the process. If the story goes somewhere you didn't expect it to go, or you can't stick to your outline, you'll have to run with it. When your muse is talking, you can't take the chance of pissing her off for even a couple of days.

6) You'll have a great excuse for skipping the family Thanksgiving with all those relatives whose politics make you despair for the future of the human race.

7) It's fun—and a great way to meet other writers all over the world. Look in the NaNo website forums for online and in-person discussions and groups.

If you decide to jump into the craziness, here are the NaNo rules:

1) Register at www.nanowrimo.org before November 1

2) Write a novel (in any language) 50,000+ words long between November 1 and November 30. "Novel" is loosely defined. They say "If you consider the book you're writing a novel, we consider it a novel too!"

3) Start from scratch. Previously written outlines and character sketches are OK—and highly recommended—but this can't be a work in progress.

4) Be the sole author. Although you can use the occasional quotation.

5) Write more than one word. No repeating the same one 50,000 times.

6) Upload your novel for word-count validation to the site between November 25 and November 30.

Chances are pretty good you aren't going to write a polished, publishable novel in four weeks (although Charles Dickens is said to have written *A Christmas Carol* in six, four of which were in November, so there's some precedent).

But PLEASE don't start querying agents or consider self-publishing until you do a serious, in-depth revision: you'll just clog the pipeline and make the agents cranky—or feed into the myth of the self-publishing "tsunami of crap"—which isn't good for any of us.

And if/when you do query, it's not wise to reveal that the book began at NaNo—unfortunately, a lot of participants send off the unedited crapola. Also, most agents won't look at a novel of less than 70,000 words, so even the Dickenses among you will have further work to do.

But if you do that work, maybe you'll have the success of NaNovelist Sarah Gruen, whose phenomenal best seller *Water For Elephants* started as a NaNo project.

And the important thing is that you'll have a draft to start revising. And you'll have finished a novel. How many people can say that?

ANNE

THE WRITERS ENEMY LIST: CRAZYMAKERS, DREAM SMASHERS, AND GROUCHO MARXISTS

"Keep away from people who try to belittle your ambitions. Small people always do that, but the really great make you feel that you, too, can become great. When you are seeking to bring great plans to fruition, it is important with whom you regularly associate. Hang out with friends who are like-minded and who are also designing purpose-filled lives. Similarly, be that kind of a friend for your friends." —Mark Twain

WHEN YOU START A WRITING PROJECT, WHETHER YOU'RE DIVING INTO the intensity of NaNoWriMo or just carving out a few hours to peck away at the keyboard on weekends, it helps a lot to get emotional support from friends and family.

But be prepared for the opposite.

Some people in your life may find your new interest threatening, and if you're not emotionally prepared, they can derail your project and undermine your self esteem. They'll work to sabotage your writing and confidence in dozens of subtle—or not-so-subtle—ways.

Here are some non-supportive types to watch out for, and tips on how to deal with them:

Dream Smashers: These are the know-it-alls who specialize in discouragement.

- They're full of statistics showing the odds against getting published.

- They'll send links to articles with dire warnings about carpal tunnel syndrome and back injuries due to long sessions with the computer.

- They have an unending supply of stories about suicide and depression in writers.

- They may appear to be supportive at first, and may even express an eagerness to read your WIP—only to give entirely negative feedback.

- They always "know" some rule that you've broken—probably mis-remembered from their 5th grade grammar class.

- They'll criticize your premise in a way that's also a personal attack: "nobody wants to read about women over 40/washed-up athletes/teenagers with disabilities."

- They'll criticize anything in your work that doesn't promote their own world view, and suggest the story would be much better if the hero were more like them.

- These people have given up on their own dreams, and want you to do the same.

- Encourage them to write their own darn books.

Crazymakers: Creativity guru Julia Cameron described these people as "storm centers...long on problems but short on solutions." They are the drama queens, emotional vampires, and control freaks who crave your full-time attention and can't stand for you to focus on anything but their own dramas. Writers are magnets for these people because we tend to be good listeners.

- You tell your Crazymaker friend your writing schedule, but she'll always "forget," and show up at exactly the time your story is on a roll. She'll draw you into a weepy tale of woe, saying you're the "only one who understands."

- Have a deadline for a difficult article? That's the moment Crazymaker will stomp into your office and confess the affair he had four years ago when you were on a relationship break.

- Got an agent waiting for a rewrite? That's the week Mrs. Crazymaker calls to beg you to babysit her sick child because she can't take time off work. After all, she has a REAL job.

Crazymakers need to be center stage, 24/7. Nothing you do can be of any importance: your job description is "minion."

Resign.

Groucho Marxists: The Groucho Marxist manifesto is, to paraphrase the great Julius Henry Marx— "I do not care to read a book by a person who would accept me as a friend." Groucho Marxists are your family members and buddies who assume your work is terrible because it was written by somebody they know.

I'm not talking about those helpful beta readers who comb through your unpublished manuscript looking for flaws to be fixed before you submit. These are the folks who feel compelled to ridicule and belittle your work, whether they've read it or not. No amount of success will convince them you're any good.

- You get a story published. Groucho can't be bothered to read it. But he's always bringing you stories by other writers in your genre, "so you can see how a REAL writer does it."

- You get your big call from that agent. Groucho will try to convince you she's a scammer. Why would a real agent represent a nobody like you?

- You sign with a publisher. Groucho has heard a rumor the company is about to go under. Look how desperate they must be if they'd publish your crap.

- You get a good review. Groucho doesn't have time to read it. But he has lots of time to research other pieces by that reviewer to show the reviewer has terrible taste.

- You win a Pulitzer. What? No Nobel?

These people are highly competitive and feel your success will make you "better than them." Remind them of their own skills and accomplishments and reassure them that any writing success you achieve won't change your relationship.

It's hard enough to live with the constant rejection we have to deal with in this industry, so when you're attacked in your personal life, it's tough to hang on. You have to erect strong boundaries and be fierce in defending them. But if you're serious about your work, the people who really care about you will learn to treat your time and work with respect.

The others will evaporate.

Chances are you won't miss them.

ANNE

ENJOY THE LUXURY OF THE UNPUBLISHED LIFE

"WTF?" sez you. "Luxury? Getting daily rejections? Living in this mousehole on a diet of ramen and generic Froot Loops? While the few friends I have left laugh at my 'delusions' of being a published writer? I'm supposed to #%&!ing enjoy this?"

Well, yes. It's the only time in your career when you will have the freedom to just…write.

OK, calm down. I know sometimes you think you can't stand this torture one more day. How long can anybody be expected to live on hope alone? Time's wingèd chariot hurries near! You're tired of the rejection, humiliation and frustration!! You're desperate to:

1) Show all those skeptical friends and relations you really do have talent. Let your significant other know all those pep talks weren't wasted.

2) Show up at Thanksgiving dinner and tell your brother-in-law who always makes digs about your "career in navel-gazing" to #%&! off.

3) Say to all those condescending customers at McChili's that you may be bussing tables now, but you're a WRITER dammit.

I know how it feels to be filled with that desperate longing to see your work published. I lived with it for over a decade. And felt the euphoria when I finally got my first book contract—I doubt there's a drug in the world to match that high. But it doesn't last long. Because after you sign is when your real work begins. And if you thought you were finished with rejection, humiliation and frustration, think again. This is what could be in store—

- Hate-hate-hating that stupid cover that makes your dashing Scottish hero look like David Lee Roth in a dress.

- Praying your new editor will see your book through after the old one leaves to start her own literary agency.

- Sending out press releases, blanketing social media sites, haunting forums, and being nice to people you've been trying to ignore for years.

- Sucking up to the local talk radio guy whose show has always pissed you off, begging for an interview.

- Groveling to the editor of the local fishwrap to get him to run maybe an inch on your launch.

- Begging bookstore managers to let you do a signing—and get enough copies into the store to make it worthwhile.

- Typing your fingers to the bone in a marathon blog tour.

- Getting your obnoxious friend who went to film school to help you put together a book trailer.

- Traveling to strange cities on crowded planes to talk to people who don't have a clue who you are and care less—if you're lucky enough to get a book tour at all.

- Checking your Amazon ranking twice a day and agonizing every time it goes down.

- Trying to wheedle reviews out of anybody you can press a free book upon.

Ah yes. Reviews. Begging someone to do a review is daunting. But dealing with a bad review is soul-torture.

If you had trouble dealing with that guy in your critique group who hated your heroine because she didn't get herself a blunderbuss and smoke that cheating hound of a duke, wait until the trolls hit your Amazon page and give you a few of those clueless, nasty one-star appraisals that bring down your ratings.

And remember—all the time you're launching your new career in marketing (yes, every single author has to be a marketer these days), you'll have to be writing a second novel. Probably in less than a year. While still bussing those tables.

Won't you be happy you've got all those rejected novels stacked up in your files? Think of them as inventory. A novel that might not be the break-out blockbuster to launch a career may make a nice follow-up once you're established.

So revel in the luxury of writing in your mousehole. With no marketing responsibilities. Or the public humiliation of bad reviews. While you build inventory.

But tell off your brother-in-law anyway. And let those condescending people at table three know you really are a writer, published or not.

PART 9

AFTER PUBLICATION: THE AUTHOR'S CHANGING ROLE IN THE 21ST CENTURY

CATHERINE

THE BLOG TOUR

THE AUTHOR TOUR IS DYING. ONLY THE VERY PRIVILEGED FEW WILL BE sent on tour by their publishers. Are you sorry to receive this news? That tells me something about you. You've never been on an author tour.

But you dream about it. Don't you?

In this dream, you glide smoothly into the bookstore under the watchful and adoring eyes of the crowd of fans who've gathered. They beg you to read. A bookstore event manager hovers over you, determining what kind of Sharpy you like best and assuring you'll never have to be shocked by witnessing the bottom of your bottomless latte. And the applause! Oh, yes. The applause.

I've been on some author tours. That's why I'm happy they're dying.

Wrap your imagination around this instead.

You arrive at your hotel at 9:00 p.m., but you're from California, and this is the east now. So your body thinks it's only 6:00 p.m., and you can't go to sleep. You're scheduled to be on the local morning news in the 5:30 time slot, which means you have to show up at 4:50. Which means meeting your media escort in the hotel lobby at 4:30. Camera-ready. Which means you have to get up at 3:00 a.m. Which your body thinks is midnight.

The local news has double-booked and forgotten you, so by the time they come running down to get you, you literally have to run up the stairs to the studio, and when they mic you up and go live, you still haven't gotten your breath back. Later your publicist will say you looked "dour" and quietly assign a media coach to save you.

But you can go back to the hotel and sleep when you're done. Right? Oh, no. You are on a book tour. You do not sleep on a book tour.

You have local radio interviews all morning, only one of the four conducted by an interviewer who actually read the book. But it's okay, because the others will have you right there to answer the question, "What is your book about?"

You spy a moment of downtime in the schedule, and naively assume you'll climb into the complimentary hotel robe and grab a nap. But instead your escort introduces you to "stock signings." She drives you to every bookstore within a 20-mile radius, so you can sign whatever copies of your book they may have on hand.

Three. They have three. If you're one of the lucky ones.

By the time you make it to your evening signing, you are exhausted enough to occasionally lose track of where you are. Not to mention who. And what. Not to mention losing your train of thought.

There are only four people there to notice.

One of them buys your book. One is a homeless guy who just came in for the warmth and free lemonade. The other two were browsing the stacks when they heard you announced. Try not to look hurt when they shuffle off again.

Oh. And did I mention they fly you coach?

Now try this on instead.

You roll out of bed in the morning, at home. Hour not relevant. You put on your lovely, homey robe and fuzzy bunny slippers (I don't own fuzzy bunny slippers, but I'm leaving room in the imagining for those of you who do). Brew an aromatic cup of coffee or tea. Sit in your easy chair, assuming you have a laptop. Start typing.

You are riding the newest wave in book promotion, the blog tour.

Wonderful book bloggers host "stops" for you on their blogs. They review your book, and/or give away copies in promotional contests to draw traffic. You provide them with guest blogs, interviews, excerpts, sometimes deleted scenes or new scenes you write just for them.

In your jammies.

Of course, you also have to provide them with copies to review or give away. If you have a publisher to do this for you, no trouble or expense. If not, it may sound troublesome and expensive. But consider this: in that case, you also don't have a publisher to pay for the plane tickets and hotels. Do the math.

I'd say, "You choose," but you probably won't get a choice. Unless you are one of the privileged few or willing to pay for your own travel, the author tour is probably out for you. Make friends with the blog tour. Every one of those little (or medium, or big) blogs will be seen by far more than four people (many have hundreds or even thousands of faithful followers). You're well-rested, your dog/cat/family is happy, and you never had to change out of your fuzzy slippers.

What's not to like?

ANNE

HOW TO BE A GOOD BLOG GUEST

GUEST POSTING ON BLOGS CAN BE A GREAT MARKETING TOOL. Whether you're on a book launch blog tour, promoting an editorial service, or simply building platform, it's an effective way to reach potential new readers in a personal way—and it's free.

If you're with a big publisher, you may be assigned a publicist who will book the guest visits for you. (Not always a great idea— more on that below.)

Guest blogging can be a lot of fun. You can meet fascinating new people and learn new blogging techniques. I'm so grateful to the wonderful bloggers who have hosted me. I didn't know all the ropes at first myself, so have to admit I've learned some of these rules the embarrassing way.

Unfortunately, a lot of the information on the Web about guest posting isn't specific to publishing/ writing blogs. You may hear that you should search for blogs that contain certain keywords and mass query them—or only approach bloggers with a high traffic ranking. This advice can end up wasting your time.

And, um, make you look like a doofus.

You wouldn't believe how many emails I get like this: "Hello Blogger: I see your blog, ANNE R. ALLEN'S BLOG has an Alexa rating under 300,000, and you once wrote a post on topic X on ANNE R. ALLEN'S BLOG so I (or "my client") would like to guest blog on ANNE R. ALLEN'S BLOG next week. We're offering this content free of charge, Blogger."

Those get a quick "thanks but no thanks." For one thing, my blog only has four posts a month, so every piece has to be fresh, hooky, and content-rich enough to draw the usual 10,000 or so readers each week. I also book guests way in advance to drum up interest in the visit.

And frankly, requests like that get my hackles up. They suggest I don't have enough good content, so I'll take something out of the blue, sight unseen. And—try a little Golden Rule stuff here, publicists—who do you know who likes to be addressed as a generic cypher by some robot?

Here are some tips on how to avoid annoying the bloggers and get the most out of guest-posting:

1) Don't judge a blog by Alexa rating alone. You'll only get a small piece of the picture. Alexa is a Web analytics company that rates websites globally according to traffic. (You can download your own rating icon by going to Alexa.com.) Google rates a 1. Amazon has an 11. Top publishing sites like Nathan Bransford's get around 140K. Mine hovers around 300K. Most author sites are in the millions.

But if you're an author with a southern vampire saga, a blog with a small readership of Sookie Stackhouse fans can reach more actual readers than a major blog that focuses on SciFi or Christian Romance.

But: If your own blog has an Alexa rating of 5 million, it's not smart to approach somebody with a rating of 500K and expect them to welcome you with open arms unless you've got some spectacular content to offer. If you want to blog in the big leagues, you need to show you're up to the job.

2) Don't expect a blogger to be impressed with "free." That isn't going to impress a blogger any more than it would impress the staff of *The New Yorker*. Most successful blogs have a very specific style and audience and not everybody is going to be a good fit. And most author blogs are not monetized, so we're all working for free.

3) Don't offer "content" that's just an advertisement for your business or your book. Offer something of real value to the reader.

4) Make sure your content is up to the expectations of the audience. A post on my blog gets an average of 3000 readers. But a mediocre post can permanently lose some of that audience.

5) Address the blogger by name. And, um, if the blog is called "Anne R. Allen's Blog" this shouldn't strain anybody's brain cells.

6) Make requests by email, not Tweet or FB DM. Those get lost and people can't find you again.

7) Um, READ THE BLOG! And it helps a lot if you've

commented a few times so the blogger knows your name.

8) Conform to the blog's tone. My blog is lighthearted and fun. Doom and gloom and a "boot camp" mentality will totally annoy my readership.

9) Don't offer off-topic content. Just because I once made a joke about airport security doesn't mean I want to run a blogpost on the evils of the TSA. It's a writing blog. If you don't have content for writers, don't query.

10) Always follow the blogger's guidelines. Some bloggers are very kind and post them. I don't, because we take so few guest bloggers and we don't want to get anybody's hopes up. But I always let guests know how soon I need the material, and what the word count needs to be. (This varies widely, so always ask.)

11) Include pictures, bio and links (and a short blurb for your book, if you're promoting one) with your post copy.

12) Offer a free copy of your book as a give-away to readers. Not every blog does a give-away, but be prepared to offer one.

13) Plan to be available to respond to comments on the day of the post and check in for several days after.

14) Promote the guest post on social media. Tweet, FB, and link from your own blog. You want people to read it, right?

15) Remember to thank the blogger, either in the comment thread or a follow-up email.

CATHERINE

WHAT TO SAY IN RESPONSE TO A BAD REVIEW (HINT: NOTHING!)

THIS IS A SITUATION THAT'S POPPING UP EVERYWHERE THESE DAYS. I have fiercely strong opinions about it, and I just can't keep them to myself any longer. I don't know if I can do much to change it, but I'm going to speak my piece. If one author (big or small, indie or traditionally published) reads this and thinks twice before hitting "send" or "post," it will be worth it. If not, may these opinions be some small solace to besieged reviewers.

Recently I tweeted the following message. "Dear authors, Here's what you say to a negative review: NOTHING!"

I stand by that advice. In fact, I'd like to elaborate.

No one has a right to argue with anyone's assessment of a book. There is nothing to argue. If the reviewer didn't like it, that's his or her opinion. You can't change it, nor should you try. Any attempt to make others feel their opinion is wrong will backfire, and just make you look like a sore loser.

Case in point: two self-published authors (two cases went viral—how many more are hiding out there?) publicly flamed out recently while trying to make blog reviewers look like fools. The reviewers came out with their reputations intact. Better than ever, in fact. The authors didn't fare so well. A cautionary tale if ever there was one.

Yeah, bad reviews hurt. I know. I like to vent about them, too. But in private, to a friend. Not on Twitter. Not in the comment thread of the review. Get it out of your system privately and move on. People have a right to hate your book. In fact, a reviewer has a right to be snide in his or her hatred of your work. I wish no one would be snide, too, but there's no such thing as the snide police. Did you really think you could enforce a no-snideness rule?

Trouble is, in the examples I've been seeing lately, the reviewer was not snide. Just honestly unflattering.

I once had a print review in a big newspaper that got many facts about my book wrong. Wildly wrong, as if the reviewer hadn't read it. It wasn't a particularly negative review (which is unfortunately often the case in these public flameouts). It just had some take-aways, and some weirdly inaccurate portrayals of the plot and other details. I talked it over with my editor who said, "It's a selling review." (Translation: nothing in there to stop people from buying it.) "Forget it." I did. It rankled. But, you know what I said to the reviewer? NOTHING! Not because I didn't long to. Because I knew no good could come of it.

I've also had reviews that were not "selling reviews." That were unselling reviews. I said nothing. Because no good could come of it.

Blog reviewers are an unfortunately easy target. Unwise authors view them as independent and small, and figure they can attack their credentials as reviewers. "If they're not authors, what do they know?" "Who are they, anyway?" These are paraphrases of actual questions authors have asked in public.

I have an answer for you. They're readers. Who could be more important than that? If you make a living as an author, your reader is your employer, in a manner of speaking. Without your readers, you're out of a job. Every reader has a right to form an opinion of your book. If you think you have any control over that, or need to find some, this line of work will make you deeply unhappy. Try to learn acceptance. If you can't, think twice before walking further down this tough road.

But it's not only blog reviewers. A couple of years ago a well-known author (I'm naming no names) went off on a professional print reviewer. The review had been mixed. Really not negative on the whole. But this author trashed her reviewer on Twitter, even posting the reviewer's email address and phone number so others could do the same. The result? The author lost her Twitter account, and the respect of many. Myself included. And more attention was drawn to the negative aspects of the review.

Offering a book for review is something like giving away a free sample of a product. You're betting that the product is good, so the sample will bring you more business. But, like any bet, it's not guaranteed to pay off. If it doesn't, you have no recourse. Just send off more review copies and hope other reviewers like it. If nine out of ten reviewers like it, be happy. That's about as good as it gets. Do not try to use it to prove that the tenth is wrong.

Even responding to positive reviews can be overdone. They are not favors. Your opinion is not terribly relevant to them, either. Most reviewers enjoy being thanked. And if the reviewer did a particularly thoughtful job, "got" your book in just the way you were hoping readers would, it can't hurt to say so. But be careful of the line here. Your book is your business. Their posted opinions of your book are not.

How many authors need to test these theories in public before the lesson is learned?

CATHERINE

DO BOOK SIGNINGS SELL BOOKS?

Sure they do. Usually. But not always. Well…sometimes not very well at all.

I think the better question is: do they sell enough books to make them worth your time and expense?

A very subjective question, but I'll give you the answer as I see it.

No. They don't.

Like so many of these e-age subjects, I can say (being very old) "Oh, there was a time." Yes, there was a time when meeting an author was a treat. People stood in line for the privilege. And one can always point to instances where they still do.

For somebody.

But I get to honestly call myself a bestselling author, an international bestselling author, and an award-winning author. And they sure as hell don't stand in line for me. And my guess is that they might not for you, either, although I'll be very happy if you prove me wrong.

The last couple of times I was on tour, I was lucky to get eight or ten people in the audience. And that's lumping in the staff who come sit their butts in a few of the chairs to make you feel a tiny bit better.

Take all this personally if you want, but I had a media escort who dropped the name of one of the biggest platform authors in the business and then told a story of eight people at her signing.

And it wasn't too surprising, considering the venue. When she told me this story we were at a good, well-known indie bookstore whose schedule boasted a minimum of three author signings *a day*. How long is meeting an author going to hold its shine with that parade of talent ever available?

So, I have to say…no. They don't sell enough books. Not like they used to.

In the past, my publicist—the one assigned to me by the publisher—would always try to put this in a larger context. She'd say, "Maybe you won't sell many books that night. But it's bigger. The staff gets to know your name. They get to meet you personally. There's a sign in the store for a week with your picture and book cover on it. Lots of people see it, even if they don't attend. And then there's the event listing in the local paper."

Yeah, yeah. True, I suppose. But does that really make up for days of travel all over the country? Airline tickets? Hotel bills? Expensive room service?

Apparently not, because the author tour is all but dead.

I think the idea of book signings selling books made more sense in the non-digital age. I agree they were created to fill a hugely important vacuum. There is no doubt that the more a reader feels as though he or she knows you, the more likely you will make a sale to that reader. So before the advent of social networking, reading, speeches and signings were the happening thing. Now, I contend, you can make many more impressions with far less wear and tear on your wallet, your family, and your soul...right, you guessed it. Online.

This is not to say that all book signings are a bad idea.

Let's say your publisher wants to tour you. And is willing to pay for it. Tour. You have nothing to lose. (Except bits of your health, I'm afraid. Not to mention your ego. But do it anyway.)

Another good use of book signings would be local events.

1) **A launch party:** your friends and colleagues will likely enjoy a book party celebrating your release date. It can be held in a local book store, or a local bookseller can bring books to sell at a different venue. Wine and refreshments help. You can go to the trouble of sending personal invitations, as well as placing listings in the local media. This, I expect, will be well worth your time.

2) **Speaking to special interest groups:** volunteer to speak at a gathering that will be of interest to residents of the area in which your book is set. Or birdwatchers, if your main character is one of them. Special interest is always a good bet for draw, and you can plan a brief talk that ties your book together with their interests.

But if you're on your own with these expenses...well, it's up to you. Ten or 15 years ago, writers created big platforms and good sales numbers by filling a van with books and driving to every bookstore that would have them, stopping to do interviews on local TV and radio. For months at a time.

Then again, this is not 15 years ago. And that was always a bit more grueling than most writers were willing to take on.

Admit it. Social networking is sounding better all the time, isn't it?

Yup. Thought so.

Welcome to the e-age.

ANNE

THE LAWS OF THE (AMAZON) JUNGLE: EIGHT RULES AUTHORS SHOULD FOLLOW TO STAY SAFE

WE'VE TOLD YOU A LOT ABOUT HOW WE USE SOCIAL MEDIA TO MARKET our books, so we thought we should also warn of the dangers.

Here's the thing: the Internet is still the wild frontier. And it's so huge nobody knows how to police it. According to mental health professionals, 4% of humans suffer from anti-social personality disorder. When you consider how many millions use the Internet every day, you've got to expect to meet some pretty scary folks—who can be even more dangerous when they run in packs.

Big, unregulated social media sites seem to encourage the worst in human behavior. Facebook allows people to make hate pages for celebrities with happy abandon, and the comments in forums can make you want to wash your eyeballs.

Even literary sites can become more like jungles full of feces-throwing monkeys than places for civilized discourse. Bullying and cruelty abound.

I know respected reviewers who have stopped posting to Amazon because of reviewer-on-reviewer attacks and harassment by angry authors. A seasoned Hollywood screenwriter was hounded so mercilessly she had to unpublish her books and change her name. Even a retired army sergeant has been terrified into silence.

Newbies need to learn how to avoid gang-infested neighborhoods and stay off the radar of the criminals, terrorists and vigilantes.

Unfortunately, marketers sometimes tell us to go into those neighborhoods and do the very things that will set off attacks. I've seen "marketing handbooks" that are the equivalent of sending children into gangland wearing a rival gang's colors.

Part of the problem is that the rules of the online book world bear little resemblance to the conventions of the staid, gentlemanly publishing industry most of us know.

That's because the laws of online activity come from the people who were here first: hackers and gamers.

So when you enter the online culture, it can feel like stepping into a game of "Grand Theft Auto." It's a young, aggressive, competitive universe. Everybody is trying to eliminate the enemy. And the enemy could be you. Naiveté is punished and ignorance is no excuse.

"Gaming the system" is a constant activity for some, and because people tend to judge others' characters by their own, the system-gamers think every innocent newbie is gaming the system too. (If someone accuses you of gaming the system, he's telling you a lot about himself.)

Probably the most infamous Internet menace was the sociopath called Violentacrez, who slimed up the forums of Reddit with threats and hate speech masked as "categories" with names like "chokeabitch" that were technically within site guidelines but invited misogynist rants, child pornography and hate.

Violentacrez was finally outed by *Gawker* last year, but thousands remain—and plenty of them lurk in the literary world.

So don't give them an excuse to terrorize you. Follow the rules. Nobody deserves to be bullied, but you're safer if the bullies don't notice you.

If the mini-Violentacrezes catch you breaking rules—even unwritten ones—they will feel they have license to destroy your career and reputation with all the self-righteous sadism of the Taliban slaughtering a schoolgirl.

Here are the rules we've learned by trial and error. Lots of error.

Rule #1 Don't Spam

Easy to say; harder to follow.

What is spam? It's defined differently on every site, so we've got a separate chapter on HOW NOT TO SPAM.

It's good to be aware that some sites have created a weird us/them dichotomy of readers vs. writers. Yes, I know that in real life, authors are voracious readers, but remember this is a videogame in some people's minds, so they need an enemy. Mention you write, and you're it.

Some authors have spammed and gamed the system so badly that we're all paying the price.

Rule #2: Never Trade Reviews

NEVER. It's against Amazon's Terms of Service. A violation can get you kicked off Amazon.

One of the tricks of the early Amazon-gaming authors was to give a book a 5-star review, then contact the book's author and demand a 5-star in return. If the author refused, the 5-star would be reduced to a one-star.

Not all trading of reviews is the result of blackmail. Lots of authors drop hints they expect a *quid pro quo* when they've written a good review. Do not fall into this trap. Even if you love the book, you could be violating the terms of service.

One of Amazon's rules is that you can't review a product if you will benefit from the proceeds. That's why your mom can't give you a review. You also can't review if you have a "rival" product. This has been interpreted recently to mean "any author who writes in the same subgenre"—even if that review is positive. But Amazon has recently clarified that policy and it is again acceptable to review books in your own genre.

In the huge Amazon review purge that followed the purchased-review scandal of 2012, thousands of reviews were removed, some of which were solid, honest reviews, so you need to avoid any hint of impropriety.

If you love the book of an author in your genre who has given you a positive review, and you're afraid you might seem to be trading, give him a spotlight or interview on your blog. You can also offer a blurb to be included in the "editorial reviews" instead of appearing to trade.

Rule #3: Don't Pay for Customer Reviews

As I mentioned above, buying reviews is a major no-no. Not only will they be removed, but your career can take a big hit. When John Locke got caught doing it a year ago, he got hit with hundreds of one-stars and his sales slowed considerably.

It's OK to pay for a professional review from Kirkus, Publisher's Weekly, or other respected publication like the Midwest Book Review. But those reviews can't be posted on Amazon as "customer reviews." You can paste a quote into the "editorial reviews" section. But a customer review is not supposed to be for sale.

Even a free book is considered "payment" by some, so book review bloggers are now required to post disclaimers when they review a book they have received from the author or publisher, although free review copies have always been a standard practice in the industry.

Rule #4: Never Respond to Your Reviews

Never for any reason (see Catherine's chapter on the subject).

1) Do report a "review" that's obscene, a personal attack, or contains an ad for another author's book. But do not write anything in the comments of a negative review of your own book.

2) One-star review attacks, called "swarming," are against the rules, so report them. Character assassination by "review" is one of the more heinous misuses of Amazon, but they won't know it's happening unless you get people to report it.

3) If a review says "I hate this genre," accept that you can't do much about it. I've seen plenty of review pages by people who apparently do nothing but troll Amazon for books in genres they hate so they can write one star reviews. Unfortunately, they have that right.

4) Accept that people review books they haven't read. Even if it's obvious the reviewer only read the "peek inside" sample or never read the book at all, live with it. Unfortunately, there is no rule you have to read a book to review it.

5) The bestseller lists are targets for nasty reviews. Sometimes it's sour grapes from wannabes and sometimes it's sock puppets (other authors with fake id's) trying to get you "out of the way." But sock puppetry is hard to prove. If the person has no other reviews and/or mentions a "rival" book, report abuse and hope the 'Zon elves will give you a hearing.

6) Free books are magnets for cruel reviews. It's one of the reasons free books aren't working as well as they used to.

NOTE: Giveaways of free paper review copies are being gamed, so I no longer recommend them. Every day I see authors complain that their expensive paper books are immediately sold on book sites as "new" and they get no review, or worse, a one-sentence one-star.

Only send a paper book if it is requested by a book review blogger or established reviewer. Always query a book blogger before sending a copy and for goodness' sake, read the blog!

7) Your readers can usually spot a troll review and nice people may even buy the book because of it.

And guess what? There really are a lot more nice people than nasty ones.

One way to fight all this is to be one of the nice people. Writing honest reviews of books you like is the best way to fight this behavior.

Rule # 5: Always Report Abuse (and take a screenshot)

What's a screenshot? If you're a Boomer like me, you may not have heard of them. But it turns out there's a way to take a photo of what's on your screen. I could really have used it when I witnessed abuse in the past.

But since then, I've found this great thing called Awesome Screenshot that puts a button right on your toolbar—and it costs nothing to download one for your browser at AwesomeScreenshot.com. You just click on that button and then, voila! You can capture the whole page, the visible part or a partial. You can even make red circles around the pertinent spots.

As of this writing, here are ways to report abuse:

1) On Facebook, there's a little downward-arrow to the right of the post that will bring up a menu. One of the possible selections is "report abuse." Unfortunately the trolls have found it too, and they love to report people for abuse when they haven't done anything. Then you can write to appeals@facebook.com.

2) On Twitter, click on "***more" in the lower right corner of the tweet. This brings up a menu for "share", "embed" or "report". "Report" brings up a new menu where you can simply block, mark as spam, "compromised" (for when your Tweep has been hacked) or "abusive". "Abusive" brings up a form to fill out. It's more hoop jumping than they used to require, but that's to prevent trolls from reporting random innocents for abuse, as has been happening on FB.

3) On Amazon there's a prominent button for reporting abuse. Use it, especially if you see abuse on another author's page. Amazon will pay more attention if it's from somebody other than the victim.

4) On Goodreads the button for "flagging" abuse is harder to find. If you click "See Review" it will open into a new page. At the bottom of the review and each comment is a "Like" button. To the right of that in a tiny light gray font is the word "flag." If you hit this button you can report abusive content. You can also report abuse to the administrators via support@goodreads.com

Even if you don't see an immediate result, things could be happening behind the scenes. Site admin usually pays attention to abuse reports only after they get a lot. So report.

Rule #6: Never Argue with a Drunk or a Fool

Internet trolls are both. They are literally high on their own rage. Rage can trigger endorphins that create a high similar to cocaine or meth.

How far do you think you'd get using reason and logic with a crazed tweaker on the street? Right. Then don't do it on the Internet.

When cybermonkeys start tossing verbal feces around a forum or blog, treat it like any other pile of poop.

1) Carefully walk around it.

2) Realize you don't have to tell people what it is. Its own stink will give it away.

3) Call maintenance.

4) Move to a cleaner spot.

You might want to send private messages of support to victims, but don't stand up for victims in cyberpublic no matter how much your inner Atticus Finch is hurting to speak. It can backfire.

Rule #7 Stay Out of Rough Neighborhoods

Absolute Write is no longer recommended. I used to suggest looking there for info on bogus agents and scam publishers. These days, you'd be safer with the scammers.

Amazon Forums: The Deadwood of the publishing frontier. Brutally anti-author and out of control with vigilantism.

LinkedIn Writers Groups. Some may be safe, but I've unsubscribed from all the ones I belonged to. Way too many rageaholics.

Goodreads: *Mean Girls* meets *Lord of the Flies*. This site has been desperately in need of adult supervision for a long time. Recently, they have made big steps in cleaning up the site, but I'd still suggest you stay in safe, author-oriented groups. If you want to be really safe, follow the advice one agent gives her clients: "Go to Goodreads to put up an author profile. Link to your blog. Log out. Never go back."

Rule #8: Change Your Definition of "Review" and Don't Take Online Reviews so Seriously

1) It's an urban myth that Amazon requires a certain number of reviews or stars or "likes" on your author page to "move you up the ranks."

Only one thing does that: sales.

Some advertising newsletters like Kindle Nation Daily, E-Reader News Today and BookBub do require tons of 5-star reviews, but I think that encourages gaming the system so I use advertisers that don't, like EBook Bargains U.K. (which advertises to something like 18 countries as well).

For actual readers, it's much more important to have a few good reviews and some good editorial reviews from well-known authors. So don't obsess.

2) Angry reviews say more about the reviewer than your book. And they put you in excellent company. I know yours hurt like a physical wound, but it helps to read some of the idiotic one-stars of the classics.

3) An online product review is nothing like a traditional book review. When most of us think of a book review, we think of something in *the New York Times,* or a thoughtful assessment of a book written by a sincere book blogger who has read the book and done some careful thinking and writing.

But online product reviews—as established in the early days of the Internet—are essentially comments, like the comments you see at the end of online news stories or a blog.

4) A lot of people view retail site reviews as a place for comic relief. Some can be hilarious. Actor George Takei recently made "top reviewer" status on Amazon for his reviews of odd products. I dare you not to laugh.

5) Amazon also has an ultra-competitive "top 500/100/50 reviewer" program and you can get caught in their games. According to many reports, Grand Theft Auto mentality is rampant there. Reviewer-on-reviewer bullying and competition can be toxic. I've heard reports that they use review comments and "useful" voting buttons to harass each other. Or they give one-stars to books their rivals love. With the author or vendor getting caught in the middle.

This is obvious breach of Amazon rules, so clicking the "report abuse" button usually solves the problem, but it can be traumatizing for the baffled author.

6) Online review sites do not require reviewers to read a book and often allow people to rate a product even before it's available to anyone.

This is a convention of the gaming world. It's something videogame companies did in the early days to gauge interest in a new game.

Now, unfortunately, it's become a convention in online bookselling. There's nothing we can do about it but realize those star ratings mean very little.

7) Most people who write product reviews and comments are sincere, helpful customers, and some Amazon book reviewers are old school literary experts who could be published in any upscale magazine.

The best way to clean up the review system is add your honest reviews to the mix. Join the ranks of the sincere and helpful!

I know that sometimes it seems as if nastiness on the Web is getting worse, but according to some, it's actually turning around. In the May 2013 issue of *Esquire*, Stephen Marche said:

"The Internet has reached peak hate. It had to. At every other moment in history when there has been an explosion of text — whether through social change, like the birth of a religious movement, or technological change, like the advent of print — a period of nasty struggle ensued before the forces of civility reined it in."

Let's hope for it soon.

CATHERINE

THE BIG ADVANCE BITES YOU IN THE ASS

EVERYBODY WANTS THE BIG ADVANCE, RIGHT? IT'S WHAT WE ALL dream about.

"More tears are shed for answered prayers than unanswered ones." This is a quote I've heard attributed to both St. Theresa of Avila and Truman Capote. (Are they back together as a team?)

To put it as simply as possible, be careful what you wish for.

Simon & Schuster paid a big advance for *Pay It Forward*. In the sales meetings, they said, "We can sell a million of these." Well. Not quite. They sold about 60,000-70,000. Of course, the paperback went on to sell extremely well, but that didn't seem to impress them, because that was Pocket Books, a whole floor down.

I was a disappointment.

Now, if they had given me a small advance, and printed, say, 10,000 hardcovers, and we'd sold over 60,000, they'd be carrying me down Avenue of the Americas on their shoulders.

But I was supposed to sell a million.

In response, they put very little into the follow-up books (in addition to the colossal mistake of trying to pass me off as writing Christian fiction), and when I parted ways with S&S, I was in a very bad position to start over with another publisher. They look at sales records. Recent ones. If the recent ones are skimpy compared to the older ones, that's not good.

So my career was…not good.

It was really the switch over to Young Adult that broke me out of my slump, because my only book that could be considered YA was Pay It Forward. And those sales records looked pretty good.

Then the miraculous happened. My agent sold *Love in the Present Tense* to Doubleday…for six figures! Just like the old days! How did we get around my sales figures for adult titles? They were so enthusiastic about the novel that they didn't check them until after I was under contract, and then they were so enthusiastic that it didn't change much.

The day I was in New York to promote the book on the Today Show, Doubleday bought another of my novels, *Chasing Windmills*.

The following year they dropped me—with much expressed regret—because my sales didn't justify my advances.

My agent told me that this was the problem with the big advances, the reason she has mixed feelings about pushing for them. If the advance had been half what it was, there might not have been a problem.

I was out there again, trying—unsuccessfully, for quite some time—to overcome those "numbers" and get back to publishing my adult books in the U.S. That's correct—as of this writing [note:

before *When I Found You* hit big numbers] I am publishing YA novels in the U.S. and adult novels in the U.K., but can't find a publisher for those same adult titles here at home. Even though they're somewhere on the national bestseller list on the other side of "the pond." (Thank goodness, or I'm not sure what I'd be eating right now.)

Yes, like the crazy person I am, I make my living at this.

Years ago, a friend who published with small presses told me this: "The nice thing about a small press is that they can't afford to publish a book and then ignore it." And that's a truth worth considering. Sure, the big guys have more resources, but will they commit them to your book? Maybe. But maybe not.

I think this is all especially true now that print newspapers are dying an agonizing death, print reviews are drying up, and book bloggers are taking up the slack. This levels the playing field, because it allows a book to be promoted with a minimum of travel and paid advertising on the part of the author and/or publisher. Small press books can get big attention.

I'm not telling you not to take the big advance. Only to be careful what you sacrifice to get it. Because it's an unpredictable beast. Just when you least expect it, it can turn on its owner.

Take it from someone who's been bitten in the ass. Twice.

ANNE

HOW NOT TO SPAM

AUTHORS NEED TO REMEMBER THAT SOCIAL MEDIA IS SOCIAL. IT should not be used for direct marketing. It should be used for making friends.

You wouldn't wear an advertising sandwich board to a Chamber of Commerce mixer, but a lot of authors are doing the digital equivalent.

The practice is known as "spamming."

If you've ever wondered why unsolicited advertising is named after a perfectly innocent meat product, blame Monty Python. In a famous 1970 sketch, the customers in a café are constantly drowned out by a chorus of Vikings singing "Spam, Spam, Spam, Spam... Lovely Spam! Wonderful Spam!" Conversation is impossible because of the "spammers."

But whatever it's called, don't do it.

As I said in the chapter on the Laws of the (Amazon) Jungle, vigilante groups can be cruel in enforcing anti-spam rules.

But the rules can be different for each site. And finding them can require tech savvy and knowledge of legalese (and good eyesight: they're usually written in a flyspeck font.) Here are the rules I've managed to discover, mostly by breaking them. As Catherine and I say, we make the mistakes so you don't have to.

How not to Spam on Facebook

1) Don't link to your blog from anything but your own page or a designated thread. Links to your blog or website are considered spam on Facebook, no matter how useful. They'll put you in Facebook jail (freeze you out of your own page) if you post links to your blog more than a few times a week, even in a private group.

This happened to me. Somebody in a group asks at least once a week about using song lyrics in fiction. So I used to post a link to a piece on my blog that tells you how to get rights to song lyrics (they're very expensive, so don't do it unless you're prepared to pay big bucks). Wrong. Unwritten Facebook rules say you can't do that, and a self-appointed vigilante will click the "report for spam" button and you're off Facebook for a week or more.

2) Limit "Buy this book" posts with links to retailer; one of the many promotion groups like 99¢ Kindle Deals, Authors 99¢ E-Book Promotion, Free Books R Us, Free Books 4 U, etc.; or your own pages.

3) Don't friend more than a few people a day. Even though Facebook is constantly telling you to "friend" people, it's a trap. If you actually do what they say, you'll end up in Facebook jail.

4) Don't post a promotion of your book in a group without reading the rules first. Many groups will kick you out for it.

5) Posting promos on somebody else's Facebook page is serious spam. It's a violation of personal space. It even makes me see red.

6) Never market through a direct message. Never use personal messaging for advertising a book or service. Only message people you already have a relationship with.

How not to Spam on Twitter

1) Never send those automated direct messages that say, "Now that you've followed me, go like my Facebook and author pages, follow my blog, buy my book and pick up my dry cleaning." Not only are they against the Terms of Service, they'll usually result in an auto-unfollow from most Tweeps.

2) Do NOT send any automatic direct messages. Even a "thanks for the follow" can annoy a lot of people.

3) Don't tweet your book unless you have news like a great review or a sale or freebie run.

4) Don't tweet somebody else's book link just because they ask. Make sure it's in a genre your Tweeps will enjoy. (DO hit the button that says "I just bought [title] by [author] on Amazon when you do buy a book. That's a great way to recommend it.)

How not to Spam on Amazon

1) A link to your own book in a review is spam. It can get you banned from Amazon. You can have a title in your signature and post as "Susie Scrivener, author of Scribblings," but without a link.

2) Do not mention your book in the Amazon Forums. Better yet, don't go there. They're not author-friendly.

3) In Kindleboard forums, only link to your blog in a designated thread, even if your blog is full of useful information to writers. I learned that the hard way.

How not to Spam on Blogs

1) Never subscribe to a blogger's newsletter just so you can hit "reply" and send an ad for your book. It's happened to me a couple of times. It's insulting and pointless. The ad doesn't go to the mailing list. It goes to the blogger—who will put you on their list of authors to avoid. Remember this is about making friends, not enemies.

2) Don't link to your "buy page" from a blog comment. I don't mind links to a blog or webpage—in fact I find them useful—but some people don't like links of any kind from a blog comment, and they'll delete the comment as spam, so be wary.

3) Don't ever take a commenter's email address and add it to your newsletter without permission. This is a serious breach of blog etiquette.

4) Don't talk up your book or blog in a comment unless it's relevant to the conversation.

"I respect your opinion, but I have a different take on this over at my blog" with a link is fine.

"This reminds me of my book, Fangs for the Memories, a zombipocolyptic Vampire Romance, $3.99 on Smashwords." Not so much.

How not to Spam on Forums

1) Lurk. Every forum is different. So never say anything in a forum until you've unearthed every rule and hung out for a good long time.

2) Beware "share" buttons. I made the mistake earlier this year of sending out my blog link to a number of sites via the "share" button Blogger provides. This apparently sent it to forums where it should not have gone on Reddit, StumbleUpon and Digg. A nice moderator from Reddit informed me all my posts had been deleted as spam.

3) Better yet, stay out of forums altogether, except small, well moderated, author-friendly ones like Nathan Bransford's, She Writes, Red Room, Critique Circle, or Kristen Lamb's WANAtribe. The bigger and older the site, the more likely it will have trolls, bad-tempered vigilantes and anti-author groups.

How not to Spam on Goodreads

1) Don't join a group just to promote your book. Spend a long time talking about other books before you bring up your own. In fact, on Goodreads, it's best not to mention you're an author at all. Take off your author hat and discuss books you've read, not ones you've written.

2) Don't send mass friend requests. This is true on almost all sites. You will be flagged as a spammer.

3) Don't thank a reviewer or someone who has put your book on their "shelf." The new Goodreads author guidelines prohibit it.

4) And especially: never engage with somebody who has given you a bad review or put you on a hate "shelf." Not for any reason. Goodreads reviews are notoriously unpleasant, unhelpful, and snarky. But authors need to learn to live with them.

CATHERINE

THE EYE OF THE BEHOLDER

I USED TO READ AMAZON'S (AND OTHER ONLINE BOOK SITES') READER reviews of my books. When they were good (which was usually) I was happy. When they were bad, I was depressed for days, even though they were usually good.

"Don't read them," my friends said. Well, that's a silly bit of advice, I thought. How can I not read them? They contain valuable information on how I'm being received. I have to know how I'm doing, right?

The comments below were taken from actual reader reviews, all from Amazon, and all for the same book. *Pay It Forward*. I repeat: *all of these reviews are for one book.*

Read them for yourself and see how much good, solid information they contain to tell the author how she's doing.

I liked the characters, they were very well thought out, and each was very dynamic.

———

The character development is a bit weak, as Hyde tends to tell rather than show her characters. This minor flaw is easy to ignore.

———

Pay it forward is a wonderful piece of work. Catherine Ryan Hyde did a marvelous job putting you in the shoes of the characters.

———

The characters were a bit shallow—Trevor a little to good to be true, mother a little to typical, teacher typical chip on his shoulder man but it didn't stop me from enjoying the story.

———

This is such a wonderful story, it has everything. The characters are amazing.

———

It is extremely interesting especially in the format. The author uses different perspectives to tell her story. She includes letters, Trevor's diary entries, as well as first and third person narratives. This keeps the readers attention because the book doesn't get boring. You always have a different point of view to hear from.

———

I actually thought the movie was better, which is rare. The book was also very good, but in a different way. It has the same heart and inspiration as the movie, but it gets a little lost in the side stories. The writing was good, but the storyline jumped from person to person a little too much.

———

Written any other way, this book would not have been as inspiring. It was written from a point of view that I could understand and sympathize with—the outsider point of view. Had the book been written entirely in third-person, it would not have had the profound impact on me that it did.

———

This book is sort of hard to follow, and it's quite lengthy, but once you start reading it, you can't put it down. Everything does come together in the end.

———

It is easy to follow and keeps the reader interested.

———

"Pay it Forward" wasn't very good. The story was saccharine sweet.

———

Pay It Forward is inspiring, funny, tearful...I couldn't put it down. It's not sappy either.

———

...very unrealistic dialogue. A great example of the horrible dialogue was when Trevor referred to Chelsea Clinton as a "major babe." I'm sorry, but I just don't believe that most 13-year-old boys think of Chelsea Clinton as a "major babe." Oh, and every other word out of Trevor's mouth was "cool." My teacher is cool, my project is cool, Bill Clinton is cool, and every damn thing is cool.

Another problem with this book was the love story between two of the main characters. They just didn't seem like they were really in love.
-Steven

———

Pay it Forward is one of my favorite all time books. I was so annoyed when a saw a review written by a certain person called Steven, whoever he is, who said that Pay it Forward was unrealistic.

It is a wonderful book packed with imagination, cliffhangers, humor and even tragedy! The ending had me crying! You get to know the characters so well, that it almost makes you want to scream when anything bad happens to them!

Guess what? I don't read the Amazon reader reviews anymore. I just keep track of how many stars each book has. It's better for my blood pressure.

CATHERINE

WHAT COULD POSSIBLY GO WRONG?

You're published! You have an actual book, and it's in bookstores. It even got reviewed in *Publishers Weekly* and *Booklist*. If you went to the trouble of looking this up at the library, you could probably find your name in *Books in Print*.

Your years of struggling are over. Publishers will *want* to see your next book. Your publisher is even asking you what you plan to work on next.

Damn good to have all that behind you. Isn't it? You have arrived!

There's just one problem. The publishing world is in constant motion as it flexes to keep pace with current technologies and a constantly changing marketplace. How can you have arrived at your destination when your destination never holds still?

You'd better just plan on arriving every day.

Here is a very short list of things that can go wrong:

You could get an advance that turns out to be too big compared to your sales, in which case you'll be looking for a new publisher (from a severely handicapped position). Been there.

You could get a small advance from a small, hungry, sincere publisher who promptly goes belly up, leaving you looking for a new publisher. Been there.

Your publisher could position you to an entirely wrong audience, damaging your ability to sell books, leaving you looking for a new publisher. Been there.

You may have to reinvent yourself as an author. Done that.

I'll never forget a walk I took in Central Park one winter. I can't even remember why I was in New York. But, boy, do I remember that walk!

It was post *Pay It Forward*, post *Electric God* and *Walter's Purple Heart*. Post Simon & Schuster, or at least, the end of that story lay in plain view. I had faced all the "too corny" criticism I felt I could bear. (Interestingly, I was initially told I was "too dark and literary." After *Pay It Forward* that switched to "too feel-good and sentimental." Which just goes to show that critics will always try to shove you into a box. It just might not always be the same box.)

More to the point, I wasn't selling.

In a mood to consider every alternative, I actually thought about going into a new line of work. Not because I didn't think I could fight my way back (hell, if I got there the first time…), but more because I wasn't sure I wanted to.

My answer to myself? I would always write. I had to write. Even if I didn't publish, I would write.

I decided to make some changes in *what* I write.

A number of elements contributed to my decision. The fact that *Pay It Forward*, though written and published for adults, had landed on the ALA's Best Books for Young Adults list, and I now had something of a YA following. The fact that every time I had an interview, someone asked me to name my favorite books…and I was still naming the ones I'd read when I was 14. The fact that an editor told me that the strongest characters in my adult fiction were coming-of-age (the young Ella Ginsberg in *Funerals for Horses*, the young Hayden Reese in *Electric God*). The woman in a bookstore who summed up what I could not put into words when she said YA fiction afforded "the freedom to be sincere."

I reinvented myself as a Young Adult author.

Then, of course, my adult career took off again, too. But that didn't matter. What mattered was that I adapted. Not driven by where I thought the money really lies in this business, but by where I thought I truly belonged.

If I'd gone with a sequel to *Pay It Forward* I'm sure I'd have a day job right now.

You will never be able to rest on your laurels in this business. Keep writing. Keep learning. Keep adapting. There will be more hard punches, even after your big break. Many more. Roll with them.

Remember the advice a screenwriter friend once gave me, lowering her voice into gangster ranges and quoting from *The Godfather*: "This is the business we have chosen."

ANNE

HOW TO QUERY A BOOK REVIEW BLOGGER

PUBLISHING INSIDER ALAN RINZLER SAID RECENTLY THAT TRADITIONAL book marketing is no longer working.

"That $50K space ad in the *New York Times*?" he said. "Forget it. It's only for the author's mother...not even an appearance on the Today Show can guarantee more than a brief spike in sales. The old ways don't work, and smart people in book publishing know that and say it openly now."

So if the *New York Times* and the Today Show are no longer the best places to find out about new books, where does a reader go?

Increasingly, people are going to book review blogs. That's why getting a good review from a prestigious blogger in your genre can be the best way to launch a book.

So how do you find the right book bloggers? And how do you approach them?

The best way is to check similar books in your genre—especially those who have been recently released. Do a search for those titles with the word "review" and read as many reviews as you can. Make a list of the reviewers you like and read the review policy. They don't all take ebooks—and some only take traditionally published or indie books—and they usually have very specific genre requests, so read carefully.

Then you send a query—pretty much the way you approach other gatekeepers like literary agents and editors. This means you send a professional letter—not a Tweet or wall post on Facebook.

Here are some general rules for scoring a review:

1) Read the guidelines carefully.

2) Then, um, follow the guidelines carefully.

3) Never send an unsolicited book: query first.

4) Don't query with books outside the prescribed genre. Even if the blogger agrees to do a review, you won't reach the right readers. People don't go to a Chick Lit review site to hear about the latest zombie gore-fest.

5) Personalize the query.

6) Keep queries short and intriguing.

7) Don't take it personally if they turn you down. Reading takes a lot of time and most of them are swamped.

8) Understand the review is for the READER, not the writer, so

negative reviews happen.

9) If you get a less than stellar review, mourn in private and move on.

Who are the worst rule breakers? According to book bloggers I've talked to, it's marketers, publicists and other publishing professionals who don't get social networking. Those are the people who blast generic review requests into thousands of bloggers' inboxes only to get thousands of deletes.

According to agent and former reviewer Danielle Smith of the blog "There's a Book", the best way to approach a book blogger is to keep your query professional, but show some personality:

1) Make sure you address the blogger by name.

2) Include a two to four sentence synopsis—no longer.

3) Keep personal information to a minimum. And don't guilt-trip.

4) Attach an image of the book cover.

5) Give the age range of the intended audience.

6) Include the page count (for print books).

7) Provide the publication date and expected time frame of when you'd like to see the review posted for scheduling purposes.

8) Don't ask for a review outside the blogger's genre.

9) Don't query if you don't have a website or a blog. That screams "unprofessional" to a blogger.

In other words, treat the book blogger like a professional and she will reciprocate.

CATHERINE

BOOK BLOGGERS ARE THE FUTURE—
TREAT THEM RIGHT!

I THINK I'VE MADE IT AMPLY CLEAR THAT I RESPECT BOOK BLOGGERS AS an invaluable puzzle piece in the modern book business. But of course that business is rapidly changing. A whole new model is becoming the norm—maybe not erasing the old model, but probably displacing it in terms of sheer popularity and volume. It will have its advantages, and a definite down side. I'm optimistic, however, and I'll tell you why. I think it will work. But here's the linchpin of the whole deal: with the help of book bloggers, I think it will fill the needs of readers/book consumers. Without them, it could be a nightmare.

The self-published ebook, along with print-on-demand technology, has opened a floodgate that has not only been shut, but carefully guarded, for decades. Anyone can get published now. This, of course, is both the good news and the bad news, all rolled into one big news flash.

The upside: that brilliant new author who was traditionally a little too literary, too controversial, too ahead of his or her time—the one publishers haven't taken a chance on since they were gobbled up by enormous watch-the-bottom-line corporations—will get published now.

The down side: so will that really bad author who never took the time to learn the trade, never bothered to get the damn thing edited, and really can't see why it's not as good as anything else out there (when it's obviously not).

So, do I think it comes out a draw? Oddly, no. I think it's better the new way. For a simple reason. We can forego anything badly written once it's published. But we can't go into the brilliant new authors' desk drawers and find what was being rejected. All we need to make it a great system is somebody to help us tell them apart. Without book bloggers, Amazon becomes the literary equivalent of the agents' depressing slush piles. With it, it's a new world where anything goes, where ideas do not have to conform to finances, where the little guy has as much chance as the big guy. Where cream rises to the top.

Print reviews will not step in and save the reader in this new book future, because print media is drying up. The Internet will have to fill that need. It's hard to imagine, looking back, that anyone had the lack of foresight to call a book blogger "unprofessional," as it's their amateur status we should be celebrating. They are doing this for love. They are doing this even though it's a model that may never earn them a living. And, let's face it, every platform gets fairer and more honest when you de-monetize it.

But if readers buy too many ebooks that are not edited or proofread (or well-written) because reviewers (under pressure or out of a sense of obligation) tell them the writing is "fine," the whole system could turn into a quagmire.

So, not to beat a point to death, but…we have to encourage blog reviewers to tell the truth as they see it. A greater measure of respect from authors would be nice, too. I know I've said it before, but I'll probably keep saying it until more authors wise up and start treating them like the future of this business.

CATHERINE

HOW TO SURVIVE THE BIG SCREEN ADAPTATION (AKA: A WRITER'S MOST DESIRABLE PROBLEM)

YES. THIS IS POSSIBLE. LIKELY, NO. BUT POSSIBLE.

If your book takes off and enjoys great sales, a big film company might step up and ask to option the rights. Which does not mean the movie will ever come to a theater near you. Hundreds of properties are optioned yearly for every film that's released. But it happens.

If you're wondering how to make this happen, I'm sorry to say I'm not sure you can. It's a bit like being struck by lightning (and often similarly painful). Lightning strikes happen to hundreds of people every year. And yet, if you're looking for such an experience (you're not, but go with me on this tortured simile) there's no special path to finding it. My only advice is to stand outside in a lot of rainstorms. Lightning rarely strikes those sitting inside by their comfortable wood fires.

Maybe you have a film agent, or your literary agent has a

subagent for film. And said agent is shopping it around. Good. That's the equivalent of standing outside in a storm. Now all you need is a whole universe full of luck.

And then, in most cases, somewhere in the adaptation process, authors begin to wonder just how lucky they really are.

My novel *Pay It Forward* was adapted for film. I am commonly asked what I think of the movie version. My answer is always the same.

"I thought the book was better."

Then again, I would, wouldn't I?

When I say that, just about everybody says the same thing: "Oh, the book is always better than the movie." Which leads me to wonder why, as a society in general, we see so many movies and read so few books. But that's another rant for another text.

I have theories as to why the book is always better.

Theory #1. The author is not a person responsible for recovering an investor's fifty million dollars (or hundred million these days), and so spends less time second-guessing him- or herself. (Isn't it nice to know there's somebody on the planet doing more second-guessing than the writer?)

Theory #2. Most books have only one author. A Hollywood movie is like the textbook definition of too many cooks in the kitchen.

Theory #3. People don't seem to realize that Hollywood will make whatever kind of movies we will support, and that we "vote" with our box office dollars.

If I had singlehandedly made the movie *Pay It Forward*:

a) The world would actually have changed at the end.

b) Reuben St. Clair, my African-American Viet Nam vet protagonist would have appeared in said film (Eugene who?).

c) All the gay, transgender, physically large, or minority characters would not have turned thin, white and straight, or disappeared entirely (ah, Hollywood is a magical place!).

d) I would have made sure that the only black and (arguably) Hispanic characters left were not gang-bangers and knife-wielding thugs.

Ah, you say. But it will be different with me. Because I will retain control.

Really? You think you can control a Hollywood film?

I'm not so sure.

First of all, if you're not J.K. Rowling, attaching script approval might very well relegate your project to a shelf forever. But let's say your work is hot, and you get what you want: script approval, or even collaboration on the screenplay.

Screenwriters do not control Hollywood films.

The director leaves fingerprints on it, calling it "A Fill-in-the-name-of-the-big-director Film" and making insane choices based on ego to prove it. The actors come in with "script notes" (i.e., I just can't see my character saying that). The bigger the actor, the harder it is for anyone to say no to the often rotten ideas. New writers can be brought in to make new changes. Even if you could conquer those forces, a film editor can completely transform the feel of a film in post production. For better or for worse.

No matter what it says in your contract, a film is going to be out of the novelist's control.

So, if I had it to do over again, would I still sell them the rights? You bet I would. In a Hollywood minute.

Let's face it. This is what you call a high-end problem.

I know other fortunate writers will face similar happy disasters (I want to go on record as saying I wish this problem on each and every person reading this), so I'll offer some tidbits of advice for the adaptation experience.

1) A useful mantra: "It's not my hundred million dollars."

2) A great quote from Jacqueline Mitchard: "Where I come from, you can either take the money or you can moan about the process, but not both." My advice? Take the money. Moaning is not all it's cracked up to be.

3) Remind yourself that they are not, as people will suggest, "changing your book." Go back and read your book. You will find it blissfully unchanged. This is not your book, it's their movie. Separate the two in your brain for purposes of continued sanity.

4) If your problems feel overwhelming, complain to your writer friends who are still struggling to get published. (Example: "Boo hoo. They cast Kevin Spacey in my movie instead of Denzel Washington.") They will help you regain perspective. Trust me. They will.

373

Just promise me that you won't be that writer who gets everything he or she ever wanted, and is still unhappy. A big screen adaptation is the brass ring. It boosts your name recognition (and I don't mean boosts like a booster seat, I mean boosts like a booster rocket via NASA) and sells more books. That title, plus your backlist if you have one, plus every other book you'll ever write.

And let's say they make a bad film. I mean a really bad film. Not like *Pay It Forward*, which I think of as a flawed film. I mean hold-the-nose-and-ask-for-your-ticket-price-back crappy. Then what will people say? They'll say, "Oh, don't even bother with the movie. The movie sucks. Read the book. The book is much better." And this hurts the writer how?

Once Hollywood comes calling for your book, nothing they can do to it will ever be as bad, in my opinion, as the hurt caused when they don't.

There are some very well-known writers who simply refuse to option their work for film because they know Hollywood is going to ruin it, and they know it's going to hurt when they do. I'd advise you not to be one of them. This is the kind of pain we should all be happy to dive into. Put on your best grown-up suit and be prepared to let go.

As my old mentor Jean Brody used to say, "We should all have such problems!"

CONCLUSION

CATHERINE

MAKE SURE YOU KNOW YOUR DEFINITION OF SUCCESS

IN LATE 2003—NEW YEAR'S EVE, IN FACT—I WAS MULLING OVER A short author's note. I was writing it to accompany a story I was fortunate to have published in *Glimmer Train*, a terrific all-story literary magazine. I'd been submitting to them without success for years. Then, acceptance. Was it the tenth submission? The fifteenth? No idea. I just know it felt good.

Unfortunately, not much else in my life did.

My novel *Walter's Purple Heart* had come out in spring of 2002, but I hadn't sold anything to a publisher for two or three years. As mentioned, Simon & Schuster and I had parted ways, very little of their attention seemed to go into that final novel together, and sales reflected that.

It put me in a terrible position to start over with a new publisher.

They might as well have thrown the last few clods of dirt over my career.

The money to pay basic bills was running out.

So I guess I had issues of success—and its polar opposite—on my mind when I wrote my little author's reflection for Glimmer Train's "The Last Pages" section. I put the words together in my head while out on a day-long hike, the only hike I've ever taken where I got so lost I needed help getting found.

Coincidence?

You tell me.

Here's what I wrote:

"Whether fortunately or unfortunately, I have passed through an odd series of events that the world seems to define as success. I know what's on the far side: Your life, much as it was on the near side. And a downward slope. As an avid (rabid?) peak hiker, I accept that any ascending trail will crest, then descend. And maybe, if you trudge along tirelessly (though this works equally well if you trudge along tired, by the way), it may crest again.

"Or not.

"No matter. I now have a very different definition of success: Trekking from the South Rim of the Grand Canyon to the Colorado River, and then back again, all in one grueling, magnificent day. Landing a 28-inch ling cod while perched on a 12-foot sit-on-top kayak, bobbing in the open ocean. Doing work you love, whether anybody pays you for it or not.

"To whomever may be reading this, I wish you great success."

Sounds like a nice requiem for a career, doesn't it?

Then the aforementioned good fortune.

By February, my agent got me a big-money, two-book deal with

Knopf Books for Young Readers for *Becoming Chloe* and *The Year of My Miraculous Reappearance,* launching my young adult career. By June, she'd resurrected my adult career with a six-figure sale to Doubleday for *Love in the Present Tense.* A year later Doubleday purchased *Chasing Windmills* to follow it.

Two years later, neither YA had earned out, and Doubleday had dropped me because my sales didn't justify my advances.

My career remained in a deep slump, mitigated only by my U.K. success, for so long that I was willing to accept that damn few people (Brits excepted) seemed to want to read what I wanted to write.

Just as the money ran out again, *When I Found You* made its amazing run up the charts, and about 100,000 people downloaded it in less than a month.

What do all these eras have in common?

During each and every one of them, I was a success. By whose definition? By my own. By the definition I had initially set for myself.

Fortunately, I'd always been clear on my goal as a writer. I formed my notion of success while I was first struggling for any kind of publication at all.

It went like this:

All I wanted was to make enough money from my writing to allow me to continue writing. I just wanted the writing to support my writing habit. I just wanted not to have to get a day job to pay the bills.

I've been mighty close to the line of not meeting my bills. On more than one occasion. But 14 years later I'm still here, with no day job. This leaves me with a choice. I can focus on the fact that I never stay cleanly in the black for long enough, and that it's a hand-to-mouth existence. Or I can look at the figures on how many writers can survive without a day job, and realize how fortunate I am.

As for the formulation (or revision) of *your* goals, I want to share a couple of pieces of wisdom I've received over the years.

The first was from my mother, who unfortunately passed away less than three weeks prior to this writing. I was a teenager when she told me this, and we always remembered she was quoting someone, but could never figure out who it was.

She said, "The problem with a fallback position is that you tend to fall back."

Now. I don't want to be the one to tell you to walk the high wire of this business without a net. It's dicey advice, and people can and do get genuinely hurt. But I can tell you this, with some certainty: If your goal is to stay on the wire, consider that the cushy net below *does* make you more likely to fall. Because you can afford to.

Make your own wise decisions here, as I don't want to be responsible for anyone else's injuries.

Another great thought. This one was given to me by fellow author Christopher Moore, in a letter of encouragement he wrote me, back when I had not one publication credit to my name.

He said, "Take joy in the work, for it may be all you get."

Wise words.

I can't guarantee you will ever make money doing this, and, if you do, I can't guarantee it will stay. But I can guarantee that if you find joy in creating and polishing a story, and you spend your life doing so, your life will be filled with joy.

On the other side of the equation, aim high. Why shouldn't you?

But you only hurt yourself with goals that are completely unrealistic.

For example, I would advise against a goal like, "All five-star reviews." Nobody gets that. And if that had been my goal, my average of 4 ½ stars would bring me nothing but sorrow.

If my goal had been for every one of my books to hit #1, I couldn't have celebrated when three of them hit #3, #9 and #12 on various important national lists. I would still have been a failure.

If there's one thing I'm quite sure Anne and I have impressed upon our readers in the previous 200 or so pages, it's that making a living as a writer is one of the hardest things in the world to do. There's only one possible reason to be a writer, in my opinion: Because, in your heart and your gut, you know you'll never be happy doing anything else.

If you think you could be happy as a writer, but you're also interested in selling real estate, I strongly recommend the real estate. Your odds of eating regularly are infinitely better. But if you honestly feel you were put on this Earth to write, ignore the odds. They mean nothing to you. Put your energy and attention where they will do some good—into the work.

Your plan at this point is simple. Not easy, but simple. Be the one who doesn't give up and go home.

I can't guarantee what you'll get, but if you love what you're doing, I can guarantee you a life of loving what you do.

You could do worse.

I wish you great success.

ANNE

THE BEST TIME EVER TO BE A WRITER IS NOW

THIS MAY SEEM A TERRIFYING TIME TO BE LAUNCHING A WRITING career. Everything in the publishing industry is in upheaval. Bookstores are closing all around us. Publishers and online retailers are battling each other in the courts.

The rules keep changing. "Experts" don't agree on anything. Us/them, either/or arguments of self-publishers vs. traditional publishers can be toxic. What you read one week is out of date the next. Half the things you read in this book will probably be obsolete a year from now. (You can check for the latest industry news on my weekly blog at annerallen.blogspot.com.)

Change can be very scary. It's like trying to go about normal business in the middle of an earthquake. There's nothing solid to hang onto.

But you know what's scarier than change?

No change.

Before the electronic revolution, publishing was a calcifying industry. New writers were finding it tougher and tougher to break in. Successful career authors were dropped if they couldn't produce annual blockbusters in spite of no marketing budget. The antiquated system of returns—in which every bookstore is a consignment shop—means publishers have been wasting a huge amount of money shipping books back and forth to warehouses and eventually pulping them.

The ebook is changing everything. Ditto social media.

Don't be afraid of the electronic revolution. It's not killing the book culture. More people are reading now than ever before. It's not destroying our literature with a "tsunami of self-published crap." It's helping us all grow in new directions.

I love this joke from social media guru Kristen Lamb: "Great, thanks to that Gutenberg jerk, everyone can be published."

Just as Johannes Gutenberg took power from the ruling priestly caste and gave it to the people—who could then read the Bible and find out for themselves what it said—ebooks are taking power from the ruling publishing caste and letting the people decide for themselves what they want to read.

This means more power is now in the hands of readers and writers than any time in history. Thanks to ebooks and social media marketing, writers can now go directly to readers with fresh, innovative ideas and stories.

If they want to.

Here's the thing: the revolution doesn't mean everybody has to self-publish. But the self-publishing option changes the playing field for everybody.

Your life is being changed for the better by the electronic revolution right now:

- Even if you've never touched a Kindle—and you don't intend to until they pry the world's last moldering paperback from your cold, dead hands.

- Even if you'd rather endure waterboarding during a tax audit than try to make sense of a Twitter stream.

- Even if your idea of Hell is being pleasant on a daily basis to a bunch of strangers on the Internet.

- Even if you stopped keeping up with technology when your last VCR went to that Great Techno-dump in the Sky.

That's because you now have choices that never existed before. And new choices are opening up all the time as the industry processes new ideas. Whatever path you take, you have the choice to turn around and try a different one.

- If you try traditional publishing and get offered a rotten contract—you can walk away.

- If you self-publish and then St. Martin's comes calling with a seven figure deal—you can jump on it.

- If you publish with a small press, you can still work at getting an agent who might make you a super author-friendly deal with one of the new Amazon imprints.

Everything is possible.

You can choose to self-publish. Or not.

You can choose to blog/Tweet/Facebook. Or not.

Don't let anybody push you onto one path or the other.

Everybody has a different tolerance for technology. You can mix and match as you wish. I've read that Twitter god Neil Gaiman writes his first draft with a #2 pencil. I know successful Kindle authors who swear by their manual typewriters. Try things out, take your time, and make your own choices.

Remember it's people who are most insecure in their choices who will seek to control yours.

What Catherine and I have tried to do with this book is let you know what some of your possibilities are, so you can make the choices that will work best for your own career—and your sanity!

ABOUT THE AUTHORS

Catherine Ryan Hyde

CATHERINE RYAN HYDE IS THE AUTHOR OF 25 PUBLISHED AND forthcoming books.

Her newest releases are *Where We Belong, Walk Me Home, Subway Dancer and Other Stories, When You Were Older, Don't Let Me Go, When I Found You, Second Hand Heart, The Long, Steep Path: Everyday Inspiration From the Author of Pay It Forward, Always Chloe and Other Stories,* and *365 Days of Gratitude: Photos from a Beautiful World.*

Forthcoming in 2014 are *Take Me With You* and *The Language of Hoofbeats* (Lake Union/Amazon Publishing July and December '14 respectively). *Pay It Forward: Young Readers Edition,* an age-appropriate edited edition of the original novel, will be released by Simon & Schuster in August of '14. It is suitable for children as young as eight.

She has two forthcoming new novels due out in 2015 from Lake Union/Amazon Publishing.

Other newer novels include *Jumpstart the World, Becoming Chloe, Love in the Present Tense, The Year of My Miraculous Reappearance, Chasing Windmills, The Day I Killed James,* and *Diary of a Witness.*

Her bestselling 1999 novel *Pay It Forward* was made into a major Warner Brothers motion picture starring Kevin Spacey and Helen Hunt. It was chosen by the American Library Association for its Best Books for Young Adults list, and translated into more than two dozen languages for distribution in over 30 countries. A special 15th anniversary edition will be published in 2015.

Both *Becoming Chloe* and *Jumpstart the World* were included on the ALA's Rainbow List. *Jumpstart the World* was chosen as a finalist for two Lambda Literary Awards, and was honored with Rainbow Awards in two categories. *Love in the Present Tense* enjoyed bestseller status in the UK, where it broke the top ten, spent five weeks on national bestseller lists, was reviewed on a major TV book club, and shortlisted for a Best Read of the Year Award at the British Book Awards. *When I Found You* spent two weeks dominating the US Kindle charts in the top three. *Walk Me Home* was #1 in Kindle at the same time as *When I Found You* held the #3 spot, causing Catherine to jump to #1 in Amazon author ranking, just above JK Rowling. *Where We Belong* won two Rainbow Awards in 2013.

Older works include *Earthquake Weather and Other Stories,* and the novels *Funerals for Horses, Electric God,* and *Walter's Purple Heart.* These backlist titles rereleased digitally in October of 2012.

More than 50 of her short stories have been published in *The*

Antioch Review, Michigan Quarterly Review, The Virginia Quarterly Review, Ploughshares, Glimmer Train, The Sun and many other journals, and in the anthologies *Santa Barbara Stories and California Shorts* and the bestselling anthology *Dog is my Co-Pilot*. Her stories have been honored in the Raymond Carver Short Story Contest and the Tobias Wolff Award and nominated for Best American Short Stories, the O'Henry Award, and the Pushcart Prize. Three have been cited in Best American Short Stories.

She is founder and former president (2000-2009) of the Pay It Forward Foundation. As a professional public speaker she has addressed the National Conference on Education, twice spoken at Cornell University, met with Americorps members at the White House and shared a dais with Bill Clinton.

Anne R. Allen

ANNE R. ALLEN IS A BLOGGER, HUMORIST, AND THE AUTHOR OF SIX Romantic Comedy-Mysteries: *Food of Love, The Gatsby Game, The Lady of the Lakewood Diner,* and The Camilla Randall Mysteries: *The Best Revenge, Ghostwriters in the Sky, Sherwood, Ltd.,* and *No Place Like Home.*

She teaches blogging and social media. Her blog, *"Anne R. Allen's Blog...with Ruth Harris: Writing about Writing. Mostly"* was named one of the Best 101 Websites for Writers by W*riter's Digest* and a finalist for Best Publishing Industry Blog by the Association of American Publishers.

Social media guru Kristen Lamb, author of *We Are Not Alone: the Writer's Guide to Social Media,* said "Anne Allen is an amazing author advocate. Her blogs are a treasure trove of the best information in an ever-changing paradigm…Anne is one of the strong voices of the Digital Age."

Stanford University creative writing instructor and former *Chicago Tribune* columnist Terry Galanoy said, "I am urging the students in my Stanford course Master Class in Professional Writing—professors and all—to make Anne's blog mandatory reading."

Blogger O'Brian Gunn says, "Author and 'writer mother' extraordinaire Anne R. Allen gives us a breakdown of what's currently taking place in the world of self-publishing and the impact it will have on the future… Anne gives her readers honest, straight-forward facts without pussyfooting around. She also has a way of making readers feel better about the tumultuous changes taking place in the publishing business. She's a true businesswoman, and I highly recommended following her blog."

From 2002-08 Anne wrote the "In Her Own Write" column for *Freelance Writers Organization—International.* Her fiction and poetry have been published in numerous print and online journals. Her poetry and short work appear in *Compose* literary journal, *Opium, Martini Madness, Indiestructible, Indie Chicks Anthology, Genre Wars,* and *Notes from Underground.* She's published nonfiction in many journals including *Writer's Digest* and *Talking Writing,* and on more blogs than she can count.Anne grew up in New England, graduated from Bryn Mawr College, and has been an actress, teacher, bookseller, antique dealer, and general office serf—as well as serving as the artistic director of the Patio Playhouse in Escondido, CA.

36323405R00228

Made in the USA
Lexington, KY
14 October 2014